Thames and Hudson

Richard Hamilton

Collected Words

1953–1982

Published in Great Britain by Thames and Hudson Ltd,
30–34 Bloomsbury Street, London WC1B 3QP

Published in the United States by Thames and Hudson Inc.,
500 Fifth Avenue, New York, New York 10110

By arrangement with Edition Hansjörg Mayer, Stuttgart, London
Copyright © Richard Hamilton

Library of Congress Catalog Card Number 82-50573
ISBN 0-500-01293-8

Printed and bound in West Germany by Staib + Mayer, Stuttgart

Photo: Henri Cartier-Bresson 1971

Preamble

When I first tried to put words together the results were embarrassingly incomprehensible (some say they still are) yet I persevered because it seemed to me that the things I wished to express were not likely to be said by anyone else. I felt it necessary to justify what I was doing, or at least describe how certain things had come about, even though I was very conscious that written explanations of paintings by the painter must reveal a doubt in his ability to make himself understood by graphic means: I said to myself often enough, if the paintings don't make sense in themselves, words won't help them.

Perhaps it was impatience, or maybe a distrust in other people's capacity, or willingness, to read the personal symbols that an artist has necessarily to create. It could have been an over-eager wish to be understood by others when I barely understood what I was trying to do myself, and writing things out certainly made things clearer for me. Even so, it is unlikely that I would have made the effort had it not been for requests. It was an odd phenomenon of the fifties in London that the most adventurous minds were those young architects who found an outlet through Theo Crosby when he edited Architectural Design. *He also persuaded several painters and sculptors among the Independent Group to gain access to an audience through print that was denied them by the galleries. Indeed it was as a result of Theo Crosby's invitation that I wrote on Duchamp for the first time for* Uppercase, *and another, longer, effort* Urbane Image *for* Living Arts *which proved a turning point; interest in my work was established among a small group of London cognoscente solely by this publication and it produced an invitation to exhibit that had been refused me for eight years. This success was convincing enough to encourage the writing of my own catalogue notes; a habit that persists.*

The somewhat fragmentary parts of this book fall neatly enough into groups. There are articles and odd scraps on Duchamp, few of which have not been published and many done less from an internal need than from compliance with requests to provide this or that for one or another purpose. Writing about Duchamp gave me an opportunity to rationalize my devotion to him and to his

extraordinary work. I have been asked to write on Dieter Roth, Roy Lichtenstein, Emmett Williams and Marcel Broodthaers. None of these writings on other artists are in any sense 'art criticism'; all that I could hope to do was to put down on paper my understanding of what these artists were doing and why. The short list, while not arbitrary since I like to think of them all as good friends, does not indicate an exclusivity in my enthusiasms for I admire and have learned from the work of many of my contemporaries and, of course, artists of the past. There are texts coming under the heading of 'Design' or 'Teaching' and other subjects that engaged my attention over the years. Some of the published pieces have had the benefit of editorial polish but I rarely let a typescript into the hands of an editor without first pestering good and patient friends to correct spelling and punctuation and point out baffling grammatical constructions. There were lectures that were not written down at all and manuscripts that are lost. Those that survive drop into their allotted sections easily enough.

The writings which refer to my own paintings have proved more recalcitrant. There are one or two self-contained texts but mainly the commentary tends to be a string of extended captions, many of which have appeared in slightly different forms on different occasions. Some are concerned with specific paintings or drawings or, as often as not, subjects; some are purely autobiographical. In order to give coherence and continuity to the bits and pieces it has been necessary to add some linking passages. To make a distinction between them the existing material in this section is set in roman and the additions are in italics.

The 'Selected bibliography' at the back includes most of the published items and the references which appear under a column indicate previous uses. Oddities of · typesetting in the later parts of the book relate the sections back to their original publication, or non-publication, and also to their subject matter. A piece written for the Sunday Times *or* The Times Educational Supplement *looks plausible set in Times Roman. An unpublished text is likely to appear in the more intimate italics. A general lack of conformity helps to isolate and identify segments of a sporadic and diverse output.*

Schooling

Lack of a 'formal' education was no obstacle to a prolonged schooling in art. At the age of twelve my interest in painting was strong enough for me to attend, illegally, adult education evening classes conducted by an itinerant art teacher for the London County Council in Southwark and Millbank. Mr Smith, whose distinguished manner and discreetly artistic personality I revered (I never saw an example of his work), lived by maintaining the size of his classes above the minimum required by the LCC with every possible subterfuge. It was well-known around the London doss-houses that Mr Smith provided free tea and buns in the school canteen during breaks; numbers stayed nicely constant with a floating population of down and outs and two or three talented misfits. His adoption of a twelve-year-old enthusiast who wandered in one evening as a result of seeing a beautiful calligraphic notice placed in a Westminster public library was completely altruistic, an act of purest generosity since I could not be numbered on his lists.

After two years of evening classes, which I attended three or four times a week, I was sufficiently adept at bravura charcoal drawings to be recommended to the notice of Sir Walter Russell, Keeper of the Royal Academy Schools. He suggested that in view of my tender years I should wait a while and apply for admission when I reached the age of sixteen; I should fill the time between leaving primary school and my application with further study. Life classes at St Martin's School of Art, at Westminster Technical College and at the Reimann Studios provided a grounding which led to my acceptance in the Royal Academy Schools in 1938 where I studied happily until its wartime closure in 1940. Some drawings and etchings from that time survive and some have been exhibited, though they hang strangely in the eyes of their maker on the walls of a museum. Adolescent fumblings may have some small interest for those curious to know what indications they hold for the future. Eclectic explorations of recent art history (appropriate in the academy of art but pretentious when displayed in a retrospective exhibition) may well throw some light on the more personal contribution which could emerge from such studies. Curiously enough, it may be that earlier drawings have a self-assurance and

a sense of conviction that is absent from those later. There are several factors that might contribute to this. Student work can be less ambitious intellectually than that produced from maturity. Youth can afford the luxury of facility while age may bring an appreciation of the maladroit as a reaction against the confidence of young accomplishment.

Too young for conscription when the RA Schools closed, I was sent by the Labour Exchange to learn engineering draftsmanship at a Government Training Centre. By the sheerest good fortune the job I landed afterwards happened to be as a 'jig and tool' designer, a 'reserved occupation' which kept me out of the army. After the sickening events of Nagasaki and Hiroshima and the capitulation of the Japanese in 1946 I learned that the RA Schools were to reopen; there was every reason to resume art studies. My long awaited return to the RA was not the joyous experience I had anticipated.

In the years immediately preceding the war, studying the nude in Piccadilly had the added bonus of the Bond Street galleries. Guernica and all the studies were exhibited in the Burlington Gallery, where the great Surrealist exhibition had been displayed. There were memorable shows of fresh-smelling canvasses by Picasso and Man Ray in commercial galleries which were visited and discussed by the students. Under the pernicious influence of the new president, Sir Alfred Munnings, the Schools had taken on a burlesque atmosphere in the knock about style of the Crazy Gang. Sir Walter Russell had been replaced by Phillip Connard. Thomas Monnington had been appointed a teacher. Sir Alfred was wont to stride through the corridors in jodhpurs and hacking jacket thwacking his booted calves with a riding crop. Cringing students were loudly accosted with such questions as 'Are you one of those buggers that talks about Picasso?'; if anyone was unwise enough to nod Sir Alfred would yell 'Well get to hell out of here!' and storm off.

Munnings was frightening but Monnington could be hilarious. His deadpan delivery of the line 'Augustus John could knock spots off Cézanne' was masterly. Another time I fell off my drawing donkey laughing at what I mistakenly took for broad humour – 'They're not even good honest Frenchmen, they're a lot of fucking

Bibliography: 59. The change to roman denotes the use of a previously published text. Its source is listed in the selected bibliography.

Nude study made in Reimann Studios life class, 1937

dagos'. My open amusement at these antics got me into difficulties and I was expelled for 'not profiting from the instruction being given in the painting school'. While the judgement was unarguable it seemed a trifle hard that the expulsion also gave the Ministry of Labour the opportunity to insist that, since I was no longer a student, I was liable for military service. Eighteen months of confinement in army camps delayed serious study further until, when finally released, I applied to the Slade School. William Coldstream interviewed me; he regarded my expulsion from the RA as an excellent recommendation and I was accepted. Three years at the Slade brought my total studentship to ten – it had taken seventeen years to accomplish that.

It is often the case that the value of an education is derived from other students. I certainly learned less from 'teachers' than from my fellows. Nigel Henderson, also at the Slade after long wartime delays, disposed of his knowledge of the world of Modern Art with an easy wit and charm. He introduced me to two masterworks that charged my batteries for the coming years. The first of these was d'Arcy Wentworth Thompson's great book on morphology On Growth and Form. *It was Nigel also who drew my attention to a copy of Marcel Duchamp's* Green Box. *He suggested one day that, since we were near, we might drop into the Penroses for tea, and there made free of Roland's library for my benefit.*

Growth and form seemed an ideal subject for another involvement of that time, exhibition design. By the turn of the century the 'exhibition' was beginning to be understood as a form in its own right with unique properties. My meeting with Roland Penrose was propitious because he commended the idea of an exhibition on Growth *and* Form *to the Institute of Contemporary Arts. The result was that a good deal of the time nominally spent at the Slade was devoted to finding the financial resources, researching, designing and, in part, making the exhibition which was to be the ICA's contribution to the Festival of Britain in 1951.*

Extended studentship has, with the modern grant system, become a way of life, almost a profession. As a student I made my own way, except for the Slade period, when I became eligable for State aid.

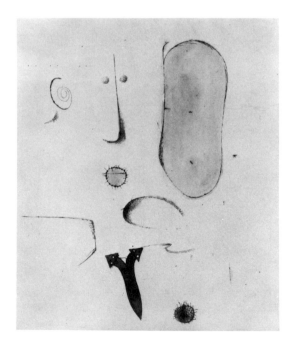

Self-portrait, 1951

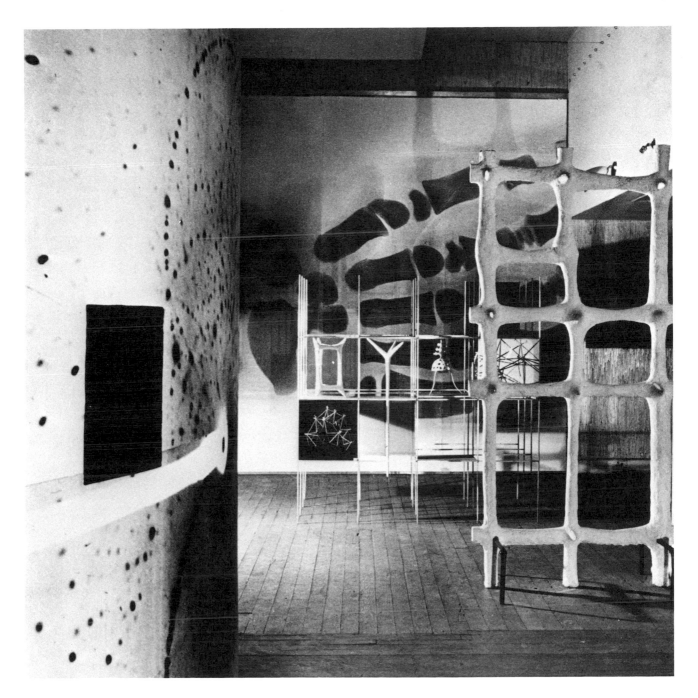

Growth and Form, Institute of Contemporary Arts, London, 1951

The belated period of studentship at the Slade Schools (1948–51) had been largely spent drawing from the nude though it also gave me an opportunity to return to an old love, etching, in the department run by a wonderfully warm and sympathetic teacher, John Buckland-Wright. Siegfried Giedion's Mechanization Takes Command *became a primary source book immediately after its publication in 1948. It was particularly significant for me in that it complemented* On Growth and Form, *which deals with the natural world in just the wide-ranging manner of Giedion's perception of technological form and process. Agricultural machinery was seen by Giedion to be at a crucial interface, the boundary at which technology meets nature. The initial stimulus for a series of about twenty* Reaper *engravings, made at the Slade, undoubtedly came from Giedion's chapter on this farm implement.*

My paintings at this time were 'abstract'; a few surviving examples demonstrate one clear preoccupation – the use of minimal elements to articulate the picture surface. These paintings took a major characteristic of Cézanne's method, that of structuring the surface through straight linear relationships, and investigated it in a very narrow sense. The theoretical arguments justifying the primacy of the painting as surface had been much discussed in the early part of this century – considerations which had led to an assumption that the logical consequence of Cézanne's example must be a commitment to the perfect integrity of the painted surface; so 'abstract' painting was granted its motivation.

In my own student musings on these questions this hypothesis appeared, by observation, to be fallacious. It was evident that no single mark, not to mention agglomerations of marks, could hope to stay put optically, on a surface. The picture plane could only triumph as a monochrome – preferably white. Paintings and drawings made during the latter part of my studentship used little stick-like units which are located by a consideration of the plane and its given edges, but which happily accept the three-dimensional implications that inevitably arise.

Perspective is the dominant clue in our interpretation of any image. The human eye will read diagonal marks as

having spatial connotations even when they are contradicted by other clues. The Ames experiment in which perspective was so perverted as to propose a giant human being in one corner and a midget in another corner of a logical-seeming room proved this convincingly. Having an unfashionable (at that time) predisposition towards an illusory representational space it was likely that perspective would form a major part of my student interests.

Bibliography: 59

Induction study, 1950

Chromatic spiral, 1950

Motion/Perspective

So-called 'Analytical Cubism' (with its avowed debt to Cézanne) held a keen interest for me in this context of surface integrity and represented form. Cubism purported to express a multiplicity of viewpoints in a single representation of the subject. My own attempts to rationalize the great Picasso paintings of the 'Analytical' period were frustrated by a growing awareness that the word analytical as used here, is one of many terms beloved by art critics that function nicely as labels but which turn out to be somewhat misleading semantically. If the Cubists were finding ways to describe the experience of moving around a subject then intuition played a greater part in their notations than analysis and logic. This is not a value judgement I hasten to say. The 'Analytical Cubist' period produced some of the greatest paintings of this century; certainly they would not have been greater paintings had they been more analytical.

A student can be forgiven for questioning the language and ideas of a previous generation. But there was one 'Cubist' painting that did have an analytical logic about it and that was a painting specifically rejected by the party leaders as nonconformist. Duchamp's *Nude descending a staircase* was this exception. If the one 'Analytical' painting to come from the Cubist circle was judged to be heretical by that circle then the inference was that mainline Cubism might not be all that analytical. In fact the Duchamp painting was soon recognised to be closer to Futurism than Cubism; not only more systematic but also unorthodox in its programme, for it is the subject that moves – the nude descends to the artist who watches immobile. Cubism was, ostensibly, about spectator motion in relation to a static subject. Futurism was about subject motion in relation to a static observer. It so happened that subject motion was much more susceptible to schematic representation – it had already been submitted to analytical procedures by means of the camera in the chronophotography of Muybridge and of Marey with, in the one case, exposures on multiple plates and in the other, multiple exposures on one plate. Visual description of spectator motion is more complex than subject motion because, when the observer moves, everything in his perceptual field moves relative to everything else. There was no equivalent precedent of

Bibliography: 59

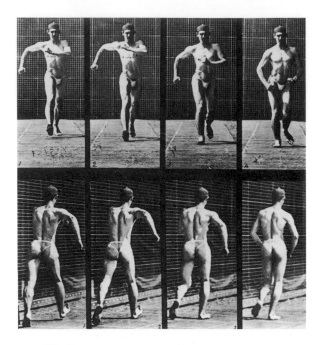

Man walking, from *The Human Figure in Motion,* Edweard Muybridge

Chronophotograph, attributed to Marey

photographic research into camera motion. No wonder the Cubists' favourite subject was the 'Still-life'.

The transitional period between leaving art school and returning as a teacher was a suitable moment for me to review the situation. My paintings were becoming progressively more figurative and I was curious about the part that ideas concerning movement had played in 20th century art, in particular its expression in Cubism and Futurism. Several paintings and etchings in 1953 and '54 attempted, in a quite pedantic manner, to clarify the distinction for myself.

Classical perspective requires a fixed viewpoint; to be more specific, it depends on one rigidly locked eyeball. In any perspective construction it is not only necessary to define the spatial location of each element of a scene but also the height and distance of the eye in relation to the subject. It is possible, if not particularly rewarding, to superimpose basic perspective layouts in such a way as to determine the graphic results of moving through a series of varying relationships to a space. For example, notations can be devised which will plot lateral movements of an eye parallel with the picture plane, or movement toward a subject, that is to say, at a right angle to the picture plane, and so on. Such diagrams can also inform about vertical changes in the terrain.

My first studies of spectator motion were purely diagrammatic, with only the merest whispers of subject matter. As the description of form was schematic, even simplistic, so was the use of colour. A spot of blue watercolour could be a token for sky, or distance, as well as recording some key intersection. Generally speaking these were blank and empty spaces, and necessarily so because the marks standing for spatial organization served a dual purpose in referring also to the proportions and edges of the picture itself – the Cézannesque integrity of the surface precept; a complication obliging 'minimal' treatments. These empty notations invited habitation and my reaction was to populate the diagrammatic space with token life forms abstracted from primitive organisms often taken directly from material researched for the *Growth and Form* exhibition. Some drawings and etchings of the early fifties (such as *Self-portrait*) were compounds of organic material without the perspective setting.

After Muybridge, 1953

At the same time I found it helpful to use Muybridge photographs to examine the differences between subject and spectator motion. In Muybridge's *The Human Figure in Motion,* motion is represented by sequences of photographs showing progressive stages of actions performed by nude human figures. One etching is a drawn superimposition, or coalescence, of successive stages of a 'man walking' series. The movement, in this case, being in a direct line towards the camera. By making drawn superimpositions of the separate Muybridge photographs the image was, coincidentally, taken closer to Marey's multiple exposures on the same negative. The result is the creation of new volumes – the forms generated include time as a factor. It was interesting, also, to see the way Boccioni's sculpture of a figure moving through space formalized these temporal progressions. The directly illustrative nature of the drawings deriving from Muybridge photographs as compared with the abstract character of the perspective chartings of those concerned with spectator motion, clarified the problems well. It is really quite difficult to find graphic means to communicate the complexities of that alternative possibility – an eye moving relative to a subject as intricate as the human form, or a still-life, or a rich spatial environment. These three areas constituted the next group of paintings and associated studies.

A landscape, *Trainsition,* took a particular visual phenomenon of motion perspective, the apparent rotation of a visual field around a point of focus when the eye is moving significantly in relation to a space. In a mobile situation, the only fixed point, that is to say visually static in relation to the other forms and locations, is the point that the observer focuses on at any moment; change focus to another position, closer or further away, and the direction of movement of objects and surfaces in front of and behind relates to that new visual fulcrum. The extent of displacement of any point is a function of its distance from the point of focus and the distance the eye traverses. *Trainsition* examines the consequences of a big displacement as in the experience of focusing on a middle distance object (a tree) from the window of a moving vehicle (a train). *Still-life?* took a group of bottles in the studio as a subject and moved sequentially towards it in a series of steps.

Still-life?, 1954

Because the bottles are below eye level, on a table, there is an apparent progressive tilting of the surface on which they are standing.

The most ambitious endeavour was the application of these principles to the female nude. Several life drawings and studies resulted in a painting. I cannot do better than to repeat a description of the procedures involved in the making of *re Nude* written for a catalogue in 1972: A classically 'still' subject, an art school nude, is approached in three stages. Moving a large easel to and fro was too cumbersome a procedure. It was necessary to make a watercolour drawing to provide information that could be transferred to the painting in the model's absence. It happened, by chance, that the blank white panel was behind the nude when the drawing was begun. After the first life session a start was made on the painting. On returning to work with the model, I found that the subject had changed, because the results of the previous session had become part of the painting's subject. Each phase of work fed into and complicated the subject further. The three shifts towards the model were a constant but the three stage painting was itself expanded by three shifts, so that, finally, the figure appears twelve times; three as the nude plus three times three in the nude in the painting in the painting.

An etching was made during the course of work on *re Nude*. It was the beginning of a practice that has become a norm in subsequent work – to make a print either as a sketch study for a painting or as a recapitulation of the theme in the later stages of its development. It is a combination of intaglio and relief printing. The etch, in large and open areas, is sufficiently deep to permit colour to be rubbed into some of the lower parts while the raised linear drawing was rolled up with black. Colour was applied to the plate individually for each proof so there was only one passage through the press. Only three prints were made because the inking procedure was tedious.

Bibliography: 49, 52

re Nude, 1954

When I went to teach in the University of Newcastle in 1953 it had been my hope that the opportunity to work at painting, without the distraction of trying to scratch a living by teaching part-time and undertaking any commercial job that was going, would enable me to produce a sufficient number of paintings to make an exhibition. The masterplan went on to anticipate success, giving up teaching, becoming a professional artist and living happily ever after. Everything went like clockwork, up to a point. Two years of intensive effort gave me the body of paintings I needed to approach the Hanover, one of the best galleries in London, and be given a show in 1955. The only trouble was the lack of success, almost nothing was sold in spite of a moderately favourable press reception. I found myself commuting to Newcastle for eleven more years.

1955 also saw the opening of another didactic exhibition, a follow-up to Growth and Form *called* Man, Machine and Motion, *this time made with the help of students. I carried with me to Newcastle an enthusiasm for the exhibition form as well as an idea for a subject.* Growth and Form *dealt with the natural world. A survey of appliances invented by men to overcome the limits imposed on them by the physical attributes provided by nature would complement the earlier show. Lawrence Gowing rewrote my introduction to the catalogue so that the language soared like the men in their flying machines. He was generous enough to suggest a joint signature.*

Clem (Batman) Sohn, from *Man, Machine and Motion* exhibition

Man, Machine and Motion

The devices which man makes to extend his physical potentialities are the oldest and the newest things we know about him. From the tool and the weapon that first added to the natural power of the hand to the optical, electric and electronic inventions which now extend the range of the senses, they are the essential material of history. This exhibition is devoted to machines which extend the powers of the human body in a special way, the machines which increase a man's capacity for autonomous movement. In particular, the exhibition is concerned with the documents, largely photographic, which record these machines in use.

We have found that these documents have a special character of their own. A photograph of an early aeroplane standing unattended has a distinct and separate beauty: the elaborate geometry of it engages the eye. The look of it in use excites us in a different way, both more intimate, less abstract, and more unexpected. The conventional aesthetic appreciation of machines – the view that the beauty of a machine lies in a harmonious fitness for its function – does not prepare us for this new excitement. The aeroplane was indeed, in the light of later experience, often wildly unfit to fly. Often it was a fantastic sport of aeronautical evolution, doomed to extinction, yet the photograph of the aviator in his spidery web moves us none the less.

There is something fabulous in this aspect of modern history; the men are acclaimed heroes and the machines, as they quickly become obsolete are consecrated, not only in museums, but in the affections of the public. There is a characteristic expression on the faces of the men in these photographs, one of pride, determination, faith. However optimistic the invention may be, the inventor-operator shows no sign of doubt when faced by the camera: even in failure he cannot be made to feel ridiculous.

The atmosphere of the photographs is a strange one. No human being before was ever portrayed in quite this situation: no contraption made by man before had the unique potentialities of this materialisation of an historic dream. The photographs in fact discover man in a new relationship. It is a relationship as cherished and as full of feeling as that earlier relation, familiar in

Bibliography: 3

art, between a horse and its rider. The realtionship is now different, and more profound. The new rider has not merely exchanged the potentialities of one creature for those of another. He has realised an aspiration which lies deeper than thought, the longing for a power with no natural limits; he finds himself in real life the super-human inhabitant of his dearest fantasy.

That the fantasy is dear to us we cannot doubt. Movement is often an end in itself – there is little justification for the existence of roller-skates other than that some people delight in using them – and an element of such delight enters into the motives for every use of the machinery of movement. The machines have evolved almost of their own accord. Often it would have been hard to say whether science, sport or economics had prompted the latest development; or whether all three were not at the service of a profound and communal obsession. The aeroplane, which evolved with the illogical wastefulness of biological evolution, was born of a myth. It was a fantasy for centuries before any man flew. Even now, in the interstellar spaces, the myth, the fiction, is again ahead. Another exhibition might have been made out of such historic dreams – and this one glances backward at such things as Leonardo's flying machines and Francesco di Giorgio's diving suit. But this exhibition is chiefly concerned with a fantasy still hardly articulate with the dream-like life which men and machines live together, the life which is with us now.

The relation between man and machine is a kind of union. The two act together like a single creature. The ancient union of horse and rider, fused into a composite creature with an unruly character of its own, always potentially anarchic and fearsome, never entirely predictable, was symbolised in the myth of the centaur. The new union of man and machine possesses as positive a composite character and liberates a deeper, more fearsome human impulse. This new affiliation, evoking much that is heroic and much that is terrible, is with us, not only in the sky, but in every street where a boy joins magically with his motor-bicycle, his face whipped by the wind and stiffened by a passion for which we have no name. Like the machinery of motion, it is with us for all foreseeable time. It creates, as we watch, its own myth. The myth, the poetry, is needed: man has no other means of assimilating disruptive experience to the balanced fabric of thought and feeling.

It is the purpose of this exhibition to examine the beginnings of just this process, and to isolate some of the visual material on which new myths are based. At first sight a collection of such documents may look eccentric, by turns rather comic and, incongruously, menacing. Looking again we realise that the quest they illustrate has itself been bizarre, as odd as anything attempted by mankind. The achievement itself is fantastic.

LG, RH

The exhibition consists of approximately 200 photographs and photographic copies of drawings. The exhibits, mounted in 'Formica' sheets, are fixed within 30 open frames all 8 feet × 4 feet made from ⅜ inch square section mild steel. These standard frames are assembled in four distinct groups one for each of the four main categories of subject matter: Aquatic, Terrestrial, Aerial and Interplanetary. Examples of underwater devices are contained in a group of five screens making an 8 feet square block 4 feet high. Aircraft are displayed on an 'H' group of frames suspended 4 feet from the floor. Space travel is carried on a suspended canopy of four frames extending from the air section and roofing the underwater group at 8 feet. Surface locomotion is located in vertically placed frames surrounding the central groups. A gallery with a floor area of 800 to 1000 square feet is required for the full display. When stacked together the screens occupy a space of 8 feet × 4 feet × 1 foot and weigh approximately 6 cwt.

Victor Pasmore was appointed to head the painting department in Newcastle not long after I began to teach there – we teamed up to work on a first year course which would operate for all students. He saw the Man, Machine and Motion *show and commented that 'it would have been very good if it hadn't been for all those photographs'.*

A technical specification of the show was circulated to a few museums. In the event, the 'travelling' exhibition didn't get further than the ICA in London.

Man, Machine and Motion, Hatton Gallery, Newcastle upon Tyne, 1955

Man, Machine and Motion, Hatton Gallery, Newcastle upon Tyne, 1955

Commuting weekly from and to London together with long university vacations, enabled me to retain contact with my friends in London, in particular with the members, if that loose association of unlike spirits can be said to be a membership, of the Independent Group. I always tried to arrange things so that I could attend IG meetings at the ICA. Indeed, Man, Machine and Motion *would have been a different affair without the collaboration of Reyner Banham (an IG convenor) who wrote the catalogue notes with not only encyclopaedic knowledge but a flair and sparkle uniquely his.*

No sooner was Man, Machine and Motion *out of the way than the stresses and strains of* This is Tomorrow *were upon us. Nothing breaks friendship like collaboration but* This is Tomorrow *was more like civil war. The tougher the aggro the more productive the enterprise seems to become. With some thirty-six artists and architects divided into twelve three-man teams, all screaming for self-expression, it took a genial genius like Theo Crosby to maintain the flow of oil on the troubled waters. Inter-group rivalry was no less bitter than the battles within each group. I was fortunate in that John Voelcker, the architect of my group, did a brilliant job of designing a structure and performed magnificently in the strenuous work of fabricating it with us (my wife Terry was a dab hand with a saw as well as an anonymous contributor at every level of the project), but he did so with unruffled equanimity. The aggravation, in my group, was produced by absent friends. John McHale went to the US for a year and returned to London to make himself available for work two weeks before the show was due to open in Whitechapel, too late to add creatively to the few acrimonious contributions which arrived by post.*

Our section of the exhibition was in two parts; divided by John Voelcker's ingenious structure which not only provided several closed spaces but two interestingly different adjacent spaces within the rectangular area which housed it. To the left was a narrow corridor of constant width and to the right a large wedge-shaped area which opened up to the main hall and the other exhibitors. This division was useful in that it allowed for a distinction to be made between the two fields of concern that we had listed as requiring representation: Imagery and Perception. The closed spaces of the structure held aspects of both.

Imagery

Journalism
Cinema
Advertising
Television
Styling
Sex symbolism
Randomization
Audience participation
Photographic image
Multiple image
Mechanical conversion of imagery
Diagram
Coding
Technical drawing

Perception

Colour
Tactile
Light
Sound
Perspective inversion
Psychological shock
Memory
Visual illusions

This is Tomorrow, Whitechapel Art Gallery, 1956

A double spread in the catalogue defined these interests with, on one page, a demonstration of a classic visual illusion in which either the black form is read or the negative, white form; an either-or situation in which the choice must be made for they cannot be perceived simultaneously. Imagery was represented by a collage, Just what is it that makes today's homes so different, so appealing?, *which was also determined by a prescribed list of interests:*

Man
Woman
Humanity
History
Food
Newspapers
Cinema
TV
Telephone
Comics (picture information)
Words (textual information)
Tape recording (aural information)
Cars
Domestic appliances
Space

The image should, therefore, be thought of as tabular as well as pictorial.

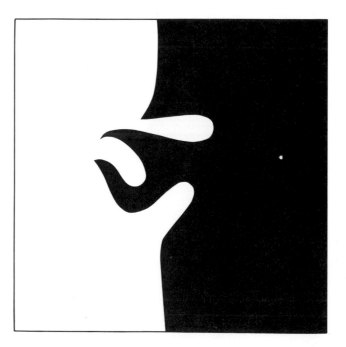

Visual illusion from *This is Tomorrow* catalogue

Just what is it that makes today's homes so different, so appealing?,
1956

Victor Pasmore, who had been involved with another group in This is Tomorrow, *approached me with the idea that we might collaborate on an exhibition in Newcastle. Remembering his comment on* Man, Machine and Motion *I proposed that we might make a show which would be its own justification: no theme, no subject; not a display of things or ideas – pure abstract exhibition.*

The structure consisted of 4 feet × 2 feet 8 inch acrylic panels (three from a standard 8 feet × 4 feet sheet) of various colours and degrees of translucency which could be distributed at will on a 1 feet 4 inch module with the minimum of visible support. Lawrence Alloway was brought in to verbalize the notion.

an Exhibit was first shown at the Hatton Gallery, Newcastle upon Tyne in June 1957. The exhibition was envisaged as a work of art operating throughout the 1000 square feet of available floor space. A kit of suspended components was devised which would allow empirical construction – the panels could be freely placed and all decisions could be taken on the site. When assembly was completed marks were collaged onto the panels – an individuation[1] of otherwise anonymous elements. The panels were static but new experiences of panel groupings were available to the spectator passing through them – his mobility gave him the opportunity to generate his own compositions. A second showing of the exhibition was made in London at the Institute of Contemporary Arts with a completely new organisation of the same elements. In 1959 the panels were integrated into an existing demountable grid system (the remains of the, *Man, Machine and Motion* exhibition) to make a self-supporting exhibition, this was called *Exhibit 2*.

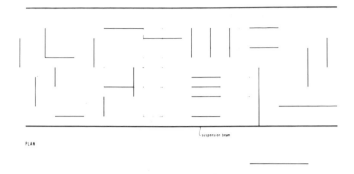
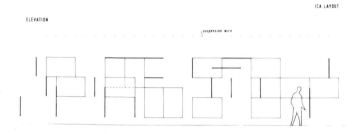

This description of the exhibitions was written as a press hand-out for *Exhibit 2*.

[1] 'Individuation' was largely the work of Victor Pasmore for *an Exhibit*. It was done jointly on *Exhibit 2*.

an Exhibit, record of installation at Institute of Contemporary Arts, London, 1957

an Exhibit, ICA, London, 1957

an Exhibit, Hatton Gallery, Newcastle upon Tyne, 1957

Exhibit 2, Hatton Gallery, Newcastle upon Tyne, 1959

It was only a few months after This is Tomorrow *that the subject of exhibition came up again. Peter and Alison Smithson put it to me one evening that it might be worth considering the possibility of a show which could develop the valuable experience gained by the participants at Whitechapel. The following letter was sent to them a few days later:*

16th January 1957

Dear Peter and Alison

I have been thinking about our conversation of the other evening and thought that it might be a good idea to get something on paper, as much to sort it out for myself as to put a point of view to you.

There have been a number of manifestations in the post-war years in London which I would select as important and which have a bearing on what I take to be an objective:

Parallel of Life and Art
(investigation into an imagery of general value)

Man, Machine and Motion
(investigation into a particular technological imagery)

Reyner Banham's research on automobile styling

Ad image research (Paolozzi, Smithson, McHale)

Independent Group discussion on Pop Art – Fine Art relationship

House of the Future
(conversion of Pop Art attitudes in industrial design to scale of domestic architecture)

This is Tomorrow
Group 2 presentation of Pop Art and perception material attempted impersonal treatment. Group 6 presentation of human needs in terms of a strong personal idiom

Looking at this list it is clear that the Pop Art/Technology background emerges as the important feature.

The disadvantage (as well as the great virtue) of the TIT show was its incoherence and obscurity of language.

My view is that another show should be as highly disciplined and unified in conception as this one was

chaotic. Is it possible that the participants could relinquish their existing personal solutions and try to bring about some new formal conception complying with a strict, mutually agreed programme?

Suppose we were to start with the objective of providing a unique solution to the specific requirements of a domestic environment e.g. some kind of shelter, some kind of equipment, some kind of art. This solution could then be formulated and rated on the basis of compliance with a table of characteristics of Pop Art.

Pop Art is:

Popular (designed for a mass audience)
Transient (short-term solution)
Expendable (easily forgotten)
Low cost
Mass produced
Young (aimed at youth)
Witty
Sexy
Gimmicky
Glamorous
Big business

This is just a beginning. Perhaps the first part of our task is the analysis of Pop Art and the production of a table. I find I am not yet sure about the 'sincerity' of Pop Art. It is not a characteristic of all but it is of some – at least, a pseudo – sincerity is. Maybe we have to subdivide Pop Art into its various categories and decide into which category each of the subdivisions of our project fits. What do you think?

Yours,

Parallel of Life and Art; an ICA exhibition by Paolozzi, Henderson, Smithson, 1953. The Smithsons' *House of the Future* was an exhibit commissioned by the *Daily Mail* for their *Ideal Homes* exhibition, 1956.

At the time the letter was written there was no such thing as 'Pop Art' as we now know it. The use of the term here refers solely to art manufactured for a mass audience. 'Pop' is popular art in the sense of being widely accepted and used, as distinct from Popular Art of the handcrafted, folksy variety.

The letter was unanswered but I used the suggestion made in it as the theoretical basis for a painting called Hommage à Chrysler Corp., *the first product of a slowly contrived programme.*

The above Pop inventory was the frame of reference for the proposed study. Were any of these qualities incompatible with fine art as I, and indeed most people, had conceived it to be? A glance through the history of art will show these characteristics as very evident: Rubens was big business, Boucher's paintings are sexy, Hogarth and Duchamp are witty. I did find one exception, 'expendable'. I could not think of an artist of the past who meant to make expendable art, it seems a self-defeating goal. Warhol later disproved this exception – defeated less by intention than by museum officials who, realizing the extravagance of the idea and the rightness of its execution, had not the slightest difficulty in preserving his work. Warhol is perhaps the great exemplar; take any item on my list and Warhol is it, extremely so.

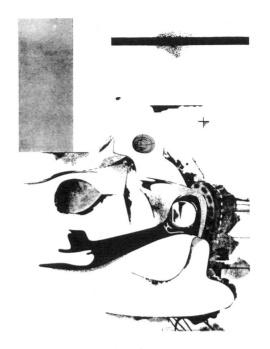

Hommage à Chrysler Corp. (version for line reproduction), 1958

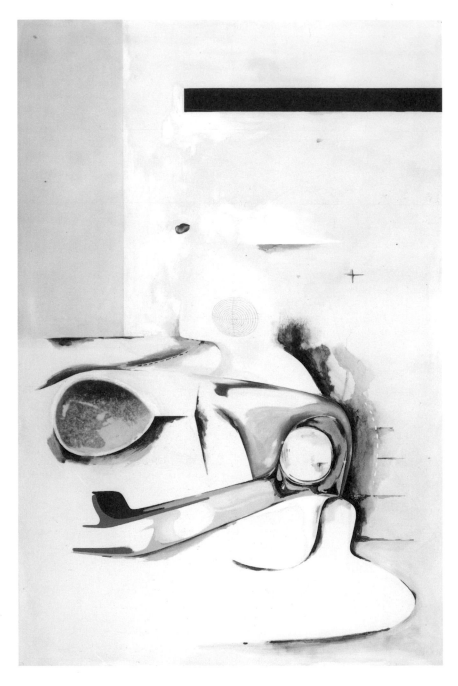

Hommage à Chrysler Corp., 1957

In 1957, as well as teaching and working on exhibition projects, I embarked on a typographic rendering of Marcel Duchamp's Green Box so progress on painting was gradual. It was also slowed down by the tentative, uncertain, unrewarding nature of the exercise – the work was very isolated in comparison with other ventures. While discussion at Independent Group meetings had been eagerly polemical there was a reluctance to look art in the eye at a social level. It would have been bad manners to discuss a painting in the studio so friends tended to avert their gaze. The outright rude question put to Lawrence Alloway on the staircase at the ICA one evening 'what do you think of my new paintings?' provoked the even more outright answer 'I think they're stupid'.

Lawrence had been propounding an aesthetic theory at the ICA with which I felt in complete accord. His idea was of a 'fine/pop art continuum'; it was a linear rather than a pyramidal concept. Instead of Picasso sitting on top of an ever-widening heap of inferior activity, with Elvis Presley and Henry Hathaway somewhere below him, all art is equal – there was no hierarchy of value. Elvis was to one side of a long line while Picasso was strung out on the other side. What I evidently failed to understand (if I didn't misunderstand him altogether) was the proper plotting along that line of the various categories of creativity. The heresy was to pull things out from one point along the continuum and drop them in at another, then stir well – the fine/pop soup alternative.

This is Tomorrow came at an opportune moment to assess the thinking that had taken place in the Independent Group at the Institute of Contemporary Arts in the preceding years. For myself it was not so much a question of finding art forms but an examination of values. My statement in the TIT catalogue put it this way:

We resist the kind of activity which is primarily concerned with the creation of style. We reject the notion that 'tomorrow' can be expressed through the presentation of rigid formal concepts. Tomorrow can only extend the range of the present body of visual experience. What is needed is not a definition of meaningful imagery but the development of our perceptive potentialities to accept and utilize the continual enrichment of visual material.

Bibliography: 27, 4

There was a mood of the late '50s felt both in London and New York, which made some painters strive for the unique attributes of our epoch – the particular character of our community as it was to register its identity on social history. Those affected by such recurring pressures sought to fabricate a new image of art to signify an understanding of man's changing state and the continually modifying channels through which his perception of the world is attained.

A quest for specific aspects of our time and the contribution that new visual tools make to the way we see our world certainly generated my few paintings of that time. Coupled with an obsessive interest in modes of seeing at a purely technical level is a strong awareness of Art. TV is neither less nor more legitimate an influence than, for example, is New York Abstract Expressionism. The wide range of these preoccupations (eclectic and catholic as they were) led to a wilful acceptance of pastiche as a keystone of the approach – anything which moves the mind through the visual senses is as grist to the mill but the mill must not grind so small that the ingredients lose their flavour in the whole.

Homage?

Hommage à Chrysler Corp. endeavoured to come to terms with just this engagement with life at a banal level without in any way relinquishing a commitment to fine art.

Partly as a result of the Man, Machine and Motion exhibition, biased by the Pop Art preoccupation of the Independent Group at the ICA and using directly some material investigated by Reyner Banham in his auto-styling research, I had been working on a group of paintings and drawings which portray the American automobile as expressed in the mag-ads. The painting Hommage à Chrysler Corp., is a compilation of themes derived from the glossies. The main motif, the vehicle, breaks down into an anthology of presentation techniques. One passage, for example, runs from a prim emulation of in-focus photographed gloss to out-of-focus gloss to an artist's representation of chrome to ad-man's sign meaning 'chrome'. Pieces are taken from Chrysler's Plymouth and Imperial ads; there is some General Motors material and a bit of Pontiac.

The total effect of Bug Eyed Monster was encouraged in a patronizing sort of way.

My sex symbol is, as so often happens in the ads, engaged in a display of affection for the vehicle. She is constructed from two main elements – the Exquisite Form Bra diagram and Voluptua's lips. It often occurred to me while I was working on the painting that this female figure evoked a faint echo of the *Winged Victory of Samothrace*. The response to the allusion was, if anything, to suppress it. Marinetti's aphorism 'a racing car . . . is more beautiful than the *Winged Victory of Samothrace'* made it impossibly corny. In spite of a distaste for the notion it persists.

The setting of the group is vaguely architectural; a kind of showroom in the International Style represented by a token suggestion of Mondrian and Saarinen. From a number of rather more direct references which were tried, a quotation from Marcel Duchamp remains. There are also a few allusions to other paintings by myself.

A lush situation

In the American magazine, *Industrial Design,* which has an annual review of automobile styling, the analysis of the '57 Buick ended with: 'The driver sits at the dead calm center of all this motion: hers is a lush situation.' My painting derives from this text. It was a problem of composition in terms of the finest art as well as an essay into a new ideology. Shallow relief was applied to convey something of the pressed steel quality of automobile bodies; it was sprayed and sanded to a car finish.

The idea of using relief emerged from an etching done at the same time – a hole cut in the plate produces a raised embossed area in the print. This was made early in relation to the painting for which it is a study. It is a good example of the kind of interaction that can take place between one medium and another. In the drawn studies for the painting one enclosed form assumed increasing importance in the composition. Its dominance was affirmed further in the etching by being cut right through the plate as a shaped hole. A hole in the plate produces an area of raised relief in the print and the raised portion invariably looks whiter than the surrounding print. I simulated this effect on the painting by applying a raised panel to the surface, also heightening the whiteness by using a different kind of white. Many of my paintings since then have had shallow relief components. The *Guggenheim* relief is a more sculptural extension of that projection of the picture into the spectator's space. Perhaps I attribute too much to this print as the germ of later work, but my affection for it is strong and so is my faith in the role of print-making as part of an artist's total activity rather than an adjunct or side issue.

The glamour of the source material for both this and *Hommage* demanded enrichment of the print with colour and metal. The few proofs made were 'tarted up' by hand.

Bibliography: 27, 49

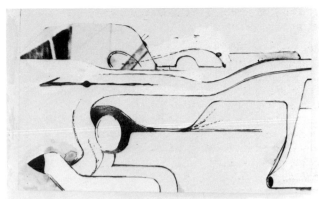

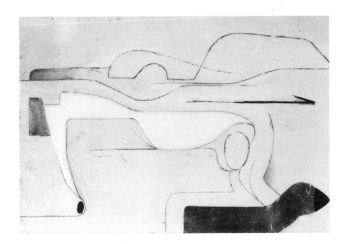

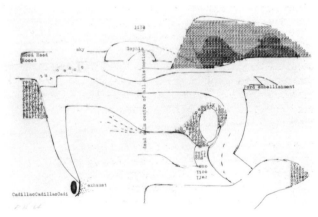

Hers is a lush situation – study, 1957

Hers is a lush situation – study, 1957

Hers is a lush situation, etching, 1958

Hers is a lush situation, text, 1963

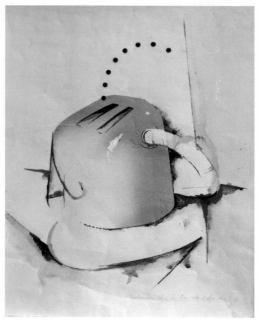

Study for '$he', 1958

Study for '$he', 1958

Study for '$he', 1958

Toastuum, 1958

An exposition of *She*

Impressionism looks like 1890, Cubism does not look like 1910, Surrealism looks like 1920, Tachism does not look like the 1950 environment. The reason for these differences is simple enough: those great styles of the past which strongly evoke the period of their birth portray objects and visual atmospheres specific to their time; those great styles which do not build in a date tag tend to avoid specific figuration or adopt appearances of other times or material which is 'classical' and therefore dateless.

The 'fabulous fifties' have produced their own strong image in the plastic arts but it is not a picture of the age itself. This '50s image is placed within its period because it is part of its time not because it portrays it. Figuration is rare and when it does emerge it operates at a crude symbolic level; Head (usually male), Woman (usually all), Landscape (differentiated from head by being horizontal). The best figurative work of the fifties – by de Kooning, Dubuffet, Paolozzi – falls into these categories as does a good deal of the run of the-mill stuff.

Strangely enough, when the environment contributes directly to the image the effect is often archaic. Human figuration sometimes comes back as pseudoman – robotics is the background for the mechanomorphic image. Paradoxically, although robots have only recently become technologically feasible, in art they are realized nostalgically as old mechanical men – as though we are looking at the artefacts of a past civilisation from a society that far exceeds it.

Contemporary art reacts slowly to the contemporary stylistic scene. How many major works of art have appeared in the twentieth century in which an automobile figures at all? How many feature vacuum cleaners? Not only the mainspring of our twentieth century economy but its most prolific image-maker the automobile industry is well with us, its attitude to form colouring our lives profusely. It adopts its symbols from many fields and contributes to the stylistic language of all consumer goods. It is presented to us by the ad-man in a rounded picture of urban living: a dream world, but the dream is deep and true – the collective desire of a culture translated into an image of fulfilment. Can it be assimilated into the fine art consciousness?

Bibliography: 22. The text was edited for its first publication – cuts have been replaced. A paragraph was pasted up incorrectly at the layout stage, that error is corrected.

In an old Marx Bros. film (and this is the only memory I have of it) Groucho utters the phrase 'Women in the home' – and the words have such power that he is overcome, he breaks the plot to deliver a long monologue directed straight at the camera. Sentiment is poured towards the audience and is puddled along with devastating leers and innuendos. This vague recollection of Groucho was revived when I began to consider the frequency with which advertising men are faced with the problem of projecting the w. i. t. h. image. 'Women in the home' was a possible title for *She*, which is a sieved reflection of the ad man's paraphrase of the consumer's dream.

Art's woman in the fifties was anachronistic – as close to us as a smell in the drain; bloated, pink-crutched, pinheaded and lecherous; remote from the cool woman image outside fine art. There she is truly sensual but she acts her sexuality and the performance is full of wit. Although the most precious of adornments, she is often treated as just a styling accessory. The worst thing that can happen to a girl, according to the ads, is that she should fail to be exquisitely at ease in her appliance setting – the setting that now does much to establish our attitude to woman in the way that her clothes alone used to. Sex is everywhere, symbolized in the glamour of mass-produced luxury – the interplay of fleshy plastic and smooth, fleshier metal.

This relationship of woman and appliance is a fundamental theme of our culture; as obsessive and archetypal as the western movie gun duel. **1–6** reveal some basic features. **1** The caress. Characteristic posture: inclination towards the appliance in a gesture of affectionate genuflexion. Possessive but also bestowing. She offers the delights of the appliance along with her other considerable attributes. **2** A job, like Dad's. Mum too has a uniform, discreetly floral apron equals pin-stripe or grey flannel. Bell provides the communications system to plug her into the home industry network. **3** Empire builder. Stockpiled cake mixes filed for easy reference: she commands the lot. **4** and **5** Is it *me?* The appliance is 'designed with you in mind' – but are you the girl next door in a party hat or the svelte job that goes with the 'Sheer Look'? Within a few years the Frigidaire image of itself can change quite a bit. **6** The source of the overall layout of *She* is this

1

2

3

4

5

6

brilliant high shot of the cornucopic refrigerator – a view that uses a photographic convention from the auto ads. The Cadillac-pink colour of this particular model of RCA Whirlpool's fridge/freezer was adopted with enthusiasm for the painting. The woman is an interesting deviation from the norm – matronly, if not downright motherly – she contributed little.

In spite of their contrived sophistication my paintings are, for me, curiously ingenuous (like Marilyn Monroe). At first sight it is easy to mistake their intention as satirical, it looks as though – and some of the references to the first six illustrations may seem to confirm the view – the painting is a sardonic comment on our society. But I would like to think of my purpose as a search for what is epic in everyday objects and everyday attitudes. Irony has no place in it except in so far as irony is part of the ad man's repertoire. My woman may seem exotic but, thanks to mass reproduction and wide distribution, she has become domesticated. She owes much to **7**, an *Esquire* photograph of 'starlet' (?) Vikky Dougan in a dress concocted by her publicist Milton Weiss. Miss Dougan specializes in modelling backless dresses and bathing costumes. The only pin-up I can remember making a greater impact in art circles was Brigitte Bardot spread piecemeal through *Reveille* (October 1957) – the gimmick of make-your-own-lifesize-BB gave it an understandable edge. I first saw Miss Dougan decorating a wall in the Smithsons' home. I gained my copy from a students' pinboard in the Interior Design Department of the Royal College. Lawrence Alloway gave me the data on her – the photograph had impressed him sufficiently to regard it as a fileworthy document. It turned up again recently as one of a group of pin-ups in a painting by Peter Phillips.

Miss Dougan's back, although too good to miss, was not quite what was needed; a rotation of the figure gave the best of both worlds plus. The shoulders and breasts, lovingly airbrushed in cellulose paint, were done with one eye on **7** the other on the Petty[1] girl. Her breasts can be seen in two ways, one reading provides a more sumptuous profusion of flesh than the other. The cleavage on the backside suggested an apron effect in negative; this was nice – an apron, however minute, is fundamental to the woman-in-the-home image. This area is in shallow relief, ⅛ inch, ply sanded down at the

[1] Petty, the signature of an American magazine illustrator renowned for his masterly airbrush work on stockinged legs in his pictures of girls.

7

8

9

10

lower edge to merge into the panel. The relief retains some subtleties of modelling which are not perceptible in the photograph – in fact, they can best be explored by sensitive fingers rather than the eye.

A supplementary detail from the double-spread ad which contained **6** was of the automatic defrosting system **8**. This was photographed, blown up and pasted into the painting.

Two other advertisements, **9** the Westinghouse vacuum cleaner and, **10** General Electric small appliances, combined to make the remaining feature of $he, the device in the foreground compounded from toaster and vacuum cleaner. The refrigerator stands for major appliance, the small mobile units were incorporated to extend the range to minor. They also provide the opportunity for a plastic elaboration which gratifies my own aesthetic needs. The ad for the Westinghouse vacuum cleaner demonstrates an endearing characteristic of modern visual technique which I have been at pains to exploit – the overlapping of presentation styles and methods. Photograph becomes diagram, diagram flows into text. This casual adhesion of disparate conventions has always been a factor in my paintings. I want ideas to be explicit and separable, so the plastic entities must retain their identity as tokens. The elements hold their integrity because they are voiced in different plastic dialects within the unified whole.

The picture was worked on for about two and a half years on and off. Towards the end, Herbert Ohl from Ulm visited me in London bringing a little gift from Germany for the English pop-artist – an advocate of what, at the Hochschule für Gestaltung, they strangely termed the 'blau-jinx philosophie'[1]. It was a winking plastic eye and within minutes of its arrival it was sellotaped into position on the painting, waiting to be inlaid and carefully sprayed to smear the rectangular block into the surrounding surface. The wink, unhappily, is impossible to reproduce – **11** and **12** are details of eye open and closed.

[1]What I should have been hearing was 'blue jeans philosophy'.   11   12

She, 1958–61

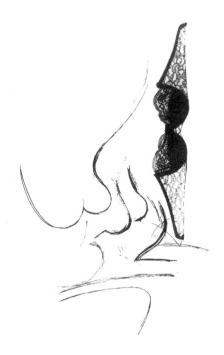

Pin-up

Girlie pictures were the source of *Pin-up;* not only the sophisticated and often exquisite photographs in *Playboy* magazine, but also the most vulgar and unattractive to be found in such pulp equivalents as *Beauty Parade.* All the paintings have references to fine art sources as well as Pop – in this case there are passages which bear the marks of a close look at Renoir.

There were five preliminary sketches for *Pin-up* which show a slow accumulation of the features that make up the design of the final painting. The habit of blotting out failings with white gouache often helped to determine the composition in a positive sense. For example the centre of the figure was obliterated in one drawing so, when rehashing the theme, the effaced area was retained as a kind of negative form. It wasn't until the gap between the breasts and the knees loomed large while painting the big version that I was forced to return to the problem and developed a solution in the drawn and collaged study of the bra and breasts.

R B Kitaj is liable to assemble disconcertingly disparate styles in his paintings (an extreme case is *Certain Forms of Association Neglected Before).* He has said of these jumps that they are, among other things, 'a change of pace'. Mixing idioms is virtually a doctrine in *Pin-up* – less perhaps to change pace than to preserve the identity of different sources; though a diversifying of language is, I like to think, a mutual objective.

Study for *Pin-up,* 1961

Bibliography: 27, 49, 52

Work in progress on *Pin-up*

Pin-up, 1961

For the Finest Art try – POP

In much the way that the invention of photography cut away for itself a chunk of art's prerogative – the pictorial recording of visual facts – trimming the scope of messages which Fine Art felt to lie within its true competence, so has popular culture abstracted from Fine Art its role of mythmaker. The restriction of his area of relevance has been confirmed by the artist with smug enthusiasm so that decoration, one of art's few remaining functions, has assumed a ridiculously inflated importance.

It isn't surprising , therefore, to find that some painters are now agog at the ability of the mass entertainment machine to project, perhaps more pervasively than has ever before been possible, the classic themes of artistic vision and to express them in a poetic language which marks them with a precise cultural date-stamp.

It is the *Playboy* 'Playmate of the month' pull-out pin-up which provides us with the closest contemporary equivalent of the odalisque in painting. Automobile body stylists have absorbed the symbolism of the space age more successfully than any artist. Social comment is left to TV and comic strip. Epic has become synonymous with a certain kind of film and the heroic archetype is now buried deep in movie lore. If the artist is not to lose much of his ancient purpose he may have to plunder the popular arts to recover the imagery which is his rightful inheritance.

Two art movements of the early part of this century insisted on their commitment to manifest the image of a society in flux: Dada, which denied the then current social attitudes and pressed its own negative propositions, and Futurism with its positive assertion of involvement. Both were fiercely, aggressively propagandist. Both were rebellious, or at least radical, movements. Dada anarchically seditious and Futurism admitting to a core of authoritarian dogma – each was vigorous and historically apposite.

A new generation of Dadaists has emerged today, as violent and ingenious as their forebears, but Son of Dada is accepted, lionized by public and dealers, certified by state museums – the act of mythmaking has been transferred from the subject-matter of the work to the artist himself as the content of his art.

Bibliography: 18, 52

Futurism has ebbed and has no successor, yet to me the philosophy of affirmation seems susceptible to fruition. The long tradition of bohemianism which the Futurists made their bid to defeat is anachronic in the atmosphere of conspicuous consumption generated by the art rackets.

Affirmation propounded as an avante-garde aesthetic is rare. The history of art is that of a long series of attacks upon social and aesthetic values held to be dead and moribund, although the avant-garde position is frequently nostalgic and absolute. The Pop-Fine-Art standpoint, on the other hand – the expression of popular culture in fine art terms – is, like Futurism, fundamentally a statement of belief in the changing values of society. Pop-Fine-Art is a profession of approbation of mass culture, therefore also antiartistic. It is positive Dada, creative where Dada was destructive. Perhaps it is Mama – a cross-fertilization of Futurism and Dada which upholds a respect for the culture of the masses and a conviction that the artist in 20th century urban life is inevitably a consumer of mass culture and potentially a contributor to it.

Glorious Techniculture (first state), 1961

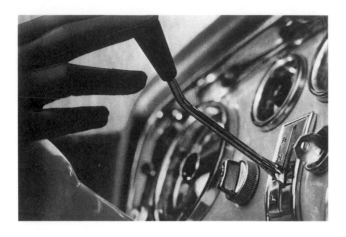

AAH!

The first sketch for *AAH!* antedates the painting by some years – it was made at the same time as the car pictures. When I began work on the panel, the subject became plainly erotic. Much of the hedonism comes from the lush visual pleasure that only photographic lenses can provide. A saga developed from an accumulation of images so that the original theme of car interior became subordinate to the overall sensuality

Exteriors of cars had been dealt with in two paintings. A car interior in an advertisement showing dashboard and gear lever invited a logical follow up. In the confined space of the car, the camera inevitably demonstrated extreme effects of blurred focus. This was one of the earliest manifestations of a continuing interest in photographic qualities and their representation in paint.

In 1963, Joe Tilson made an alphabet picture called A–Z Box, of Friends and Family, *inviting people to work on a small panel of a standard size. The vertical panels were installed in rows running from A to Z. Various friends were selected either by surname or Christian name initial.*

I was allocated 'R' for Richard but I liked the idea of 'R' for AAH! The upright panel was the wrong way round for me so I took a sidelong, perspective view of my painting. Joe didn't like undoing his picture every time I wanted my piece for a retrospective so I made a replica for my own use.

Source of *AAH!*

'AHH' in perspective, 1963

Bibliography: 27, 49. See also 'Urbane Image'. Two paragraphs on page 50 beginning 'In real close' describe the motivation and narrative of *AAH!*

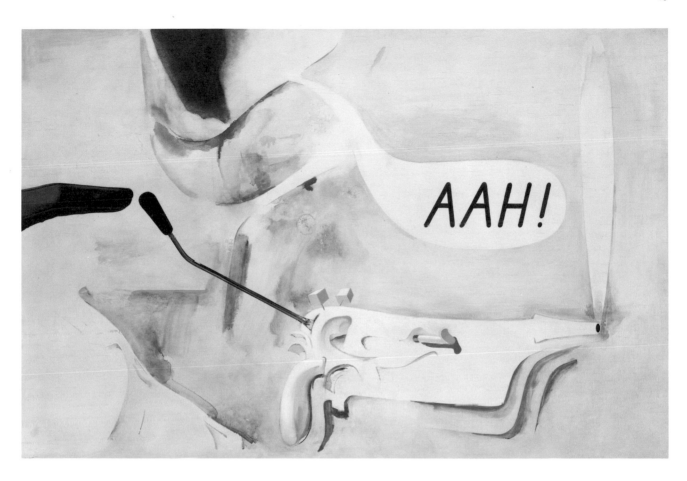

AAH!, 1962

A definitive statement

As was the case with *Hers is a lush situation* the idea for *Towards a definitive statement on the coming trends in men's wear and accessories* came directly from a fragment of text; in this instance a headline from a *Playboy* section on male fashion. The 'Towards' was added to my title because I hoped to arrive at a definitive statement but never reached a point where I felt able to drop the tentative prefix.

It became immediately apparent that fashion depends upon an occasion, season, time of day and, most importantly, the area of activity in which the wearer is involved. A definitive statement seemed hardly possible without some preliminary investigation into specific concepts of masculinity. Man in a technological environment (a) was the first area. Space research was then throwing up its early heroes, every freckle on Glenn's face was familiar to the world. J F Kennedy had made his incredibly moving speech inviting all peoples to join together in the great tasks awaiting mankind – the exploration of the stars among them.

The sporting ambiance was covered in (b). Elements from American football, motor cycle and car-racing and Wall Street were introduced.

Adonis in Y fronts attempted to catch some timeless aspect of male beauty. Certain contours were derived from the *Hermes* of Praxiteles – other parts were from muscleman pulps.

Each of the preceding three paintings contributed something to the larger working of the theme. It was found to be no more definitive than the rest. The panel may be hung in any orientation (a nul-gravity picture). One view, horizontal with the head on the right, is less favoured.

Bibliography: 27, 52

Towards a definitive statement on the coming trends in men's wear and accessories (a) sketch II, 1962

Towards a definitive statement on the coming trends in men's wear and accessories (a) 'Together let us explore the stars', 1962

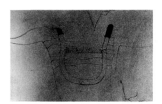

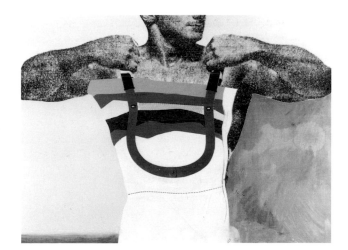

Towards a definitive statement on the coming trends in men's wear and accessories (b) sketch, 1962

Towards a definitive statement on the coming trends in men's wear and accessories (c) sketch, 1962

Towards a definitive statement on the coming trends in men's wear and accessories (b), 1962

Towards a definitive statement on the coming trends in men's wear and accessories (c) Adonis in Y fronts, 1962

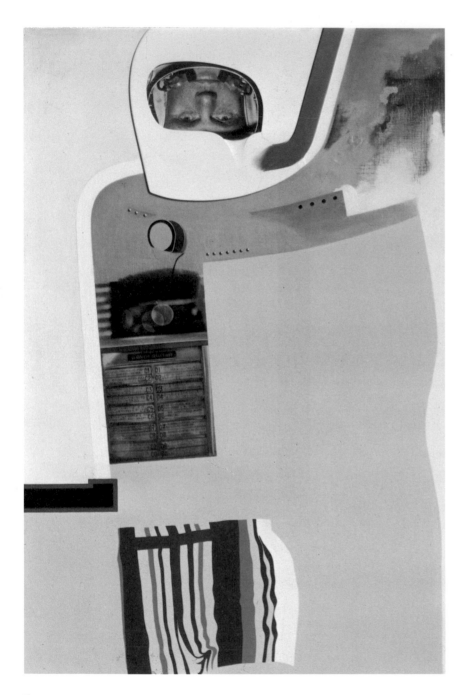

Towards a definitive statement on the coming trends in men's wear and accessories (d), 1963

Urbane Image

Chrysler Vice-President Virgil Exner models the plump detailing of the sleek 'flight-sweep' – lining the crustacean recesses of Plymouth's headlamp hood with mirror-like chrome and giving it a dark brilliance that even *Life* and *Look* can't press onto the pages of their multimillion editions. Ad-artists create a language of signs for chrome – flick and flourish to simulate the sparkle of fashioned metal. GM Vice-President Harley Earl promotes a jet technology to condition the reflexes of auto consumers while Saarinen builds status symbols for the Detroit plant.

Howard Hughes/Hawks found their answer at the drawing-board when they engineered Jane Russell's bra to set a trend in bosoms later catered to by Exquisite Form. Aware of the technological background of their product, Exquisite Form presents it as a solution to a suspension problem 'with or without floating action'. The loaded, tight shapes that feed Exner and Earl are brought full CirclOform by the ad-man (who knows his iconography), so models must learn the caress appropriate to the smooth BEM which their charms must help to sell.

As round, firm and fully packed as any, Voluptua shapes her lips for a goodnight kiss that sends us off to a dreamy TV fantasy of the sexiest machine that ever took us from point a to point b.

In slots between towering glass slabs writhes a sea of jostling metal, fabulously wrought like rocket and space probe, like lipstick sliding out of a lacquered brass sleeve, like waffle, like Jello. Passing UNO, NYC, NY, USA (point a), Sophia floats urbanely on waves of triple-dipped, infra-red-baked pressed steel. To her rear is left the stain of a prolonged breathy fart, the compounded exhaust of 300 brake horses.

At home (point b) – Vikky (The Back, by arrangement with Milton Weiss) Dougan's archetypal presence dominates even the Cadillac-pink RCA Whirlpool refrigerator/freezer, with automatic defrosting and automatic filling of ice-tray functions: major appliance if ever there was one. Westinghouse, Hoover, Singer, GE – grand new artificers – bring your bright fabrications in homage to her. Heap your gift-wrapped minor miracles (dotted line shows trajectory of the toast from the vacuum cleaner: see illustration) to her command that

Bibliography: 25, 38, 41, 52, 54

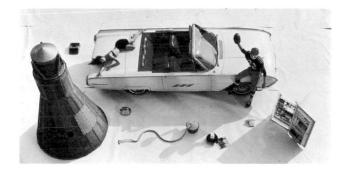

'Self-portrait' cover for *Living Arts 2,* 1963. Photo: Robert Freeman

she remain supremely housewife-mother-cupcake.

This month's playmate, however, is Miss June. Take a girl – there are plenty of good amateurs and in any case it helps to put in a biographical note. Miss Wells is a teller at the Chase Bank's Denver branch, or, a stylist at Young and Rubicam (you might come across her anywhere) just so you know she can afford her own flat, spends all her income on clothes (worn offstage), and is on the lookout for a meal ticket to 21. She's built (37, 22, 36), sociable (show a record player and a couple of highballs), intelligent (use a record sleeve with Zen in the title), available through the Bell system (Princess handset) and has friendly eyes that come out green on Ektachrome. From there on it's just a matter of technique, a photographer with his heart in his job, a good retoucher (Abstract Expressionist when he's not working), and the best blockmaking and printing facilities that money can buy concentrating all their efforts on pinky tints which filter out over bed and sand and walls and carpet and record sleeve and towel till even the words are made flesh.

In real close; what's in the finder? With a long-focus lens opened up to f2, depth of field is reduced to a few millimetres when you're not too far from the subject. Definition swings in and out along a lip length. A world of fantasy with unique erotic overtones. Intimacy, trespass yet, on a purely visual plane. Sensuality beyond the simple act of penetration – a dizzy drop into swoonlike coloured fuzz, clicked, detached and still, for appreciative analysis. Scale drifts that echo Van Vogt's pendulum swing of time; fulcrums of visual fixity that Penn engages with the twist of a knurled knob.

Of course it's not all phloo – every picture tells a story. In this case the velvet gloved finger of God energizing the Isher weapon through the power glide lever: the Varaflame ejaculation being induced in confirmation of the Dichter dictum, and the reaction a comically dribbled sigh of ecstasy.

We live in an era in which the epic is realized. Dream is compounded with action. Poetry is lived by an heroic technology. Any one of a whole range of hard, handsome, mature heroes like Glenn, Titov, Kennedy, Cary Grant, can match the deeds of Theseus and look as good, men'swearwise.

The scanned image is replacing the screened look in many fields today. Broad coloured stripes add a fashionable sporting touch to chest and loins, though two-colour full block numbering can project collegiate styling more effectively – the domed fibreglass helmet is, of course, a must for work and play.

Metals are in. Aluminium is this century's colour. Underwear in fine lustrous lamé for maximum radiation protectivity with the riveted or seam-welded corsage for external use; gun-metal, gold and platinum, however, still find support among the smart set. The trend towards electronics in male accessories is on the upgrade for outward-looking bucks styled to the needs of tomorrow and the pleasantest present.

Mr Universe takes his place by Miss World. They stand side by side, fronting camera, a dawn sun suffusing the sky with an orange glow smeared with puce and violet. As the lens zooms slowly out they recede, minute against the immense void of Space. He murmurs 'Are you ready?' Shafts of golden light radiate from them as we await the immaculately dubbed response: 'Affirmative.'

Glossary

Virgil Exner   Chief body stylist for the Chrysler Corporation from 1953 until 1961. He was primarily responsible for the 'Forward Look' introduced by Chrysler in 1956, a style in which the car sloped evenly from high tail fins to a low front end. Promoted as a 'line', in much the manner of Paris haute couture in the post-war years, it helped to reverse the sliding fortunes of the third largest automobile manufacturing organization in the US. The line is best represented by the '57 Plymouth and Imperial models. Chrysler's star dipped again in '61. Reorganization of the company by a new president found Exner among the axed executives.

Flight-sweep   Synonymous with the 'Forward Look'.

Harley Earl   Head of styling department at General Motors. He is the designer who first established the concept of fashion-styling for automobiles – Earl has long upheld the value of 'dream car' development both to stimulate design-thinking and to tease prospective markets.

Saarinen   Eero Saarinen's contributions to the GM plant are among the most restrained and elegantly distinguished buildings of the period, in apparent contradiction to the flamboyant design approach of GM products.

Howard Hughes   Hollywood film producer/director, aeronautical engineer, pilot, playboy. Produced *The Outlaw,* a film starring Jane Russell and publicized largely on the proportions of the female lead's bust. Legend has it that Hughes applied his considerable aviation design skills to the problem of a brassiere which would add lift and control to his star's biggest asset.

Howard Hawks   Brilliantly gifted film director. He worked, uncredited, on *The Outlaw* with Howard Hughes.

Exquisite Form   Corsetry manufacturing company wont to use engineering terminology in their advertisements.

CirclOform   Brand name of an Exquisite Form product.

BEM   Bug-eyed-monster in science fiction parlance.

Round, firm and fully packed   'So Round, So Firm, So Fully Packed' was a slogan used in a Lucky Strike cigarette-advertising campaign calculated to arouse the need for oral satisfaction.

Voluptua   Star of an American late night TV show intended to send tired businessmen amiably off to sleep, in which performers, cameramen and technical crew all wore pyjamas. Some use has been made in *Hommage à Chrysler Corp.* of all the above-mentioned products, personalities and ideas. Voluptua contributed the lips.

Jello   Brand name of an American jelly.

UNO   The United Nations Organization building appears as a reflection in the windscreen in *Hers is a lush situation.*

Sophia   Sophia Loren's lips form part of the female subject of *Hers is a lush situation* which has as its

theme a text derived from a review of 1956 cars in *Industrial Design.* The analysis of the Buick ends with 'The driver sits at the dead calm center of all this motion; hers is a lush situation'.

Vikky Dougan   'Starlet' who achieved notoriety as a model for backless dresses and swimming costumes.

Milton Weiss   Vikky Dougan's publicist and designer of one of her most successful stunt dresses.

RCA Whirlpool   A Whirlpool ad provided the overall scheme of *$he.*

Major appliance   Refrigerators, freezers, cookers, washers, dryers are major appliances. Smaller units of domestic equipment, toasters, mixers, polishers, for example, are minor appliances.

Grand new artificers   An oblique reference to Joyce's description of Daedalus as 'grand old artificer'.

Playmate   *Playboy* magazine contains a three page pull-out colour pin-up in each issue. She is referred to as Miss April/May/June (according to publication date), Playmate of the Month.

21   New York restaurant.

Bell   American commercial empire which provides facilities equivalent to the GPO telephone service.

Retoucher   Most advertising photographs are retouched by artists; meticulous work which demands a high degree of illustrative skill. Dick Smith tells me that he has a friend in New York, an Abstract Expressionist painter, who earns his living by retouching.

Flesh   The colour which pervades the whole of a *Playboy* pin-up, background as well as figure, perhaps because the main concern, at a purely technical level, is with the representation of these hues. This theory prompted the flesh-coloured ground of *Pin-up.*

f2   Any but the cheapest cameras have a variable opening within the lens. The different sizes of aperture are identified by f numbers. The lower the number (f2 is a big hole) the more light admitted to the film when the shutter is opened and the shorter the exposure required. The larger the opening the less will be the distance in front and behind the point of focus within which the photographic image will be sharp i.e. well defined.

Depth of field   Distance within which the subject is in acceptably sharp focus. A function of aperture and distance of focal plane from lens. The closer the plane of focus is to the camera the shallower the depth of field will be for any given aperture. *AAH!* is concerned very much with the phenomenon of photographic definition.

Van Vogt   A master of the science fiction genre; his speciality is the control of varying time scales. One of his novels is called *The Weapon Shops of Isher.* A cover to the paperback edition depicts his weapon – used in *AAH!*

Penn (Irving)   Photographer noted for his work in Vogue.

God   Almighty being. Mythical creator of the Universe. The story of Man's creation is pictured by artist Michelangelo as God touching the finger of Man-myth Adam with his own, thus bestowing life.

Isher weapon   Lethal appliance described in Van Vogt's novel. It has a remarkable built-in safety factor – it will not function as an instrument of offence.

Varaflame   A Ronson lighter fancifully associated by me with the Isher weapon.

Dichter   Ernest Dichter PhD, consumer products psychologist. Working as motivation research consultant for Ronson he explained that flame is a sexual symbol and that their advertising should express this.

Scanned image   Scanning, the technique of breaking down visual information into simple variations of intensity of a point of light which passes across and down the image in a series of parallel lines – in much the way that the reader's eyes are now scanning these lines of text – provides a significant proportion of our present visual intake, and this proportion is bound to increase. Not only is TV reliant upon this fundamental mode of seeing and recreating an image but the means of reproduction of half-tone images must now employ the method to an increasing extent.[1]

Screened look   Screening, the older process of rendering multi-toned visual information into usable components for reproduction purposes, utilizes a device which produces a grid of small black dots varying in size dependent on the values of light and dark in the subject. The image is seen all at once but broken down into units.

Theseus   Heroic figure of Greek mythology who enacted many glorious deeds. The group of pictures which carries the title *Towards a definitive statement on the coming trends in men's wear and accessories* (a label derived from a heading to a *Playboy* male fashion section) attempts to represent our mid-century myths, dreams and exploits in terms which have Hellenic correspondences.

Mr Universe   A title competed for annually by human males (at present only Earthmen) who are well-endowed with muscles and the ability to assume certain highly stylized poses.

Miss World   A title competed for annually by human females. Each contender represents her own nation's ideal of physical beauty.

Dubbed   The process of recording voices separately from the filming of the action of speech and song and then combining the two. The voice need not be that of the person filmed nor need the words be in the same language as those used by the performer.

Affirmative   Yes. Somewhat forced expression of need to conclude on a grandly positive rhetorical note. An art of affirmatory intention isn't necessarily uncritical; though I affirm that, in the context of our present culture, it will be non-Aristotelian. While value judgements are not made, the value of human thought and life and love may still be upheld – together with a desperate hope for their corny future.

[1] I am happy to note that the films for the illustrations in this book were made by a laser scanner operating at 200 lines to the inch.

  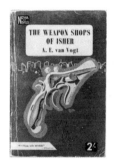 

Flight-sweep	Bug-eyed-monster	Penn photo	Scanned look
Harley Earl	Voluptua	Michelangelo's God	Screened look
Jane Russell	Playmate	The Isher weapon	Praxiteles' Hermes
CirclOform	Bell's 'Princess' handset	Ronson's Varaflame	Mr Universo

NYC, NY, and LA, Cal. USA

Epiphany, 1964

After This is Tomorrow *my activity had continued to be fragmented. At the time I was attempting to assimilate mass media, 'Pop' material into my paintings, work began with George Heard Hamilton (an introduction effected by Duchamp) on our English version of the* Green Box *notes. During the three year course of production of the typographic rendering of Duchamp's notes for the* Large Glass *Michel Sanouillet published the first edition of his collected writings of Duchamp in French (1958) and Lebel's great monograph appeared (1959); our little green book emerged in 1960. Walter Hopps was preparing for the first retrospective at the Pasadena Museum in California – its opening, in 1963, was the occasion of a public demonstration of affection for Duchamp and a warm appreciation of sixty years of creativity.*

Walter Hopps contrived the financial resources to get me to the opening, ostensibly to give a lecture on the Glass, so my first trip to the United States amounted to total immersion – New York, New Haven, Los Angeles, Las Vegas, Boston. My detached observation of the US from the other side of the Atlantic had not prepared me for the culture shock – returning to New York from the West Coast already seemed like a retreat to the old world. It had all been dreamlike. I flew West with the Duchamps on a perfect day – not a cloud in the sky, a seemingly endless grid passing below, varied only by geographical features which defeated the remorseless imposition of straight N/S/E/W lines, mile by mile sections of immaculate American folk quilting. Marcel sat beside me venturing names for rivers and mountains and cities.

This privileged introduction to the States continued into California. Duchamp was fêted royally; there were conducted tours around the galleries, to artists' studios, to collectors, to museums, with invitations always kindly extended to me – a once in a lifetime orgy of art tourism. Two memorable exhibitions happened to be in LA. There was Claes Oldenburg at the Dwan Gallery, a large, superbly installed show of great works. At Irving Blum's Ferus Gallery there was Warhol – a room of Elvis Presley pictures and a smaller room full of Liz Taylor portraits. Both Oldenburg and Warhol were in LA for their shows and for the Duchamp party at the Pasadena Museum, so I had the opportunity to get acquainted – altogether the trip initiated many friendships which were to be confirmed on subsequent visits to the States.

Among the more surprising experiences was the recognition of how widespread were those interests that I had buried myself in. Duchamp had become, in the six years that elapsed since I first became deeply involved in his work, a major cultural hero. My other enterprise, that of expressing the interests of a consumer society in fine art terms, was a named movement – Pop Art. This, with its masters and camp followers, was a band wagon which had overrun me; I picked myself up and prepared to jump on it.

One result of this visit to the USA in Oct '63 was the acquired first hand knowledge of the work of such artists as Warhol, Lichtenstein, Dine, Rosenquist and Oldenburg. The thing that impressed me about the Americans was their throwaway attitude to Art – a point of view which the European, with his long tradition of the seriousness of culture (not even Dada was that carefree), could hardly achieve. *Epiphany* is a souvenir of America. The button which is its source was bought in a seedy joke shop in Pacific Ocean Park. On my return it stood for much of what I had enjoyed in experiencing the States, but it also summed up that which I most admired in American art, its audacity and wit.

Bibliography: 27, 52

Marcel Duchamp in Los Angeles, 1963

Oldenburg's Dwan show in LA 1963

Hugh Gaitskell as a Famous Monster of Filmland

Some people, seeing earlier pictures of mine, thought that they must be satirical. They felt uneasy because they couldn't accept a title like Hommage à Chrysler Corp. *at its face value and supposed that some veiled criticism was implied. The discomfort was all the more serious because of the ambivalence of the painted image – a lyrical compilation of an adman's visual language was a very soft kind of social comment; if that is what it was. But could a painter be paying homage to Chrysler Corporation in 1957 as a fine-artist in Paris at the turn of the century might honour a patron or another artist? At times I found it necessary to explain that neither the title nor the picture were satirical. They are intended to be witty but not without a certain affection for the institutions and social mores they feed upon. They are fine art works about popular art phenomena. They are not intended to suggest that giant corporations, or the techniques of the mass media in presenting them to the public, are meritorious nor are they suggesting that they are meretricious.*

Early in '62 it occurred to me that instead of protesting that I didn't paint satirical pictures I might consider painting a satirical picture to investigate the difference. If I looked for a theme which provoked me to righteous anger where would I find it? In putting to myself the question 'what angers you most now?' I found that the answer was Hugh Gaitskell. Perhaps it isn't easy to understand, with so much time intervening, how Hugh Gaitskell could emerge as the prime subject of my disapproval for my political inclination is to the left, radical, not a party member but vociferous and demonstrative. Gaitskell, at the conception of the painting, was leader of the Labour Party – had been for seven years of opposition to Tory government. Gaitskell seemed to me to dilute constructive opposition to policies that were leading us steadily to perdition. But, most importantly, I regarded him personally as the main obstacle to adoption by the Labour Party of a reasonable nuclear policy at a time when the will of a majority within the Labour movement in Britain had been expressed in condemnation of our continuing nuclear attachment. Gaitskell's role was all the more sinister because he was leader of the left, because he

Bibliography: 29

3 *Hugh Gaitskell as a Famous Monster of Filmland – sketch,* 1963

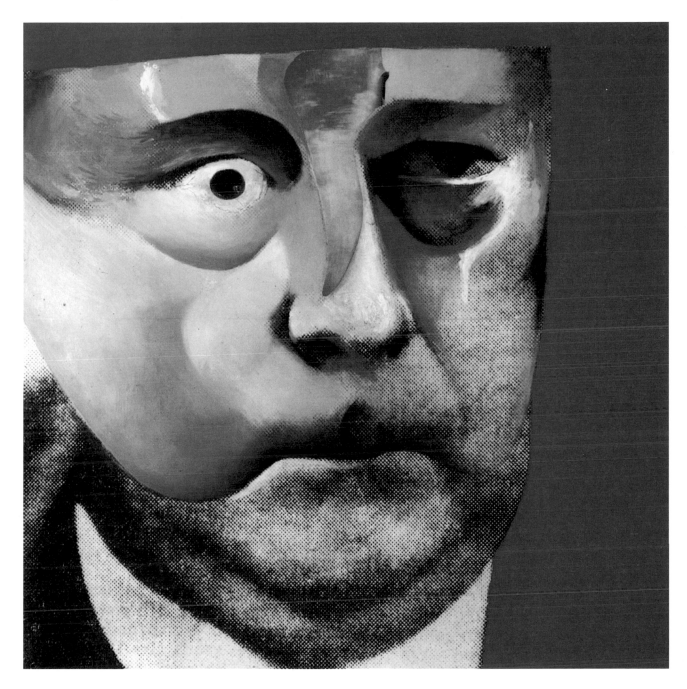

7 *Portrait of Hugh Gaitskell as a Famous Monster of Filmland*, 1964

was powerfully placed to fight his own left, and because he did so from moral conviction and not for political or economic expediency.

Hanging fire among potential pictures in my mind was another project – a painting of a monster. In the search for archetypes the monster emerges inevitably along with those other primal figures: the hero of the western, the pin-up girl, the spaceman. Hollywood and Hammer Films gave renewed life to the monster myth; with Hollywood in decline a magazine called Famous Monsters of Filmland has been gorging on its editor's collection of film stills to run into about twenty issues so far. A good number of copies of Famous Monsters had been lying around in my studio waiting to be used and identification of Gaitskell as the political monster was a natural. Portrait of Hugh Gaitskell as a Famous Monster of Filmland became the subject. A satirical painting should be topical and passionate; I imagined the picture as one to be violently executed, it should be big, the paint aggressive, the meaning awfully clear.

I began, with the help of my wife, to collect press photographs of Gaitskell, the file also included relevant headlines and newspaper cartoonists' caricatures. My wife died in a car accident late in '62; three months afterwards Gaitskell died. We were told what a great man he had been – the unifying force in the Labour Party, the only person who could have held it together through the difficult years. The painting was shelved to be taken up again a year later. It was a subject that my wife felt strongly about and, in a way, she had generated it; for her, political philosophy was something to be acted upon, so there were good reasons for suppressing any squeamishness that Gaitskell's death might have occasioned. Two images came to coalesce from the accumulated material, a press photograph of Gaitskell (1) and a cover of Famous Monsters of Filmland No. 10 (2). The FM of F cover was of Claude Rains in his make-up for The Phantom of the Opera freely painted and with a lurid red background.

The pre-figuration I had was of a panel four foot square with a close-up of the head so large that it overflowed the edges; the colour was to be violent and the handling expressionistic. The first sketch was a trial run at manipulation. It was this aspect of the painting that made me a little nervous because it had been many years since I had put on paint in any but a tight, even constipated manner; to tackle a subject that put the onus on handling was to demand reform of long habit. This first attempt with colour on paper was a disaster – very dull, mannered marks and not much like Gaitskell, too grotesquely drawn even to be a good monster. The drawing was destroyed. A second sketch (3) was made with crayons on paper with emphasis on the portrait – I tried to keep it like Gaitskell using gentle, if unlikely, colours. A bloodshot protruding eyeball from a new source (4) was tentatively introduced. At this stage I thought I'd better get back to handling problems and decided that since the paint had been visualised as juicy it had been stupid to try the first tests of myself with ink on paper, so I should try a small version with oils on a panel. I prepared the surface of a small square board and then, since the key to the identification of the Phantom with Gaitskell was the lower edge of the mask and Gaitskell's mouth, made a relief overlay for the panel – a cut-out mask of plywood modelled back to the original surface. The FM cover had a metallic look, so I put on a primer of copper paint thinking that this would shine through the oil paint and give it a metallic quality. When painting began on the copper priming, it soon became obvious that the copper was a dead loss for it killed the superimposed paint stone-cold. The oil sketch was abandoned and I started again on another trial panel, a bit larger this time, two foot square, primed with white paint.

After a few weeks of work on this new board I became despondent about the whole project. The effort of simply getting, and keeping, the Gaitskell likeness, while striving for an aggressive paint quality was getting me down. It was a feeble painting. While working on this it had occurred to me that the smaller version had been quite a nice little object before I painted on it – just as a copper coloured relief. I went back to it, scraped it, drilled two holes for eyes, carved some bags under them, and reprimed the whole panel with several coats of copper paint rubbed down

unevenly to give some textural interest and then returned to the larger panel. By this time it looked even worse. Since it was the Gaitskell likeness that proved troublesome it might be possible to overcome the difficulty by taking a given likeness and working over it. A two foot square photographic enlargement from the press photograph was ordered.

The amusing thing about the small relief panel was the way its mood changed when the board was lying against different backgrounds. The one inch diameter eye holes changed colour if it was lying on a chair or on the floor or on the wall or, with a magazine under it, on the table. While waiting for my photo enlargement I cut a circle from strawboard and covered it with a fairly random assortment of coloured papers and screwed it to the back of the little panel so that the circle could be rotated from the edge to bring a series of different colours behind the eyes. This version (5) has stayed this way (but now motorised)[1]. It isn't recognisable as Gaitskell, it isn't much like a Famous Monster of Filmland *image. There is a faint resemblance to the melancholy features of the Creature of the Black Lagoon (6) but that was a coincidence: his sweetly lovelorn overtones were a wide diversion from my purpose.*

When the photo-print arrived and was pasted down on to the panel, I began to feel that something was being accomplished. There was Gaitskell for a start and the usual pleasurable bonus of the big dot that a blown-up newspaper half-tone provides. There were disadvantages too, as I knew from previous experience, oil paint gets terribly slimy over a photograph and it's a slow process laying down colour for the sole purpose of getting a surface to work on. Another retarding factor was the need to paint in such a way that I wouldn't lose what I'd got of Gaitskell – a hasty underpainting would have lost my advantage. So the angry violent painting was curbed by these reins but an interestingly nasty paint quality began to emerge. Although it was tortuously arrived at it did begin to have a Famous Monster *feeling about it. The colour is unpleasantly reminiscent of those portraits you see in the windows of print shops and suburban framemakers of oriental ladies with green or blue faces.*

1 Hugh Gaitskell, press photo

2 *The Phantom of the Opera,* 1943

4 *Jack the Ripper,* 1959

6 *The Creature from the Black Lagoon*

The Creature with the Atom Brain, 1959

Master make-up artist Dick Smith creates *Dorian Gray*

[1] The relief was subsequently translated into a casting in aluminium and electroplated with copper. A mottled green patina was encouraged.

Enough time now has been spent on A Portrait of Hugh Gaitskell as a Famous Monster of Filmland *(7) so I shall leave it at that. It isn't a four foot square expressionistic painting of a satirically conceived subject. But I have a throw-away toy relief plus a painting which doesn't induce the depressing frustration of knowing that the end result is a total failure: in spite of the fact that it doesn't measure up to a daydream.*

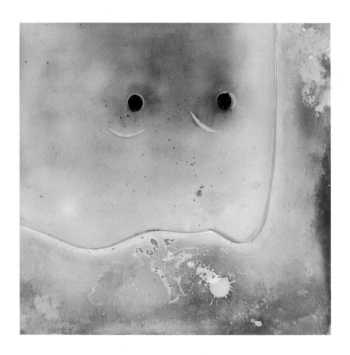

5 Study for *Portrait of Hugh Gaitskell as a Famous Monster of Filmland,* 1963–70

Desk, 1964

Interiors

One of the First Year excercises I set at Newcastle involved collecting large-scale collage material; billposting firms and cinemas were the best sources for this. After these forays the art school was littered with large poster sheets, offcuts and discarded pieces. Among the stuff coincidentally acquired from cinemas were old publicity stills and, wandering through the empty classrooms one evening I almost trod on a still from the film *Shockproof* (directed by Douglas Sirk, screenplay by Samuel Fuller) – one of dozens on the floor but this had a fascination that I spent some time analysing.

Everything in the photograph converged on a girl in a 'new look' coat who stared out slightly to right of camera. A very wide-angle lens must have been used because the perspective seemed distorted; but the disquiet of the scene was due to two other factors. It was a film set, not a real room, so wall surfaces were not explicitly conjoined; and the lighting came from several different sources. Since the scale of the room had not become unreasonably enlarged, as one might expect from the use of a wide-angle lens, it could be assumed that false perspective had been introduced to counteract its effect – yet the foreground remained emphatically close and the recession extreme. All this contributed more to the foreboding atmosphere than the casually observed body lying on the floor, partially concealed by a desk. I made three collaged studies and two paintings based on this image of an interior –ominous, provocative, ambiguous; a confrontation with which the spectator is familiar yet not at ease.

My involvement with the domestic interior theme began in the '50s with a collage entitled *Just what is it that makes today's homes so different, so appealing?* It developed in the '60s as a result of a chance encounter with a film still. I have recently resumed the subject after a long pause, though some intervening pictures did have a relationship with the genre. I made still-life paintings and these are, in a sense, interior details. Another picture that almost fits the category is *I'm dreaming of a white Christmas* but an emphatic human presence makes it more a 'portrait'. Most other paintings since those first interiors dealt with the exterior world, whether they were about people or buildings or nature.

Bibliography: 27, 62

Still from *Shockproof*

The earlier interiors relied heavily on collage of ready-made material from magazines. If something larger than its printed size was required I had to resort to photographic enlargement and that necessitated a switch to black and white. Colour printing from my own photographs was tempting since it seemed to offer a greater freedom of scale; given original transparencies or negatives I might have a more flexible source and a better control of quality. During the last two years[1] I have used a camera frequently on my travels and a few shots – made with no serious attempt at photographic quality in themselves for they were seen only as elements that might contribute to a whole – proved useful.

In the event the new interiors often played the art game, but this involvement with other artists' art, either as homage or parody, is more fortuitous than contrived. I found myself naïvely surprised that the photographs of unpopulated rooms were usually provided with their special focus and that this could often be no more than a framed picture. In the way that a human presence in a room will dominate the space with its strong psychological magnetism, a painting, or some other artistic manifestation will draw attention and command its environment; this occurs in a depicted room also, whether the treatment is highly stylised or not and it is especially true of paintings that embody a human figure, or a representation of a figure within that representation. The Berlin interior subject, initially collaged from photographs taken in René Block's apartment, has at its centre a framed picture of a man's head. It looks like a photograph but it is, in fact, a painted simulation of one by Gerhard Richter. Several friends, looking at my collage have instinctively asked 'who is the man' – on the face of it an irrelevant question but it is one which confirms my conviction of the portrait's dramatic importance.

In bringing together works that could reasonably be labelled 'Interior' I found that art was as often the subject as that they were about rooms. I happened to use part of a colour supplement feature for *Interior I*. A colourful impressionist painting in the background of the photograph, which showed Madame Manet in her own drawing room, became a series of drab greens, greys and ochres quite unlike the Berthe Morisot

[1] 1978–80

original. So a secondary concern of my painting was this transformation of a work of art into a new image by the processing it receives through photography and printing and back again into painting. Its complement *Interior II* also contains references to art, including a patch of blue to signify an Yves Klein monochrome, a trick which recurs in *Interior with monochromes*.

A different procedure operated when I was invited to contribute to a portfolio in homage to Picasso published by the Propylaen Press. Paraphrasing of Picasso's many styles was the primary idea rather than an incident in a larger context and Velázquez's great interior painting *Las Meniñas* must have been hanging around in my head waiting for some loving attention. A predilection for the interior theme no doubt lead me, unconsciously, to van Eyck for the basis of the poster to the National Gallery exhibition 'The artist's eye'.

Any interior is a set of anachronisms, a museum, with the lingering residues of decorative styles that an inhabited space collects. Banal or beautiful, exquisite or sordid, each says a lot about its owner and something about humanity in general. They can be dreary or warm and touching, on occasion, inspiring; all tell a story and the narrative can be enthralling; some even give us a little lesson in art appreciation.

Interior 1, 1964. The painting has an inlaid mirror behind Patricia
Knight's right arm. The empahtic red and blue is probably the reflection
of part of a painting in the room in which it was photographed.

Notes on photographs

I've always been an old-style artist, a fine artist in the commonly accepted sense; that was my student training and that's what I've remained. I made abstract pictures at one time until, in the mid '50s, like a good many other painters, I began to move back to figuration. The return to nature came at second-hand through the use of magazines rather than as a response to real landscape or still-life objects or painting a person from life. Somehow it didn't seem necessary to hold on to that older tradition of direct contact with the world. Magazines, or any visual intermediary, could as well provide a stimulus.

It's a matter of gaining a wider view – an extension of the landscape – that makes an artist look to the mass media for source material. The Cubists had adopted a multiplicity of viewpoint of their subject by moving around it. In the '50s we became aware of the possibility of seeing the whole world, at once, through the great visual matrix that surrounds us; a synthetic, 'instant' view. Cinema, television, magazines, newspapers immersed the artist in a total environment and this new visual ambience was photographic; reportage rather than art photography in the main.

Photography is a medium with its own conventions though we treat its products as a truth less flexible than hand-done art. Yet photographs of a given scene can be as unlike each other as each might be from a painting of that scene. Choice of lens and control of focus through aperture selection can extract widely differing images from a single viewpoint. Some of our attitudes to the camera are, even now, a hundred years after its invention, a little naïve. We tend to think of the photograph as being a kind of truth. We like to think of it as what the eye sees, but that can be far from the case. A camera is a very different optical device from the human eye, different in subtle yet significant ways. For example, camera lenses focus on a plane and an undecipherable blur can sandwich this sharp layer. Then, the print is often retouched, especially if it is to be reproduced. Somewhere in a process engraving studio a hand modifies with pigments, stains and acids. Graphic artists are continually painting the photograph to transform it into a more printable image or to bring it closer to someone's preconception. In fact, a distinction between camera work and painting hardly operates in a

Bibliography: 35, 40, 49, 52. This is an amalgam of several overlapping texts on the theme.

good deal of photographic magazine and advertising material – whether it be retouching to enforce or modify information or handcraft in the making of blocks for printing. One reason for the high cost of colour reproduction is the amount of skilled hand treatment required in colour processing. The marriage of brush and lens can be intriguing. Strangely enough, the point at which art most crucially meets photography is the area which has long been tinged with acrimony – retouching the photograph (even cropping the print) is regarded by a 'true' photographer as a dubious activity.

Artists 'copying' photographs, or using them as a ground for a painting are playing an even fouler game (the rules of the Royal Academy Summer Exhibition specifically forbid what they call 'vignettes' – painting on a photograph). The stigma attached to the use of photography by painters has faded (not without some rear-guard action – there was all that fuss about photography and screenprints some years ago) and the ground is clear for some fruitful interaction.

I often had recourse to photographic enlargements for collaged details in earlier paintings. The photographic aspect of these contributions was not, in itself, an objective – sometimes it was necessary to make an enlargement from an element that was too small in its magazine source for direct use. Occasionally there were advantages to be gained from making painted additions over the photograph before enlargement. Inevitably, with great scale increases from small originals, mechanical reproduction screen asserted their textural qualities. Sometimes photographic ideas and techniques (i.e. differential focus) were imitated with paint. A number of avenues have been followed since then; exploring the possible relationships of painted marks, and marks resulting from the interaction of light and photosensitive emulsions.

In the '60s many painters adopted photography as part of their medium. Artists were using the camera to make a frank transference of imagery onto their canvasses – as Rauschenberg and Warhol had done. Direct photographic techniques, through half-tone silkscreen for example, have made a new contribution to the painter's medium. In my own case there was a time when I felt that I would like to see how close to photography I could stay yet still be a painter in intent. I borrowed an image from Braun which was not merely a photograph but one that was also very stylish in that sense. The modifications made to it were airbrushed stains applied to the surface in such a way that the photographic quality was not disturbed, colouring it as a retoucher would to keep its integrity. *Still-life* does as little as can be to interfere with the photographic essence of the original.

At the same time there was another painting on which the marks were made in direct opposition to photographic quality. *My Marilyn* is that other extreme. Marilyn Monroe demanded that the results of photographic sessions be submitted to her for vetting before publication. She made indications, brutally and beautifully in conflict with the image, on proofs and transparencies to give approval or reject; or suggestions for retouching that might make them acceptable. After her death some were published (there was a batch by George Barris in *Town,* others, by Bert Stern, in *Eros)* with her markings – crosses and ticks, notes for retouching, instructions to the photographer, even the venting of physical aggression by attacking the emulsion with nail-file or scissors. There is a fortuitous narcissism to be seen for the negating cross is also the childish symbol for a kiss; but the violent obliteration of her own image has a self-destructive implication that made her death all the more poignant. *My Marilyn* starts with her signs and elaborates the possibilities these suggest. *Still-life* and *My Marilyn* were made concurrently, as opposites – in one case the photograph pure and intact, (at least ostensibly so), and the other an outrageous interference – the handmade mark in savage conflict with the photograph.

It's an old obsession of mine to see conventions mix – I like the difference between a diagram and a photograph and a mark which is simply sensuous paint, even the addition of real, or simulations of real, objects. These relationships multiply the levels of meaning and ways of reading. The more recent uses that I've made of photography stem from the possibilities inherent in these two works.

The contrast between *Still-life* and *My Marilyn* is confirmed in their compositional treatment. *Still-life* is, unlike the works that precede it (apart from *Epiphany),* an entity. In the earlier paintings idioms had been mixed in a self-conscious manner to retain the individuality of elements – they are anthologies. 'Still-life' is not composite in that way. The Marilyn painting is unlike previous pictures in that there is an avoidance of a unifying perspective. The individual shots are spread across the panel like a comic strip, four photographs, each repeated three times on a different scale – perspective is respected only within each frame. The painting was also an excuse for a physical involvement with paint itself. A screenprint with the same title arrived at similar plastic ends through the use of process photography and received no hand-working by me, other than masking. *Landscape* spans the disparities of *My Marilyn* and *Still-life* in one picture. There are painted marks quite unrelated to the subject; in other places the application of colour amounts to a simple phototint job. The source was a postcard remarkable only for the fact that it was hand-tinted, colour had been applied to each copy by hand and each was marginally different. There was no aggression, just a sheer abandoned dabbing on of dyes in arbitrary haste. I was fortunate enough to find the original negative in the library of the biggest aerosurvey company and ordered an eight foot long print of the area showing in the postcard. 'Painting' consisted of adding many different types of marks to the print, starting with a loose filling-in of fields with tints and on to marks which bear no relation to the photograph at all. Trees, in one part, are fabricated from paint-soaked sponge, some tiny houses are made in false perspective from balsa wood.

Postcards have their own fascination. Since *Landscape* they have provided material for several works with figures on a beach as their subject. Usually they are taken at such a distance that the people, so important in the scene, are oblivious of their contribution. One postcard, of the beach at Whitley Bay, has produced several variations, a medium-sized painting, a print on a photographic base, a postcard, a one-off 'multiple' and the cover for the March 1969 issue of *Studio International.* This particular postcard is itself a true photographic print without an intruding reproduction screen. It was examined in many degrees of enlargement for *People* dated 1965–66: it is one of a series of explorations into

My Marilyn, 1965

Still-life, 1965

Landscape, 1965

the legibility of a photographic image degraded by gross enlargement. Photographs such as this, of a heavily populated beach in the north of England, can show a random sample of humanity. When broken down and analysed they can provide an incredible amount of information about individuals and their activity. There is, however, a breaking-point, a stage at which the emulsion is too large to absorb the imprint of form. It was a search for this moment of loss that became the real subject of the series.

Small areas of photographs were also investigated for *Whitley Bay* and *Trafalgar Square* to satisfy a curiosity about the ability of certain configuration to hold a thin dilution of human personality. The process of magnification inevitably introduces doubts about the veracity of what we call photographic. In being taken nearer the carrier of the image we become more aware of its characteristics as a medium. The type of emulsion, half-tone screens, the interventions of a retoucher's hand, all become more apparent and contribute more to the quality of an image which, on a different scale, may be unquestionably photographic. Somehow these fractionated representations, grossly deteriorated through the enlarger and adulterated by processing for reproduction, retain a contact with and a power to evoke the bodies that originated them. *People* touches the fringe of that perception, the shallow edge between recognition and abstraction. *Trafalgar Square* lets the rich visual qualities of the degraded fragment provide extensions into the impressionist sensuality it parallels.

The fascination that photographs hold for me lies in just this allusive power of the camera's imagery. I find it astonishing that a flick of a shutter over a coating of silver emulsion can snatch so much information about that milli-second of activity over half a mile of beach at Whitley Bay one summer's day. As this texture of anonymous humanity is penetrated, it yields more fragments of knowledge about individuals isolated within it as well as endless patterns of group relationships. Ultimately, enlargement takes us into unreadable, abstract clumps of silver halides. The attempts of some non-figurative artists to create paintings or objects without external reference (however admirable the results) seem to me to be not only futile but retrograde. I marvel that marks and

shapes, simple or complex, have the capacity to enlarge consciousness, can allude back to an ever-widening history of mankind, can force emotional responses as well as aesthetic ones and permit both internal and external associations to germinate the imagination of the spectator.

I suppose that I am much more concerned with ideas about paint than with paint for its own sake, or even a subject for its own sake. The reason for becoming involved with Bing Crosby in the negative colour painting called *I'm dreaming of a white Christmas* was not a nostalgic affection for Bing Crosby films, rather it was that the painting was quite demanding technically and it also offered some metaphysical exploitation. It follows from a Duchampian idea about everything having an opposite. Scientific thought is now being directed at the notion that every particle has a negative particle partner and that a non-world exists adjacent to our world; that this world has as real an existence, in an opposite phase, as the one we experience. It's nice to be able to see a ready-made token of that reversal of our normal perception in the form of a photographic negative. The painting of a negative colour frame from a Bing Crosby film can take us a little closer, in a symbolic way, to that looking-glass world. The idea that Bing in negative becomes racially reversed is amusing too (the song from the film makes an apt title for the painting) – he becomes an American Negro. His clothes, colour reversed, are more bizarre; he wears a black shirt and white hat, a yellow cardigan and a light blue coat – unlikely for Bing. The change is such that we think of him as a much more racy figure than the one we know. The exterior seen through a window is lurid too, the normally blue sky is orange, the green trees red. This is disturbing but not surrealistic. In many ways the scene becomes that much more magical and mysterious and beautiful and more rewarding when meditated upon than the scene as we would normally know it.

I would like to think that I am questioning reality. Photography is just one way, albeit the most direct, by which physical existence can modulate a two-dimensional surface. Painting has long been concerned with the paradox of informing about a multi-dimensional world on the limited dimensionality of a canvas. Assimilating photography into the domain of paradox, incorporating it into the philosophical contradictions of art is as much my concern as embracing its alluring potential as a medium. It's necessary, at the moment, to pry out a whole new set of relationships. After all, photography (perhaps we should establish a broader base and think of what I am talking about as lens-formulated images, whatever the chemistry or electronics involved) is still fairly new compared with the long tradition of painting and there are many adjustments of thinking yet to be made.

Bathers II, 1967

People, 1965–66

Panavision 70 mm negative frame from Paramount's film *Holiday Inn* starring Bing Crosby

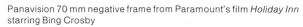

Colour negative of R H with negative colour *I'm dreaming of a white Christmas* painting, photo: Rita Donagh

I'm dreaming of a black Christmas, collotype and screenprint 1971

I'm dreaming of a white Christmas, 1967

Object/Multiple

Still-life relates to the 'ready-made'. Whereas Duchamp's ready-mades were chosen with a deliberate avoidance of concern with the aesthetic merits of the object, *Still-life* takes a highly stylized photograph of an example of high style in consumer goods to raise the question: 'Does the neutrality of Duchamp or the studied banality, even vulgarity, of the subject-matter in most American Pop Art significantly exclude those products of mass culture which might be the choice of a NY Museum of Modern Art 'Good Design' committee from our consideration? This was a factor also in the use of the Guggenheim Museum as a theme for art.

By the time I made *Toaster* the habit of working a print simultaneously with a painting was well established. The print on the toaster theme is less a version than a natural corollary of it. My interest in process, aesthetic or technical, had led me to make a series of studies and reliefs which echoed, through analogy in painter's terms, the design and construction of a building. Similarly, the *Toaster* painting equates with the appliance, and the print[1] metaphors the public relations vehicle for it. The text is an important part of this work not only for its visual quality (conjunctions of word and image are fundamental to the manner of presentation in the field depicted) but in the way it provides information and tunes the aesthetic response as only the explicitness of words can do. The text was not written by me but was compiled and adapted from Braun advertising brochures.

The Documenta print, *The critic laughs,* was initiated by a 'ready-made' object, or to be more precise in our Duchampian terminology a 'ready-made assisted'. It is an association of two mass produced objects – a Braun electric toothbrush and a giant-sized set of teeth made from sugar (a confection to be found in the English seaside resort, Brighton, which exemplifies the darker side of British humour). This conjunction immediately reminded me of Jasper Johns' 'sculpmetal' toothbrush which carries molars instead of bristles. His title *The critic smiles* seemed too mild for the grotesque shudder of electrically animated teeth – even *The critic laughs* doesn't quite accommodate this hysteria.

The electric toothbrush and vibrating sugar teeth were photographed with the help of Euan Duff. A Kodacolor

Bibliography: 35, 40, 48, 49, 50, 52

Toaster, 1966–67

[1] See page 90.

The critic laughs, offset litho etc., 1968

The critic laughs, multiple, 1971–72

print followed and was heavily retouched. From this came an offset litho print, laminated to regain the photographic character, to which additional hand-painted marks were applied. Thus there were three possible points at which paint might intrude: on the object itself, on the photographic print, and on the offset litho print. Sugar teeth are a little unhygienic for the permanent needs of art. They 'sweated' in certain weather conditions and began to crystalise and crumble away with time. They are also a little heavy for the small motor. Hans Sohm of Stuttgart, the great archivist of Fluxus and Happenings documentation (also a dentist), made an excellent model of the sugar teeth in dental plastic – chomically inert and lighter.

The laminated offset-litho version of the subject is, stylistically, in the nature of promotional material for the product. Multiple editioning of the object is an obvious development. As with all consumer products, packaging and presentation posed subsequent problems – to be solved by the design of a case, styled and made, in the manner of the box for the Braun 'sixtant' electric razor. Product, package and promotional matter is the cycle of the consumer goods industries. Nothing in my experience and practice suggests that this same cycle does not apply to that category of human activity we label 'art'.

At the time of writing the last paragraph I had not realized that an instruction book and guarantee card would be necessary to complete the analogue – of course, art usually comes without a guarantee.

After a gap of nine years I had the good fortune to extend the metaphor further and take it to a splendid conclusion. The British Broadcasting Corporation invited me to make a contribution to 'The Shock of the New', a series of programmes on art since 1880, written and presented by Robert Hughes. The interview form did not appeal to me so I proposed that the BBC should make a 'commercial' for one of my products. To my surprise the idea was approved so the scripting and filming of a short sequence in the style of a TV commercial advertising The critic laughs *was undertaken.*

This is the plot. A svelte and beautiful young lady bears the gift-wrapped multiple to the bathroom where her partner is about to shave. She carries the box ceremonially, as an Egyptian high priestess might support a sacred talisman, and presents it to her lover. Surprised, slightly awed, he lifts the lid of the exquisitely wrought case to disclose giant teeth and an electric toothbrush. They are assembled, a look of amused disbelief crosses his features as he switches on, and realizes that the vibrating object is more for Her than Him. She smiles slyly as the tip of her tongue glides sexily along her lip.

The 'voice-over' says this:

For connoisseurs who have everything. . . .at last, a work of art to match the style of modern loving. . . . .*The critic laughs* . . . .a perfect marriage of form and function. . . .created for you and yours by Europe's caring craftsmen in an exclusive edition of only sixty examples. . . .*The critic laughs*. . . .Feel the thrill of owning. . . .*The critic laughs.*

Hamilton is proud to present its new multiple. . . .

The critic laughs . . . . by Hamilton.

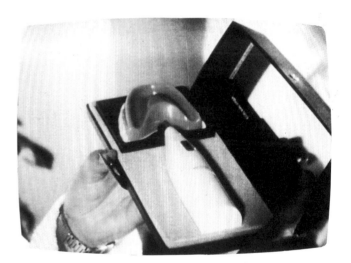

Loraine Chase as 'Her' in the ' TV Commercial' in the BBC production *The Shock of the New*, 1980

The 'product' as advertised

Lux Corporation, manufacturers of some of the finest amplifiers in the Hi-Fi market, approached me in 1973 to discuss the possibility of my making a work of art to celebrate the fiftieth anniversary of the founding of the company in 1925. The proposal was that I might clad one of their production amplifiers in some 'Pop' sculptural treatment.

After a little resistance to the idea I went to Japan to consult with Lux more directly. During the fourteen-hour journey I realized that my reluctance to become involved was due to the fact that my interests lie less in three-dimensional objects than in the representation of form on a two-dimensional surface. As a painter, it is the area of illusion and paradox that concerns me.

The first question that I asked when I reached the factory in Osaka was 'How thin can an amplifier be made?' The limiting factor, it transpired, was the length of a three-way switch that it was convenient to use. This determined a thickness of 7 cms. We decided that 1 metre square would accommodate my image and also be adequate for the components of an amplifier of 75 watts per channel. Lux wanted the operational concept to be mine also so I devised a control panel that would satisfy my own domestic needs for Hi-Fi.

Although the artwork includes a tuner it is necessary to plug in a power supply, speakers and other ancillary equipment such as phono decks, tape decks, headphones, etc. I included an 'input/output' section as part of the image. This has two advantages. First, it makes the equipment very easy to use since all connexions are accessible from the front, but I also liked the idea of 'plugging in' to a work of art festooned with links to a used environment. One of the attractions of the scheme for me was the production of a picture that might establish a sensory intimacy with its owner. Every day, perhaps every hour, I touch my radio or record player. Maybe a similar rapport could be achieved with a painting.

Built into the conception of the piece is the hope that obsolescence of the technology, or the inevitable drift towards malfunction and decay, would not affect its validity as a work of art. It remains 'art' and its durability will lie in its strength, or weakness, as such – it has an

equal chance of survival in a museum with any other of my painted images.

1975, Lux's anniversary year, has come and gone. The change in the economic climate, but also the, perhaps over-ambitious, nature of the project has slowed completion. By 1980 a prototype should be functioning.

The Lux project, begun in 1973, was intended for production in a limited edition in 1975. The scheme has been abandoned. Only a full-size, nonfunctioning mock-up and a working prototype exist.

Lux executives, world agents and R H in Osaka, 1977

Study for 'Lux 50' – II, 1976

Study for 'Lux 50' – IV, 1976

Lux 50, 1973–79. Functioning prototype

Romanticism

Soft pink landscape derives from a group of Andrex advertisements. These were very evident in the colour supplements in the early '60s introducing the new range of coloured toilet papers then being marketed. 'Soft pink' or 'Soft blue' with the particular colour quality suffusing the whole image – always that of two girls equivocally posed in a forest glade.

Nature is beautiful. Pink from a morning sun filters through a tissue of autumn leaves. Golden shafts gleam through the perforated vaulting of the forest to illuminate a stage set-up for the Sunday supplement voyeur. Andrex discreetly presents a new colour magazine range. A pink as suggestively soft as last week's blue – soft as pink flesh under an Empire négligé. The woodland equipped with every convenience. A veil of soft focus vegetation screens the peeper from the sentinel. Poussin? Claude? No, more like Watteau in its magical ambiguity.

Sometimes advertisements make me wax quite poetical. None more so than the series by Andrex showing two young ladies in the woods. I have, on occasions, tried to put into words that peculiar mixture of reverence and cynicism that 'Pop' culture induces in me and that I try to paint. I suppose that a balancing of these reactions is what I used to call non-Aristotelian or, alternatively, cool.

I was having lunch with friends in New York recently (September 1980, nine years after making the first Soft pink landscape *study and perhaps eighteen years after first encountering the Andrex ads), with Bridget Riley sitting at my side. She teased me about my habitual plagiarism – even of her work. The plagiarism is self-confessed, though I couldn't remember any adoption of Op ideas, except in* Epiphany *and that isn't exactly Bridget's style; I was really confused. It turned out that the Andrex ads of girls in the woods that I found so inspiring were conceived by Bridget Riley when she worked at the J Walter Thompson advertising agency. I've always said that some advertising showed signs of genius but who would have thought that the particular genius at work here was her's.*

Bridget Riley's haunting vision set me off on the path of romance; two classes of postcard spurred me on. Flowers and sunsets were added to the forest scene to

Bibliography: 49, 50, 53, 54, 55, 56

" UN DES EFFETS DES EAUX DE MIERS "

make a balmy triplet. Subsidiary material was fed in here and there. By coincidence, a rash of squatting girls appeared in the fashion magazines. The pose probably began as a space-filling idea – it must have been about getting a long, thin, human body into the format of a magazine without wasting too much space. The bland, empty stare used by fashion models seemed entirely appropriate to the squatting posture.

Another motif that came to my attention at the time derived from Miers. In almost any village café in the south west corner of France you might come across a postcard, in several variants, of a group of young people defecating in the woods – it's a jolly scene, picnic baskets, newspapers, parasols; skirts up, trousers down, everyone taken with a silmultaneous urge. The display of charmingly dimpled bums was designed to bring to public attention the healthily laxative waters of a small spa in the valley of the Lot.

Some resistance was encountered when the group of paintings, studies and prints was first exhibited. Nick Serota had turned the show down for the Museum of Modern Art in Oxford on the grounds that it would not be of sufficient interest to the undergraduates. Having accepted it for the Serpentine, the Arts Council cancelled the show, until I proposed that they actually ask the parks Commissioners if they would be offended by the work instead of assuming that they would – in the event, the Commissioners were less squeamish than the Arts Council. Once exhibited, the critics regarded the paintings as evidence either of a kinky sexual aberration (I hadn't thought of the work as erotic, but who knows about art critics) or an early onset of senility.

The group has its profounder meanings as well as its kitsch aspects. Among several sunsets was a sunrise postcard view of Cadaques. The giant turd, common to all of the series, smothers the church, a central feature of the small town. Jung, in his Memories, Dreams, Reflections, describes a reverie which he felt to be of great personal significance. He says 'I saw before me the cathedral, the blue sky. God sits on His golden throne, high above the world – and from under the throne an enormous turd falls upon the sparkling new roof, shatters it, and breaks the walls of the cathedral asunder.'

Andrex ad, circa 1960

Mary Quant ad

Postcard from Miers

Soft blue landscape, 1973–1980

Flower-piece III, 1973

Polaroid portraits

The first time I used a Polaroid camera was in January 1960 when I presented a lecture at the ICA in London entitled 'Glorious Technicolor, breathtaking Cinemascope and stereophonic sound' (it had the subtitle 'technical developments in the entertainment industries in the fifties'). Edwin Land had given a camera to the photography department at Newcastle University; I borrowed it on each occasion that I gave the talk and demonstrated it by photographing the audience. It was magical to take a photograph and have the instant result passed from hand to hand. It was unlikely they had seen, or heard of, the Polaroid Land camera before.

The Polaroid portraits project started in New York in March 1968. The cameras were becoming fashionable, people were buying them. It was a successful commercial product, a hit on the market in a big way. Roy Lichtenstein had his new toy which he demonstrated by photographing me in his studio and giving me the result. Shortly afterwards I went to Canada and found myself in Vancouver visiting a guy called Iain Baxter (N E Thing Co) who also had a Polaroid. Naturally he photographed me, so I had another souvenir. I was quite pleased to see that in both cases an example of the artist's own work was visible in the picture. I was seen in front of both a Lichtenstein and a Baxter work.

When I got back to London I thought that it might make an amusing project to get a Polaroid camera myself so that I could ask artist friends to 'take a photograph of me'. In the earlier requests I asked them in their own studio so that their own work would be represented in the background; even Jim Dine's photograph shows me standing in front of a Christmas tree with cut-out stars and other decorations which he regarded as his artwork. Later it seemed less important to have the artist's own work in the photograph. It may have been at the time that Barry Flanagan took one; in the picture that pleased him most I was sitting at a table with a drink, about to have a meal and there was no art around. So I began to forget about the artist's own artefact being included in the picture – the Polaroid was his work. Slowly I began to establish, to my own satisfaction anyway, that what the artist did with this very immediate tool does really present his own personality. It might be only a simple snapshot but the hand of the artist would

The above is a rehash of recorded conversations including one with G J Lischka published in *Das Sofortbild Polaroid,* October 1977, and another, unpublished, with Elizabeth Glazebrook in August 1972.

Photo: Man Ray

be revealed because it was holding the camera. The important thing was simply the association of a particular finger on the button with a particular moment.

As time went by it became apparent that other people as well as I began to read into these images a bigger significance. They would say 'Ah yes, you can see that this one is by Jasper Johns because it looks like a flag – this blue band of sky and the very horizontal stripe effect.' Maybe it was a bit silly to think of Jasper having that specific a vision when he's just holding a camera and taking a snap in a very casual, friendly atmosphere but people did read these things into the results. Finally when Francis Bacon photographed me, after saying that he had never used a camera before (he is not interested in photography as a medium for himself but is obsessed by photographic material made by others), he hardly knew which way to point the lens. He was swaying about and slightly tipsy, yet the first picture was just like a Bacon painting – accidental movement of both camera and subject produced a blurred, multi-viewpoint image. He wasn't happy with it and went on to do others. At that point it seemed clear that the artist does have a specific kind of eye, an attitude that will direct the image in an entirely personal way. Even if it is the first photograph he takes it may have some quality that is recognisably his, consciously or not. Some artists, in any case, are very aware of what they are doing when they look through a viewfinder – Jim Rosenquist revealed himself as a Polaroid virtuoso as soon as he took hold of the camera. Something seems to happen when the artist is merely holding the instrument and pressing the button. A choice is made, a thoughtful decision, even though a marginal one; that's the thing that I now find most interesting. The quality isn't so important, very few of the artists involved would think of it as a 'work' in any serious sense; in most instances it is done in a very casual way, like an autograph, but because the Polaroid is an amusing device it is more fun than making a signature with a pen.

But, it can be more serious than that too. Andy Warhol must have taken fifty photographs before he was satisfied (even then it was more a question of being sated than a realization of success). The studio floor was littered with Polaroid material, some shots were not separated and nobody knew how long they had been 'cooking' (60 second photography went by the board); there was complete chaos. He was going on because he loves making Polaroids – it's a great game and he obviously gets a kick out of being able to produce images with so little effort. Brigid Polk, who joined us for the session, is also a dedicated Polaroid artist. Andy told me that she had given up a drug habit for the Polaroid habit, she couldn't afford both. She knows the camera extremely well and has a sensitive relationship with it; a technician of a high order.

Three of the contributors to the first two volumes published are great masters of the art of photography, and it shows. It doesn't need much imagination to see that the Man Ray Polaroid has a touch of his genius. Cartier Bresson's has a characteristic unforced brilliance – he knows exactly when his subject is at ease. It takes a little background knowledge to appreciate the craftsmanship of Ugo Mulas's picture – it never fails to move me. We were old friends when I visited him in his bedroom in Milan, he was dying of cancer, kept from pain with drugs. He wanted a happy picture and his skill was such that, even in the awful circumstances that we were both acutely aware of, he was able to make me laugh at the lens. A few weeks later he was dead.

It's an easy enough thing to do, yet I believe there are some marginal decisions on my part also. You hand a camera to someone and say 'take a photograph of me'. The only influence I can have (apart from a little manipulation) is in the choice of whom I ask and when; a contriving of the relationship of one photograph to the other in the sequence; that is the only control I have, editing. Why a picture of me? There is only one common denominator in all these situations, one individual who is always, of necessity, there. I realize how silly, how banal, I often look. The same face and figure constantly reappearing (though it ages over the years); I am embarrassed by it in some ways. I can bear it because it is necessary to have a binding theme for the books and I pay the price by suffering the humiliation of being photographed, I submit to the will of the photographer rather than make the more aggressive demand of photographing him or her.

Printmaking

I have always thought of myself as a print-maker as well as a painter. While at the Royal Academy Schools in 1938 I made prints from celluloid sheets scratched with a dry-point tool. The RA had an arrangement whereby its students could attend print-making classes at the Central School of Arts and Crafts. Etching was my first love as a print medium, its rudimentary techniques were learned at the Central; by the time I left the Slade I felt something of a virtuoso. Even in the period between, my mind was not far from the medium; the studies for a set of illustrations to James Joyce's Ulysses *were conceived for etching.*

It was intended to make an engraving for each chapter of the book but the project was abandoned when no publisher could be found. Most of my drawings and watercolours are studies for paintings or prints – as the prints themselves are often studies or adjuncts of paintings. The *Ulysses* drawings are an exception in that, though fairly large, they are composed for a different, necessarily smaller, scale.

The chapters, or episodes, of *Ulysses* are treated in various literary styles by Joyce. Indeed, one chapter alone, that dealing with the maternity home (Horne's house), goes from the birth of language through a chronology of historical styles to modern vernacular. I planned to make a pictorial equivalent of Joyce's stylistic leaps.

A predilection for diversity of media from drawing to drawing, and a diversity of media within a single drawing, has established itself as an oddly unifying factor. As time goes by I become increasingly aware of the irrelevance of making a distinction between one medium and another, or one process and another, or even one style and another.

My first one-man exhibition was a show of Reaper *engravings at Gimpel Fils in 1951. These exploited a great many of the possibilities of working on copper. There were about twenty 'variations', and the idea was that they should be a demonstration of different techniques as well as being a set of variations of the physical configuration of the machine. The plates were made at the Slade – their style and treatment slots them perfectly into the pre-Festival of Britain provincial art scene.*

Bibliography: 44, 46, 49, 53

Figure composition, 1939

Reaper (i), 1949

There must be over fifty plates before *Structure,* a print which I now see as the beginning of real invention in the medium. The image relates to a student phase of painting, elementary in its plastic content, which explored the primary paradox of paint – the supremacy of surface organization of the canvas, and the inevitability of three-dimensional readings ensuing from the articulation of that surface with marks. Technically the print is quite ingenious, for the ink is held by combinations of aquatint and deeply etched cavities, some of which are asymmetrically formed to provide gradations when wiped in the right direction.

Heteromorphism coincides with the *Growth and Form* Exhibition; indeed, the print was used for the cover of the ICA catalogue. The wealth of biological material that I encountered, in a way the essential stuff of life, affected the identity of any mark made – the main purpose of which had previously been to specify a position on the rectangle. Whereas the indications of *Structure* are anonymous, skeletal components, the individual marks of *Heteromorphism,* though equally 'basic', are strongly identified as types of form (or as typical of process) and their relationship as strongly implies a space available for occupation.

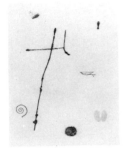

Each of the seven forms is executed with a different technical means so the print has the appearance of a sheet of samples. The 'perspective' or environmental suggestion of the total image results from placing aerial or mobile forms towards the top and the more earth bound or liquid forms at the bottom.

Done at about the same time, *Self-portrait* is a humorous comment on the Darwinian idea of very complex (both structurally and psychologically) entities evolving from the simplest life forms. A human head is compounded of features representing primitive organisms (bull sperm, sea-urchin, flat-worm, etc.). As is the case with *Heteromorphism* a variety of techniques (hard-ground and soft-ground etching, engraving, dry-point, aquatint, punches) are used to keep the elements separate and retain their individual character.

This device has proved important to me in a great deal of later work, whether print, drawing or painting. The making of a new unity of unlikely parts from different sources is the crucial idea behind collage, a key feature

Structure, etching, 1950

Heteromorphism, etching, 1951

Self-portrait, etching, 1951

re-Nude etching, 1954

of 20th century art in almost any medium. Collage, bits stuck together, is fundamental to film-making (as Eisenstein understood better than anybody); film can hardly be made in real time except as a fragment. Picasso invented an application in sculpture. It has its place in music – John Cage may not use the term but his compositions demonstrate the concept of assemblage of discrete and identifiable parts. While putting this collection of words together I've been very reliant on scissors and paste.

In 1953 I began to teach in the Fine Art Department in the University at Newcastle. There were some facilities for etching there but no one was using them, so it was natural enough to set up an evening class for those students who wished to learn the craft. While teaching I started to work again in the medium – at first, with etched motion studies from Edweard Muybridge, and others from life; a double return signalled by the title *re Nude etching.*

We had three presses at Newcastle. As well as the etching press there was an ancient lithography press and an equally old Victorian letterpress. The only lithography I had experienced was as a student at the Central School of Arts and Crafts in 1939, when a technician took away the stone after the drawing had been made and we didn't see it again until it appeared with a proof.

I've never felt happy with lithography, the slippery flow of grease on stone is the antithesis of the resistance of copper to the cut of a burin. The chemistry of lithography seems less controllable, by me anyway, than the slower bite of acid into metal.

Aided by a book I began to experiment with the litho press to get it into operation. Because of my lack of skill in treating the stone the proofs degenerated with each pull. After the first proof the print failed to give the qualities as drawn on the stone. Two different drawings of the *Hommage à Chrysler Corp.* subject were made with only a few marginally satisfactory pulls from each. The proofs were treated with collage and given some hand-coloured additions to bring back some interest. My technical failures with lithography at this time proved so daunting that I now hold an irrational grudge against the medium.

In 1963 Christopher Prater was operating a small silk-screen establishment with one assistant. He was printing posters for the Arts Council of Great Britain and generally working on the fringe between commercial printing (small-quantity prototype jobs for design offices) and art publicity material, largely through Gordon House, one of our best typographic designers and an artist of standing. He had made some prints for Gordon and a few for Paolozzi when Gordon House suggested that I might do something at Kelpra Studio. He pointed out that the *Adonis* painting might be a convenient starting point.

To obtain money to cover the cost I sent a letter to friends. It was headed:

*BARGAIN OFFER ***** SATISFACTION GUARANTEED*

and said. . . .To make 40 prints I shall have to pay the printer £80. If I were to sell 20 signed prints in advance at £4 each, a ludicrously low figure, I could pay my bill and have 20 prints left to dispose of at a higher price (about £8) and derive some income from the venture.

I am writing to 25 friends in the expectation that 20 will wish to take advantage of the bargain offer. Let me know if you wish to subscribe. . . .Prints may be returned in lieu of payment if not satisfied.

I had made a primitive attempt at half-tone silk-screen with a poster for This is Tomorrow – *preparing the screen in the textile department at Newcastle. The photographic possibilities in the hands of an expert were exciting.*

Screenprint was an altogether changed medium by the time I came to it. The older methods of 'Serigraphy' were little used, except for making reproductions. The early system relied on stencils made by painting substances directly on the screen which are later washed out from an overall filler to allow the pigment through. Stencils made by the hardening of a gelatine emulsion when exposed to light transformed the craft to an industry. A new degree of accuracy became possible, which led to the development of precisely engineered printing machinery. The process is simple and fast – additional workings can be made indefinitely. Silkscreen inks have received a lot of attention, and nylon or metal mesh screens brought many advantages.

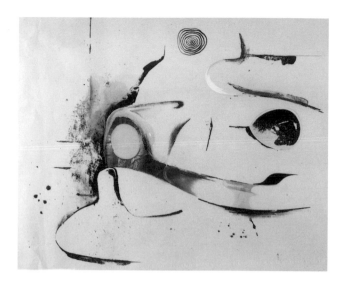

Hommage à Chrysler Corp. (b), touched lithograph, 1957

If the stencil is made by exposure to light through a film positive (today, even cutting is done on a film that will produce a positive to make a photo-stencil) then the hand will lose some of its importance in the process, and the medium will be exploited for its new potential. The appeal that the medium had for a new generation of artist print-makers was that it is less autographic than etching or litho – it hasn't their dependence on the hand of the artist and in that sense is a modern print-makers medium.

When moving among the various print media the artist will often come up against problems of polarity. Lateral reversal is the first hurdle to overcome in etching or litho. The novice print-maker is immediately confronted with the need to put down on the plate or stone a mirror image of his subject. This has been fundamental to the idea of print. The printing forme is the reverse of its imprint. Often, the print-maker will have to adjust to another contradiction, tone reversal. A painter thinks naturally in a positive sense. He draws black on white – the ground is normally light and he paints darker tones on it. Humans don't think in negative and it's hard for them to make a mental adjustment from one sense to another. The character of each print medium depends very much on inventions which utilize these relationships. The oppositions of left and right, light and dark, water and grease – these are the mechanics and the chemistry of print.

Things have changed in commercial printing. Positive plates are now made from positive films. Offset printing, becoming standard, uses laterally correct plates; a rubber-faced roller picks up the image in reverse and puts it back on the paper the right way round. The traditional craft techniques hold their old mystery.

The wonderful thing about silk-screen, as one soon discovers, is that its nature is natural. Ink isn't picked up from the face of raised metal, nor pulled from recesses cut or etched in metal, nor is it lifted from the surface of a stone or plate; it is pushed through the back of a screen, seen the right way round. When making a photographic stencil, a black drawn line will stop light from hardening the emulsion so it washes away and we are left with an opening in the screen through which the ink will pass. The simplicity of the medium, as far as the artist is *concerned, is that he gets what he sees, or what he draws, the right way round, and dark on light.*

My studio in the sixties always contained a Leica camera on a copying stand. It had a reflex attachment and bellows for extreme close-ups – basically a slide-making set-up. I became addicted to using it as a microscope to look at details of any printed material around – playing at making compositions. I looked at postcards a good deal for they are easy to handle and very available and I was less interested in subject matter than the print structure, the way the image is transmitted.

I had a Castelli poster, itself a caricature of the blow-up, for the Lichtenstein show of September '63 and I put this under the camera (just in passing, for everything was going that way). It proved surprisingly rewarding. It was possible to make interesting crops on the already magnified regular field of dots with its intrusion (at that scale) of alien marks. I made several negatives of carefully contrived selections from the print and then, as carefully, selected one of the enlargements to be converted back to a screenprint.

In a way my object was defeated. Enthusiasm for process photography had led me to suppose that the camera could do almost anything. Chris Prater soon discovered that my 35 mm negative could not produce a perfectly regular grid of dots. It was a little optimistic to suppose that the film plane would have been exactly parallel with the subject plane. The distortions were corrected by simply squaring up the grid on a drawing board and the dots (discs) were cut by hand.

The two-colour printing was not expensive so I was able to enjoy giving them to friends, always writing on the bottom *A little bit of Roy Lichtenstein for*, and then the name of the recipient.

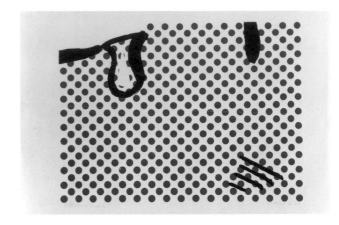

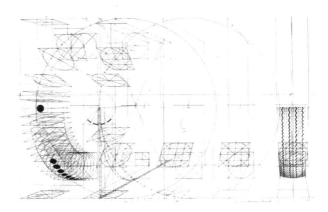

A little bit of Roy Lichtenstein for . . . . . ., screenprint, 1964

Five Tyres – abandoned, screenprint, 1964

There is a certain fascination for the artist in the way that commercial printers have succeeded in presenting a great range of colour on the printed sheet using only four inks: a yellow, a red (magenta), a blue (cyan), and black to control tonal modulation. It happens, of course, because the three colours are applied in small dots, now incredibly small, and in amounts that will mix optically to produce whatever colours are being matched in the source – the idea behind Impressionist painting techniques. The alternative method of creating more colours on the paper than pigments used is to print transparent inks, layering one flat tint over the other (see Kent State). The whiteness of the paper shines through less with every layer and colours inevitably lose brilliance.

It is tempting to try to get the maximum colour effect with the minimum of printings. Screenprinting offers both possibilities, transparent overlays as well as half-tones, but half-tone colour is essentially a photographic reproduction process. I thought that it might be instructive to try to obtain mixtures by cutting pieces of ready-made dot material and applying them to a range of drawings on film, one for each ink, to tease a little more apparent colour from the limited number of screens.

The screenprint version of the *Interior* theme starts from a black and white photograph of one of a group of collages and colour is added to give a pseudo-photographic effect of half-tone colour reproduction. I made colour separations by hand, using ready-made mechanical tints. In parts the techniques are revealed for what they are by removing the overlying black screen. The general quality of collage, the dominant method of the studies and paintings on the subject, is maintained with this use of fragments of evenly dotted cellophane, Zip-a-tone, Plastitone, Cellutint and other brands.

For the painting called *Interior* it was my intention to screenprint onto the surface of the panel to get a photographic kind of reality into the girl. My source was a black and white film still but I decided to put colour on the painting and then silk-screen the figure with black pigment on top.

To try out the method I made some trials on paper to

Interior, screenprint, 1964–65

Patricia Knight, screenprint, 1964

determine the degree of accuracy that was required and to see what effect impasto would have on the half-tone dot of the screen. I roughed out in pencil the approximate shape of the figure and painted it, then screened on top of the six variations at Kelpra Studio. It worked rather well.

Interior I was nearly complete, except for the figure, so we took the screen to my studio to work directly on the panel. In the event it seemed unnecessary to colour the figure. By this time another version of the picture *(Interior II)* was contemplated. It had not been started but I screened the figure onto a completely white panel, making a guess at what might be a reasonable position. Later decisions about the composition had to follow from her immovable fact.

The first four screenprints that I made were very much dependent on Christopher Prater at a technical level. *My Marilyn* was approached somewhat differently. The art school in which I taught accepted the need to have silk-screen facilities available for students to supplement the etching and litho printmaking equipment. I tried out our methods of screen preparation to get things functioning and proofed the *Marilyn* print myself, making screens and printing rather ineptly to produce a number of variations. Colours and even registration were changed throughout the proofing.

Since the basis of the print was a group of photographs with markings made by Marilyn Monroe's hand, it became an objective of the prints to produce a painterly result without actually making marks with mine.

One of the proofs was used as the basis for a reprinting with Kelpra Studio using my existing positives.

The painting My Marilyn *has a partner in a Braun-inspired work. The Marilyn print has its concomitant in* Toaster. *It is an early example of the readiness of the modern print to move around, to mix the media: offset litho, screenprint, and in this case, collage, not a print medium at all. Technical purity was no longer sacrosanct.*

In my travels around the print workshops of Europe and America, I have come to think of the different establishments, and their personnel, as different

My Marilyn, screenprint, 1965

Toaster, screenprint etc., 1967

instruments on which the artist plays. However beautifully constructed, the special qualities of each need to be understood by the performer if they are to give of their best. Each has a unique timbre, preferences, biases, and special skills, different machinery, papers, psychological make-up. The workshop can exert a strong stylistic pressure or respond discreetly to the artist's needs. It's an exciting relationship.

Every printer has his own way of going about things. What Domberger was able to achieve with Self-portrait *covered technical areas that Chris Prater at that time was not exploiting. Although he has always used photographic methods of screenmaking, Chris's forte then was his cutting. One has only to see the Paolozzi* As Is When *series to appreciate Chris Prater as the greatest stencil cutter around. The Domberger organization in Stuttgart was remarkable for its photographic virtuosity.*

I had been making another of my futile efforts at lithography but, as with all my experience in that medium, what I hoped for from the stone just didn't print. The lithographic quality of I'm dreaming of a white Christmas *derives from the fact that the preliminary drawings for colour separations were all made with lithography in mind. The* Self-portrait *print led me to believe that Domberger might give me the desired result from silk-screens. I arrived in Stuttgart with enough of the drawn positives to start printing and then made new positives as the need arose. The thing I most enjoy about working with a screenprinter on a small edition is the way it is possible to embark on printing an edition without a proof or even a very firm idea of the ultimate result – each additional screen being made as a consequence of previous printings.*

Many prints made since *Adonis* had employed more than one print medium, and some had hand-applied additions. Very often prints were developed on the printing table, so much so that I felt the screen was simply offering a means of repeating a gesture rather than changing the artist's relationship with the work. There was still the same kind of sequential thinking; the print would help to generate itself as a drawing or a painting does. The activity is a dialogue between the

Self-portrait, screenprint, 1965–67

I'm dreaming of a white Christmas, screenprint, 1967

statement (image) as so far established, and consideration of that fact by the artist. Sometimes the screen medium seemed a little superfluous. Is it more difficult or time-consuming to repeat a hand gesture seventy-five times than to make a screen and print from it seventy-five times? It depends on the complexity of the individual mark. Also, a hand-made mark might avoid some of the limitations of a printed mark; it can be less anonymous, richer.

Fashion-plate started as a multi-media print to investigate different values of representation. The print has, of course, a subject but the subject certainly became media in the course of its execution. The suitability of the fashion model for an exploration of the relationship between painted mark and photograph (the theme of *My Marilyn*) is evident, for the 'made-up' model is very much a painted image before the photographic stage is reached; painting, of a sort, continues after photography in the process-engraver's work.

The print was the final result of an intended three-quarter length painting of a fashion model. Three initial studies for the head revealed a need for a setting. A photograph was made in a professional photographer's (Tony Evans) studio, of a roll of background paper and lights. The photograph was taken to Milan, where an initial printing was done in grey on a commercial offset press. It was put through the press three times to soften the mechanical half-tone dot. Registration was minutely adjusted for each run so that the dots are not superimposed but occupy spaces immediately adjacent to the equivalent dot.

Collaged studies were made on some of the printed backgrounds. The only way to get a print quality similar to the fashion magazines was to make plates directly from transparencies, instead of photographing the printed page, and to use coated paper rather than the hand-made Fabriano I had made a start on. Having opted to use collage for the edition, I then persuaded David Bailey to provide me with suitable original transparencies to take back to Milan, have plates made, and print the number required on the plate-makers' proofing press. Silk-screen printings were added in London by Chris Prater and cosmetics were applied either through stencils (pochoir) or free-hand.

Multiple printings, with the involvement of several printers, hand-workings, and very large amounts of time often spread over months, means that each copy of an edition of seventy or so will be costly to produce and expensive to buy. The likelihood is that the edition will be sold at a reasonable price when published; as the prints change hands later prices can become absurdly high.

Just at the time that I was becoming aware of the economic problems inherent in the publication of small editions, Dorothea Leonhart, a Munich dealer, proposed to publish prints in very large editions. It seemed a good moment to try to cut across the situation that had developed in the print market.

It is surprisingly difficult to control the price of prints. If the work is to be of a certain quality there are factors which inhibit large numbers. A lithograph drawn on stone will not go on producing the same image indefinitely. Universal Art Editions published lithographs in very strange edition sizes; twenty-seven, twenty-three, or even less. This was not perversity but a decision on the part of the publisher to stop printing as soon as the image showed the slightest sign of deterioration or change. A copper plate will wear, etching inks are very abrasive; however finely ground, the particles of carbon bound in oil will remove the surface as fast as metal polish – which is why they are faced with a microscopically thin skin of steel to resist erosion of the softer copper. Even steel-faced plates have their limits, the steel must be removed and a new skin applied as soon as wear becomes visible. With or without the problem of wear there are still restraints.

Printing etchings is a slow procedure. It takes a long time to damp each piece of paper individually, ink and wipe the plate, pass it through a heavy hand-press, dry the print, and examine each one for the occasional flaw. A natural limit of boredom is imposed. With silk-screen the limitations are not so severe. But even that medium has its problems; physically handling the paper a great many times, drying each application of colour means space-consuming racks. Things go wrong, less from wear than from ink clogging the smaller openings of the screen. Silk-screen printing is a fast, manual, immensely strenuous business, with the additional

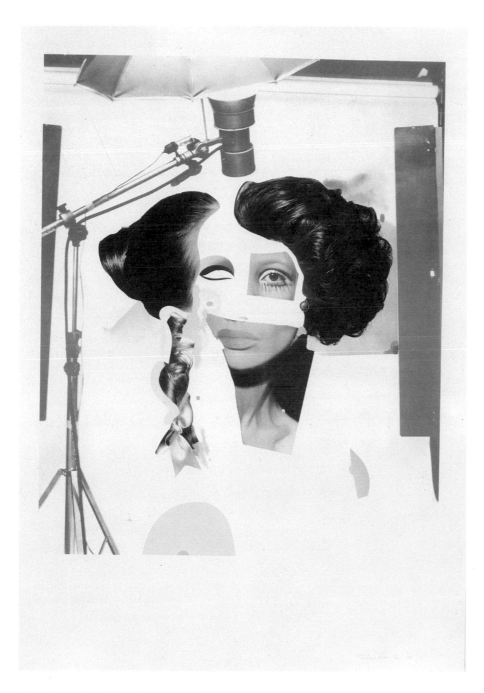

Fashion-plate, multi-media print, 1969–70

problem of nervous strain. Working is necessarily hasty but it is vital to watch for signs of incipient trouble. The screen can fill so that the smaller openings do not print, or worse, an unwanted hole appears. Every halt to the rhythm of the passage of paper beneath the screen – the washing of the screen with solvents, the patching of holes – introduces further hazard, and change, the enemy of the classic concept of printing, namely uniformity of the edition.

Given these barriers to edition size, there are other considerations. At one time the Customs and Excise Department decided that purchase tax would be imposed on any artist's edition exceeding seventy-five copies (that figure has become an average even after the change of taxation to VAT). It is a lot more effort to produce twice as many but the remuneration can be the same, or nearly so. Because a small edition is, given the present marketing set-up, more prized by collectors, they will pay more for an example. If there are twice as many they may wish to pay half as much. Should the artist regret that these commercial factors intervene between him and another audience that he would wish to satisfy, and insists that the price be maintained at an artificially low level to cater for enthusiasts with smaller incomes, the consequences are not ideal. Prints in small editions will inevitably change hands quickly; they gravitate towards the dealers and the prices rise to the high norm. There are two solutions, a) to lower the standards; the higher the quality of the work the higher the price will go, or b) to increase the number of copies; the more there are, the easier to obtain, and maintain, a low price.

An artist may not wish to work on a two-tier system, one quality for the poor, another for the rich. On the other hand, it isn't easy to achieve excellence on a large edition – so the invitation from Leonhart was an interesting challenge. An edition size of five thousand would ensure that the print could be sold cheaply and that the price would not rise unduly afterwards. The problem was to produce five thousand copies of a print that showed the same dedicated involvement of artist and printer apparent in small editions.

It had been on my mind that there might be a subject staring me in the face from the TV screen. I set up a camera in front of the TV for a week. Every night I sat watching with a shutter release in my hand. If something interesting happened I snapped it up. During that week in May 1970, many possibilities emerged, from the Black and White Minstrel Show to Match of the Day; I also had a good many news items. In the middle of the week the shooting of students by National Guardsmen occurred at Kent State University. This tragic event produced the most powerful images that emerged from the camera, yet I felt a reluctance to use any of them. It was too terrible an incident in American history to submit to arty treatment. Yet there it was in my hand, by chance – I didn't really choose the subject, it offered itself. It seemed right, too, that art could help to keep the shame in our minds; the wide distribution of a large edition print might be the strongest indictment I could make.

Kent State is the most onerous of all the prints I have made. Without anticipating the problems, I chose to layer many transparent colours over each other to build the image from the overlaps and fringes. It was an absurd procedure. The more layers of pigment the longer the drying time – it didn't take long to discover that we were manufacturing gigantic fly papers. Every small insect trapped caused an accumulation of ink with each additional colour. For an edition of five thousand we started with six thousand pieces of paper. Three thousand of these were rejected, largely as a result of insects. A new printing was embarked upon with three thousand sheets of paper. We just about made the edition; two proofing runs, two edition runs of fifteen printings, seven trips to Munich from London. I'm glad I tried it, but that kind of big edition has to be a once in a lifetime experience.

The Kent State student depicted, Dean Kahler, was not killed. He suffered spinal injuries and is paralysed. The text that I originally wrote for the subject avoids any mention of the horrible circumstances of that day in May. It coolly describes the passage of information. From the actual fact of a young man struck down by the bullets of amateur guardsmen to the eventual representation in a print, all the transformations of energy, listed remorselessly like a modern version of the tale of Paul Revere. It seems far more menacing than a sentimental registering of personal disgust.

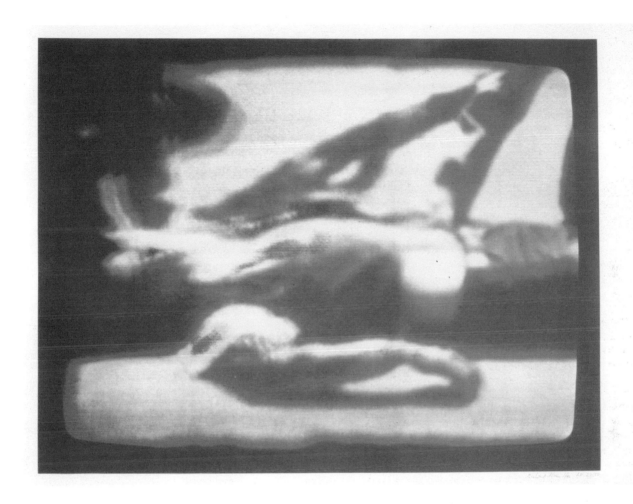

Kent State, screenprint, 1970

A cine-camera films an event on a University campus in Ohio, USA. The scene filmed, almost by chance, in conditions not conducive to rational operation, happens at a pace hardly permitting accurate exposure or focus. The information recorded in the emulsion is urgent; it is processed and put into the hands of an American TV network or News Agency which transforms the image in the film frames into electric signals, later beamed at an antenna on a satellite orbiting the earth. The satellite passes on the signals to a tracking station in the south of England and electrons are 'piped' to a recorder which duly notes the facts on a magnetic tape.

That evening, the message is re-transmitted as part of a BBC news broadcast to be detected by a TV receiver; information is decoded and divided among three guns in its cathode ray tube. They spurt out streams of electrons which excite, to varying intensities, spots distributed evenly in triads over the surface of the tube. Red, blue and green dots blink as they are scanned.

Staring at the screen is a still camera. Still, until with a sudden snap it gulps the moving picture (if it was 8 mm originally 16 frames per second scanned 25 times per second, a gulp equalled 2 frames scanned 3 times). What does the subject feel buried in a layer of gelatine in the darkness? 'There is no known way to detect a latent image in a photographic emulsion except the process of development.' Out of the chemicals into the light another, this time random, mesh of coloured particles tells the story. The same message is there – the tone of voice is new, a different dialect, another syntax; but truly spoken.

The two and a quarter inch square transparency now confronts a process camera to be sliced and layered. One slice carries no magenta, one no cyan, one no yellow, another slice holds in reverse the tonal values of all colours. Different times of exposure through these separation negatives produce different positives which, when holding back varying amounts of light from an emulsion on a nylon screen, make some areas of mesh open and leave others closed. Fifteen such screens are used to print pale transparent tints on paper. Fifteen layers of pigment; a tragic chorus monotonously chanting an oft-repeated story. In one eye and out the other.

Bibliography: 44, 45, 48, 49, 53

Kent State, still from TV transmission

Five Tyres – abandoned

A virtue of that fashionable adjunct of the visually oriented person of the '50s – the pin board – was the way it gripped certain things. Some images obstinately held the board and the mind. It was with surprise that I realized the number of years a trivial piece of advertising showing the historical development of the automobile tyre had stayed on my board.

In an issue of a magazine called *Technique et Architecture* published around 1951 (I was then nominally its London correspondent), there was an illustration of five tyres in a row. On the centre of each tread was an oval panel labelling it with a date – 1902, 1905, and so on to 1950. The picture stuck, as sometimes happens. I looked at it often, made a projection slide, used it in talks with students over the years. The attraction of the image is hard to explain. It is a squared-up half tone block in black and white from a retouched photograph of the tyres. It expresses in very simple, essentially visual terms the historical progress of a technical quest. The problem involved pattern-making – the patterns being about motion and friction (traction). These patterns are disposed in relief on a group of tori, in sharply-angled perspective, of which the perimeters (the treads) confront the viewer.

As time went by I became increasingly intrigued until, in 1963, I began to make a perspective drawing of the subject.

I proposed to make a print; an embossed relief, printed blind, so that the effect would be of the varied treads of the five tyres pressing up from the back of the paper – but in perspective.

It would have been possible to make embossing blocks directly from the linecut source, but I thought that a little too easy. I determined to make a new and idealized perspective projection of the tread types which would give me the structure anew, and more precisely.

As an exercise in perspective it is as tough as any that might be engaged in. Rectilinear objects of great complexity can be fairly easily rendered in classical perspective. Simple curves such as arches and domes are also straightforward enough, if time-consuming. There was no intrinsic difficulty in representing the tyres

Bibliography: 49, 50, 53

except that to use idealized perspective projection of a standard Renaissance type for this particular geometry was exceptionally laborious. I found one evening that I had taken two hours to establish the position of five points among thousands.

After working for a good many weeks it became clear that to continue in the rigorously accurate manner that alone made the task worthwhile would require such an abundance of time that I would have to consider whether the result could possibly merit such devotion. It was when I regretfully decided not to complete the drawing that the word *abandoned* was added to its title *Five Tyres*.

It had been my intention to plot the faces of the treads and then to etch them deeply into a copper plate like an impossible imprint in mud. The uninked plate would then have been put through an etching press to emboss paper with the forms. The paradox of a shallow relief print of a perspective projection was the main interest of the project. My original drawing of the tyres had demanded the use of coloured pencils as an aid to separating out the various overlying parts of the projection. Simplified tracings of each colour provided positives from which to execute a screen-print. A photographic augmentation which fitted the perspective scheme was added to complete the print for a group of graphics published by the ICA in 1964.

Five Tyres remoulded

In 1970 Carl Solway, an American art dealer and publisher of EYE Editions, visited my studio. While looking through some old prints he brought up the possibility of completing the *Five Tyres* project, using a computer to plot the perspective[1]. The suggestion was exciting and we decided to investigate the practicability of the technology for my purpose. Carl Solway was to try to find someone in the US competent to undertake the programming. The search narrowed down after some false leads to MIT and the Cambridge, Mass. area, and finally to Sherril F. Martin, manager of computer animation at Kaye Instruments, Inc.

Computers have been used by artists ever since they discovered that a computer can instruct a drawing machine just where to place its point and inscribe a line.

The 'remoulded' text was written to accompany the publication of a portfolio containing a moulded relief and the computer graphics involved in its production.

[1] No such technology existed in 1963.

The uses to which the computer has been put by artists most often develop out of properties peculiar to that device which enable it to use a set of instructions to effect transformations of a given image, or develop sequences of kinetic patterns. There is a tendency to ask it to perform what it most likes doing, or at least what it does most fluently, so we have come to recognise a computer graphics style. The use of a computer to make a conventional perspective projection puts no claim on its capabilities as an image creator – that is to say, the stylistic qualities are not prompted by the tool. This kind of problem might have been posed by anyone since Piero della Francesca and its solution can be precisely foreseen. What the computer provides is an inhuman speed which makes possible the formulation of a complex perspective image in its purest terms.

The objective was to take the Tyres drawing begun in 1963 to completion, following its dimensional character closely, so the first step was to provide information in a form suitable for the programmer. All the basic dimensions of the tyres and their relationship to vanishing points were to be repeated. The major part of the work, at this stage, was to convert the pattern of the treads into an accurately dimensioned development. Thus the tubular ring of the moulded tyre was imagined as cut and flattened into a two-dimensional sheet. I bought a small electronic calculator and made the conversions necessary to take the patterns from three dimensions to a flat surface.

Major computer programmes usually have wider applications than that of giving an answer to the specific problem in hand. CAPER (computer aided perspective), itself an extension of CALD (computer aided line drawing), by S E Anderson of Syracuse University, May 1967, is a general programme, written in FORTRAN. This offers the essential notions as to how instructions to the plotter may be stated, together with card-coded commands which provide the potential for the generation of any line-drawing. The presumptive space awaits the addition of specific data applicable to the particular configurations to be described. Sherrill Martin received my data and proceeded to inform CAPER so that it would tell a plotter how to draw the required perspective. A series of encoded messages was then converted into a deck of punched cards. An

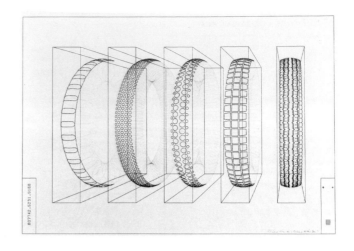

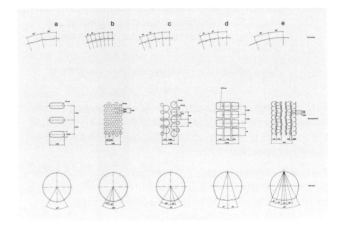

Five Tyres remoulded – computer drawing

Five Tyres remoulded, dimensional data – screenprint

IBM 360/75 computer read the deck and generated signals on a magnetic tape to control the movements of a pen on a drafting machine. In this case a Calcomp 763 was used, which co-ordinates rotary movements of the paper with lateral movements of the pen along the axis of the cylinder to produce any figure.

Because the original hand-drawn perspective of 1963 had required the preliminary projection of radial sections of the tyre casings and also lines defining the major circumferences on which to lay the treads, a network of sections was programmed for each tyre to provide these on the plotted drawing – though the final image did not demand this information nor was it required to be made explicit in the programme. Removal of hidden lines is a complication in perspective programmes, therefore expensive; excessive superimposition of front and back of the tyres was avoided, simply by plotting the treads through only 180°.

At this stage the original idea of producing an embossed print on paper was modified to a proposal to cast the relief to the treads integrally with a sheet of cold-curing rubber. I filled in the linear drawing by hand with the intention of etching a metal plate to serve as a mould. Etching proved unsatisfactory, so the mould was mechanically engraved in a brass plate. Machine cutting permitted a variation of relief. To take advantage of this, a further drawing designated depth of cut in tenths of a millimetre. The 'print' is 'cast' by spreading on the plate a silicone elastomer (manufactured as a flexible mould material), then reinforcing with a non-woven Terylene cotton fabric.

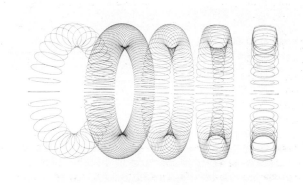

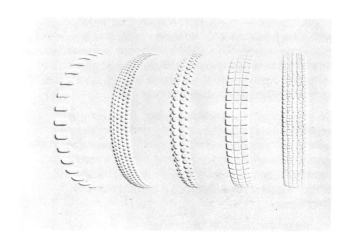

Five Tyres remoulded, radial sections – screenprint

Five Tyres remoulded – cast

Flowers

Nothing is more likely to stimulate my interest in a new subject than to notice a major pictorial genre that I have left unexplored. Over a period of twenty years or so the main classes have been covered: interior, nude, portrait, landscape, seascape, architecture, still-life, self-portrait; these were usually seen first as categories and that recognition has been sufficient justification for their pursuit.

It's surprising that such an obvious genre as 'flower-piece' remained so long untouched. The lush paint quality of *Soft pink landscape*, with its relish of romantic colour, tempted a further venture into this sweet mood with a subject hitherto unnoticed, possibly because of its easy charm.

Naturally there are inhibitions to overcome – flowery allure is an irrelevant anachronism in the context of cultural ideas in our period. It takes perversity and a touch of irony to make it tolerable. The three flower-piece paintings were made not from life but from three-dimensional postcards, the sort laminated with a lenticular plastic sheet and which create an illusion of depth. Two of the three source postcards were tampered with. One had a toilet roll added to the fruit arrangement classically combined with flower-pieces; another had some paint loosely applied and also the turd which had emerged from the association, in *Soft pink landscape,* of girls and toilet paper – glamour and shit.

This compulsion to defile a sentimental cliché was perhaps, though unconscious initially, a conformity with a well-established tradition in the flower-piece – the convention of placing, often lower right, a *memento mori:* an insect, a crab, a skull – some sinister motif which suggests that life is not all prettiness and fragrance.

Whatever the reasons for involvement with a subject, each of the major classifications has its unique technical problems. A portrait demands a 'likeness', the delineation of a building will require some investigation of perspective methods; the flower-piece genre should be, above all, about colour. Using paint to create colour effects, in this sense, is something that I have rarely found worthwhile, here it was to be the *raison d'être*. An

Bibliography: 49, 55, 56

etching on the theme was made concurrently with the paintings in which the colour interest was emphasised by introducing a technical problem, that of making colour separations by hand on copper plates.

Images on paper tend to have white borders; over the years I have taken over these vacant spaces to varying degrees and with differing aims. The boundaries of the worked area in the flower-piece paintings, like those of the print, are loose because a severe conjunction of image and edge seemed alien to the freedom of the painted mark.

The three *Flower-piece* paintings have, in the course of their completion, become a triptych. Each canvas in the group has since been subjected to a specific print medium: etching, collotype and lithography. Because colour *is* the subject, the opportunity was taken to apply 'process' colour printing concepts to traditional art printing techniques with separation being made empirically rather than through photographic filters.

Etching *Trichromatic flower-piece*

Most colour printing processes nowadays utilize three primary inks (yellow, magenta, cyan) each printed from a separate plate or block. Mixing of these 'process' colours occurs, optically, on the paper to produce all intermediary hues. A further printing, black, helps to control contrast. For very fine quality it might be thought desirable to make additional printings of colours that are hard to achieve with the three inks, but that's rather special. In process work, the colours are separated photographically with film and filters and half-tone screens are interposed to break the continuous tones into dots.

Hand-worked colour etchings rely on other means. Inks are individually mixed and applied to specific areas of the plate. The number of colours printed with each impression is limited only by the ability of the printer to push ink into certain parts and wipe the surface clean without smearing into others. It is conceivable to print twenty or thirty different ink mixtures from a single plate with one passage through the press. As many plates as are necessary can be printed in this way.

Trichromatic flower-piece is printed from three plates

Sonia Orwell, an old friend of mine and friend also of Aldo Crommelynck, visited us while I was working on my trichromatic plates. She took me aside when she saw what I was up to and advised me sadly 'You know Richard, there's more to life than shit and flowers!' It was at that moment that I became aware that 'shit and flowers' does sum up life rather beautifully.

each inked with only one colour: yellow, magenta or cyan, plus another for the normally added black. They were produced by the traditional methods of hand-worked copper: line etching, aquatint, dry-point, burin, roulettes etc.

Collotype *Flower-piece A*

The greatest problem with colour etching had been the difficulty of keeping the drawing on each plate reasonably in register with that on others, for colour mixing on the paper does appear to be a function of registration. Collotype's basic reliance on photographic films provided a simple solution to the registration problem. A black and white photographic negative was made from the painting of the subject and four full-size positives on film were produced from this. Each of these was then nominated as being, potentially, the separation for either yellow, magenta, cyan or black. The film nominated 'yellow' was brushed with acid to clear, or reduce, opacity in those areas where there was least red or blue. It was drawn on or painted with ink to add or reinforce yellow marks. 'Cyan' and 'Magenta' were treated in the same way to provide the differing colour printing values from initially identical films. The advantage of the method was that registration was exact because all of the films were derived from the same source. The problem lay in assessing colour as optical mixtures of grey tone values. Contact negatives made from the hand fabricated positives prepared the gelatine printing surface. After proofing, these negatives were further modified with acids, ink and scrapers to improve the results. Registration may have been perfect but colour quality inevitably left something to be desired, so colour highlights were added to the print by the more autographic medium of silk-screen.

Lithography Flower-piece B

In my own very limited experience of the medium I had been forced to conclude that lithography is a most recalcitrant and unforgiving medium. In some ways that may have been a misunderstanding. Of the two primary means of making marks on the stone (a) drawing with a stick of grease and (b) applying a suspension of fine grease particles in water, the second is infinitely more hazardous (this assumption was tested with four stones;

see Flower-piece B – crayon study*). Successful washes demand either a deft touch or a style that allows the free exploitation of chance. The medium won't be pushed around. But there is also a temptation to suppose that washes will yield in the print the gradations apparent on the stone and that they afford the best means of gaining a wide range of half-tones which avoid the texture of rubbed crayon.*

Even in the best of printer's hands, though Ken Tyler might argue with this, washes are likely to coarsen in the chemical processing of the stone, and subtleties harden up. In commercial lithography using photographically prepared plates, there is a technique of high quality printing in black and white known as 'duotone'. Two plates are made, one exposed specifically for the lighter tones and the other for the darks. The light plate is printed in a reduced (grey) ink and the other in full black. A greater tonal range is possible with this approach. I decided to apply the principle to colour printing from drawn stones, in other words, a duotone trichromatic. Another theoretical advantage, to my mind, was that each overlying printing of the same pigment would smooth out the characteristic graininess of stone lithography. The virtue of using more than one stone for each colour was confirmed in the proofs.

Unlike an etched copper plate, the stone won't happily tolerate meddling. A copper plate permits endless removal, lightening and adding – nothing done to it is irrevocable, each new proof is an invitation to modify; indeed, early proofs from the plates for Trichromatic flower-piece *pleaded for improvement. The need to correct the six initial stones, after the first colour proof, was frustrated by the unwillingness of stones to suffer elaborate alteration after proofing. They can be 'opened up' to receive further work but the process of opening will erode a good deal of the quality of what is already there. So my corrections consisted largely of removing marks completely, and of balancing the ink densities for each printing. Another serious consideration is that every proofing puts the stone at risk of deterioration.*

A decision was taken to persist (lavishly so) with the methods that seemed to be offering most benefit.

Three further printings of the same three colours, reduced to a faint tint, were added – but this time from plates made by airbrushing through a stencil mask. The final printing, of white rather than black, is from a crayon drawing on a plate. The printing order is therefore:

1 *Yellow stone (a)*
2 *Yellow stone (b)*
3 *Yellow plate*
4 *Magenta stone (a)*
5 *Magenta stone (b)*
6 *Magenta plate*
7 *Cyan stone (a)*
8 *Cyan stone (b)*
9 *Cyan plate*
10 *White plate*

Ken Tyler insists on calling this an edition in ten colours. I prefer to express it as a three colour triple-tone printing, plus white.

Sunsets

Jung's young dream bleeds into after-images of *Garden of Evil.* A lake of geranium; cadmium oranges, yellow as Naples. Terre verte ultra marine; indigo to violent Mars.

Bibliography: 56

Trichromatic flower-piece, etching, 1973–74

Flower-piece A, collotype and screenprint, 1974

Flower-piece B, lithograph, 1975

The Swinging Sixties

Political or moral motivation is hard to handle for an artist. My first venture into the area, Portrait of Hugh Gaitskell, *was prompted by curiosity; to see if I could do it.* Kent State *was thrust upon me by circumstances – I accepted the challenge with trepidation. There had been another attempt,* Swingeing London '67, *made without any qualm. I had felt a strong personal indignation at the insanity of legal institutions which could jail anyone for the offence of self-abuse with drugs. The sentence in the case of my friend Robert Fraser was blatantly not intended to help him through a sickness, it was to be a notorious example to others. As the judge declared 'There are times when a swingeing sentence can act as a deterrent'.*

There were several moves towards the subject at the time of Robert's arrest in '67. Gradually, the sense of outrage subsided into quiet deliberations on the technical requirements of the expression of that anger.

In the mainstream of Western painting (since the Greeks, anyway), it has been taken for granted that a painting is to be experienced as a totality seen and understood all at once before its components are examined. Some twentieth-century artists questioned this premise. Certain works by Paul Klee make most sense when scanned like a poem or a page in a comic book. Duchamp's *Large Glass* reveals its quality with two separate components – the Glass and the written notes which refer to it. The manner of apprehending an essentially visual work is often a concern of mine. *My Marilyn* requires to be read partially by cross-referencing within the picture. *Toaster*, with its text, approaches the problem differently. *Swingeing London '67* investigates the subject first at the level of pure information. The 'poster' is an application of the principle of providing the factual and psychological background in a form which can best present a multitude of small nuances of indeterminate matter. A major difficulty with painting is that the very nature of the medium demands a degree of resolution in the formal rendering. The point is pressed home in the 'poster' because it is apparent that the compilation of seemingly factual reports is full of contradictions. Form and colour are elusive. Choice is arbitrary. Decision becomes whim.

Bibliography: 44, 46, 49, 52, 53

Situated chronologically between the 'poster' and an etching on this subject, the water-colour drawing tried to reinforce the slightly blurred and evasive pictorial quality of the coarsely reproduced newspaper photograph which was the source. A few colour notes were added, but the main purpose of the drawing was to try to get to grips with the anatomy of the hands.

In becoming firmer and more explicit the drawing was unwillingly removed from the documentary language of its source into an arty stylization. The outcome of these conflicts was the decision to combine a painted quality with a superimposed silk-screen printing in the six versions of the painting subsequently completed.

A return to the Swingeing London theme was occasioned by a request from a very worthy organization, Release, to make a print – one of a group to be contributed by several artists – to help it through a financial crisis. Release was set up to provide legal aid as well as more general assistance to people in trouble with the law, most frequently through drug offences. Another equally vital and equally impoverished body, the National Council for Civil Liberties, was brought in to share benefits from print income.

Robert Fraser, my swinging art dealer, was friendly not only with Mick Jagger and the Stones but also with the Beatles. He encouraged several of his artists to undertake commissions to make record sleeve designs and got the groups involved with the artists. Paul McCartney was taking a very active role in putting together the double album called 'The Beatles', and I took responsibility for the design of the package, with Gordon House looking after the printing and Paul McCartney working with me much of the time in the studio.

The great attraction of the job for me was in that the power of the Beatles was such they could override the usual commercial niggling. My real employers, EMI and the company design officials, were out of the running. Another consideration was the size of the edition, potentially in the region of 5,000,000.

To avoid the issue of competing with the lavish design treatments of most jackets, I suggested a plain white cover so pure and reticent that it would seem to place it in the context of the most esoteric art publications. To further this ambiguity I took it more into the little press field by individually numbering each cover. The title *The Beatles* was blind, embossed in as seemingly casual a manner as possible and the numbering had almost the appearance of a hand-numbering machine. Inside the album was a give-away 'print'. Most of the design effort and expense went into this. Each of the Beatles provided me with a large dossier of personal photographs and I selected from this material to make a collage. Because the sheet was folded three times to bring it to the square shape for insertion into the album, the composition was interestingly complicated by the need to consider it as a series of subsidiary compositions. The top right and left hand square are front and back of the folder and had to stand independently as well as be a double spread together. The bottom four squares can be read independently and as a group of four. They all mate together when opened up and used as wall decoration.

I tried to think of the print as one which would reach and please a large audience, but there were some arcane touches which only the Beatles' more intimate associates were likely to smile at. Its standards are those of a small edition print pushed, with only some technical constraints, to an edition of millions.

The Beatles' print was a return to the problem of large editioning; here was the ultimate multiple image, as far as numbers is concerned. Control would cease at an early stage because printing was to take place all over the world, more or less simultaneously. Instead of sending printed paper, or even printing plates, to centres in Asia, North and South America, Africa, and several European locations, positives would be sent from a process-engraving works in Amsterdam to the various places where printing was to be done – as masters would be sent for pressing the discs. Differences occurred everywhere, and with every reprinting, more changes and deteriorations. It was really a matter of getting one proof right and hoping that the production run would not depart too much from the plate-makers' proof.

Release, screenprint, 1972

Swingeing London 67 – poster, offset litho, 1968

In the decade '63-'72, I had some thirty prints to my credit – an average of three prints a year. Not a prolific performance but I'd learned a lot about a lot of different ways to multiply an image, from silk-screen to dye transfer, through collotype and lithography to commercial offset, and an intermixing of any; even a moulded print in a new material, for which there was no precedent. There came a hankering after my old love, etching.

With many of the modern print techniques it is best to leave things to the expert. The artist is there to communicate, as best he can, the idea he has about the final state of the work. He can't operate process cameras, expose plates, push acid around on films, or even retouch negatives. These skills are not learned dabbling in a print-shop for a week or so at a time. The artist needs to be on hand, for many decisions must be made and only he can make them. One reason that I have worked away from Britain is that anything done here in a commercial printing works, rather, than an art establishment, will be subject to union problems. In England, they won't have a client inside a dark-room checking out a size under an enlarger, they won't have him standing by an offset machine saying 'a little less yellow', 'can you put a bit more red here?' If a 'client' picked up a spatula and mixed some ink for the press it would mean 'everybody out!' I would not wish to knock the print and graphic workers' unions but the fact of the matter is that a relationship between an artist and a print worker in Italy, Germany, or America, is not seen as a threat to the system but rather as a pleasant interlude from the normal run of things.

Etching and lithography are the most direct of the artist's media – why else would they be so beloved by museum curators? – but they are still dependent on craftsmen. There is nothing in the preparation of plate or stone that the artist could not learn to do, but there are very good reasons for his not doing it. Different shops have different habits, slightly different materials, different temperatures and degrees of humidity – that micro-climate is important. If an artist is working in the same place every day for long periods then he can get to know the characteristics of the stones, how fast the acid will bite, which brush has been used for sugar and which brush for varnish – a mistake can be disastrous.

Getting to know an art school print-room, or a casually run commercial shop, will mean frustration and time-consuming tests.

After a couple of plates in the early '70s good fortune befell me when the Propylaen Press invited a contribution to their portfolio *Hommage à Pablo Picasso*. My first thought was that homage could best be paid by displaying respect for the masterly craftsmanship and love of the medium that Picasso demonstrated in his own etchings.

Aping his skill would demand the collaboration of a master etcher of the class available to Picasso. My willingness to undertake a print was conditional on the agreement of Picasso's etcher, Aldo Crommelynck, to work with me. His acceptance of the proposal preceded any thought of subject.

I saw Velásquez' *Las Meniñas* at the Prado for the first time in 1972 – its reputation as being among the greatest paintings that exist is well founded. The temptation to paraphrase Velásquez in Picasso's styles proved irresistible. In a curious way the *Hommage* print is the culmination of an old obsession. From the time of the *Ulysses* illustrations until now, style and the conjunction of disparate styles, have been a major interest. The Joyce illustrations would have been a series of etchings, each one echoing the style changes in the text. *Las Meniñas* provided an opportunity to run the gamut of Picasso's 'periods' in one plate – from 'Rose' through 'Analytical Cubism' to 'Primitive' to 'Neo-Classical' and so on. The stage of Velásquez' Meniñas could carry a lot of action, and the mysterious ambiguities (it seems to contain an infinity of cross reflections with the space the picture confronts), allowed some narrative interplay with substitutions of personalities as well as styles.

Finally, the plate wraps up a long-standing concern with the many etching methods (my first exhibition was a group of about twenty *Reaper* engravings each using different, or different combinations of, etching techniques) in one ambitious combination. Most of the ways a copper plate can be pitted to hold ink for transfer to paper are utilized – sometimes separately, sometimes in combination.

Bibliography: 53

Picasso's meninas, etching, 1973

Reflections

Perhaps the most telling thing about mirrors is that they innevitably touch the ego – the myth of Narcissus says something about a particular psychological condition but it also refers to the peculiarity of everybody's relationship to reflection; we all react to our own appearance every time we see ourselves. I can't bear to sit in a restaurant facing a mirror, my reflection shocks me, it is even repellent.

While thinking about, and therefore looking at, mirrors, it seemed that there would be little distinction between a representation of a mirror and a representation of anything, in the sense that a picture of something, a photograph or a figurative painting, is a fixed reflection of a thing seen. To experience the true nature of the mirror it is necessary to be aware not only of the reflection but of the thing reflected – the more intense the appreciation of this duality the stronger the experience, and we are aware of nothing more than ourselves, hence the trip of delight or disgust.

During the course of conjecture on the 'given' theme of this portfolio, I touched the mirror surface and realized that the fact that I could see part of my physical self, as well as its reflection, made the visual experience stronger. Contact made the transition between the actual and the reflected smoother; it made the sensation more spectacular while making the plane of separation more of a barrier. It also increased the perception of depth beyond the plane. My task became a problem of recreating these aspects in the print. Reaching for a volume behind the mirror suggested that the use of three-dimensional photography might help to reconstruct that experience.

A preliminary black and white photograph, home made in my studio, established the plausibility of the composition; this was the basis for a re-enactment with the special equipement of the Vari-Vue company in their Mount Vernon plant. A unique property of the three-dimensional camera is the possibility of focussing in two senses. There is the normal photographic focus which fixes sharpest definition at a chosen distance; but, because the

camera swings radially, the locus of the arc of camera movement will determine a focus of minimal displacement. This can position the reflected form behind the picture-plane.

My concern was to define the subject in such a way that its scale would be 'life-size'. The printed image, theoretically, would recall the scale of reflection resulting from a person placing his hand on a mirror. In so far as possible, within the technical limitations of the medium, an interval of twelve inches marked on the mirror being photographed would be twelve inches on the print.

Whatever the subject or whatever the good cause, a mixed portfolio is something a publisher can get his commercial teeth into. It is a useful strategy also in his or her dealings with the artists – things get very unclear financially when a number of printmakers are involved in a package. It isn't often that I have been sucked into these uncomfortable schemes; the only benefit to be gained is in the competitive spirit that they engender – the provocation of a challenge. Mirrors of the Mind was one such, a conception of Nicolas Calas' published by Multiples Inc. Offered the seed of an idea it is possible to become obsessed until the technical solutions are found to bring it to fruition.

3-D postcards had haunted me for some time. The flowers subject derived from them and I had used a lenticular fragment in *She*. This was my first opportunity to use the technology directly.

Nicholas Calas asked me to write something about the print. All but the last paragraph was my reply.

Palindrome, 3-D print, 1974

In Horne's house, etching, 1981–82

In Horne's house

The only benefit I experienced from eighteen months of enforced detention in our post-war army was time to read. An excellent regimental library of English classics from Chaucer to Hardy provided a staple diet. I also spent many hours in the barrack room reading and re-reading my own two-volume Odyssey Press edition of *Ulysses*. It was then, in 1947, that I first began to think about the possibility of illustrating James Joyce's great novel and to make studies.

With illustration in mind, my examination of *Ulysses* was more intensive than any book I have read. The process of studying Joyce diligently was to provide me with not only subject matter, but it also demonstrated a stylistic and technical freedom that might be applied to painting. Joyce, with his mastery of all styles and his virtuosity in weaving them into a rich tapestry, was the exemplar that later gave me confidence to try some unlikely associations in paint. Each of the twelve chapters of *Ulysses* is treated differently. The language, form and subject modulate to express differing themes and personalities. None of the episodes is so complex as the 'Oxen of the Sun', in which the birth of a child in Horne's house, a lying in hospital, is echoed in the text by the birth of language, and its historic progress, in a procession of English prose styles from latinate incantation through Anglo-Saxon, Mandeville, Morte d'Arthur, Milton, Swift, Pater, etc. to the slang of 1906.

After a thirty year pause (and with the James Joyce centenary coming up) I began to think again about illustrating Bloom's odyssey. My original study for the boozy discourse in Horne's house was a paraphrase of Cubism, which I later regarded as an unworthy solution as compared with the dauntless ambition of Joyce's pyrotechnics. A *pastiche* of different historic styles of art is clearly more appropriate for the birth episode. Working over an unfinished second attempt from 1949, I completely revamped it to include the concept of a developing flow of styles from earliest to modern. One reason that I had fought shy of that approach before was my concern for the fact that the modes of perception of literature and painting are inherently unlike. A literary, or musical work is unfolded sequentially while a painting or drawing is perceived as a whole. In the meantime I had this problem licked: paintings from 1957 on and a 1973 etching called *Picasso's meninas* (which put his many periods together) gave me some confidence in the mixing of styles and in presenting them as an ordered succession of ideas.

Joyce's readiness to ape the manner of other writers and genres had long since freed me from inhibitions about the uniquely personal mark that every painter is supposed to strive for. *Ulysses* is a laborious compound of everything Joyce knew of Dublin at a precise date, and that included its past as well as its contemporary inhabitants; it is patched together with all his skill in English, his grasp of its past, its linguistic complexity and its common usage. From my early study I kept only the relationship of figures in the composition, but I allotted different styles to each of the participants and their setting: stepping from Easter Island through Egypt, Bellini, Rembrandt, David, Cézanne, Cubism, Futurism to abstraction.

Several drawn studies were necessary before I was ready to embark on the plate with Aldo Crommelynck, with whom I had worked for the first time when executing *Picasso's meninas*. The Crommelynck studio exercises a remarkable virtuosity in the laying of resin grounds, so it is tempting to rely greatly on the soft, velvety tones of aquatint when working there. *In Horne's house* is a tour de force of lift-ground aquatint. After the first delineation of the subject in soft-ground etching, the composition was elaborated with carefully-timed acid bites applied to the plate by brush and swab rather than by immersion in a bath. There is some stipple and line etching and a little tidying up with a burin.

The plate is a large, grandiose one; an edition of *Ulysses* with text pages on this scale would be preposterous. My original studies, modelled as they were on the French *livre d'artiste,* had been too large for a hand-held book and too unpretentious for a portfolio. To squeeze their density to a smaller size made no real sense – particularly in view of the difficulties of reprinting such a mighty text – so I preferred to go to the other extreme and make a self-sufficient, weighty print that could carry some dramatic flourishes, and which would reflect Joyce's daring span of history and styles.

The economics of printmaking

Portfolios with a common theme are a publisher's ploy to persuade artists to make prints. Who could say no to the Propylaen Press suggestion to pay 'homage to Picasso on his ninetieth birthday'? In any case, there are sometimes fortuitous benefits. The opportunity to work with Aldo Crommelynck (Picasso's etching collaborator for many years) opened up a lasting friendship worth any vexations. The publisher behaved impeccably but the project was bitterly soured by a go-between, Paul Cornwall-Jones.

Printmaking does have its perils – usually at the distribution end. At the beginning of the sixties print boom the print dealers were having a whale of a time. The artist might be offered a third of the selling price, and then find that the production costs were deducted from his third. It didn't take me long to realize that this kind of thing was grossly unfair. My counter-proposal was based on equality. No artist should get less for creating a work than a salesman should get for selling it. The formula of 50/50, after deduction of production costs, looked more reasonable, and it would be if it worked. In my experience it doesn't. Once the print edition is made and in the hands of a publisher, what does the artist have? Faith and hope. The publisher is better placed: he holds the work physically, he holds the income from sales, he holds the accounts. In case of disagreement the publisher can claim ownership because the printing bills were paid by him. In fact, a publisher isn't ever likely to put much 'up front'. He may pay bills with advance sales; the so-called 'subscription' strategy. It is easier to sell a new work, wet from the press; it is not only new, it is cheaper then than it will be later. Production costs are usually recovered very quickly – profits are slower. In any case, he is likely to be holding up to three months of an artist's income from other work because, at best, accounts are done quarterly.

If, for one reason or another, things are not working out in this utopian 50/50 world there is always the ulimate solution – to split the assets 50/50. It has happened often enough for me to recognise the fallacy of this ostensibly equitable scheme. The artist walks away with half the remaining stock and, because he is not, and

would not wish to be, a print distributor, he goes straight to another print dealer to offer him a 50/50 deal and ends up with 50% of 50% while the original crocodile sheds tears over 100% of his 50%.

There is a better way; a means to circumvent the artist's tactical disadvantage which I recommend to all printmakers. The artist must do all that is necessary to retain ownership of his own work until it is sold to a third party. A print publisher, is a distributor, a wholesaler, and he should be permitted to hold work only on consignment. After all, the job of an artist has been done when he has made and signed the edition; the job of the 'publisher' has been done only when he has sold a print and handed over 50% of its profits to its creator.

The arguments against my proposition are usually these. The publisher purports to have put up the 'risk capital', i.e. paid the printing costs and production expenses. As I have demonstrated, this rarely happens in effect. A publisher will also say that he performs a service in 'promoting' an artist; that he somehow adds to his status by the activity of distribution. On the other hand, it hardly happens that an artist/printmaker is encouraged by publishers to make prints unless he has already made a substantial reputation for himself, and continues to maintain it. Print dealers want the lucrative stuff. Petersburg Press, for example, have never touched an artist who didn't provide gilt-edge stock.

In fact, publishers are more likely to do damage to the print scene by overstimulating production by a small number of artists and by overpricing – real expertise and devotion to the medium is the exception. Making prints is too much like printing banknotes; the dangers are considerable. Without a strong conviction that the various print media provide the artist with unique qualities, unattainable with any other art form, it isn't worth the trouble.

A lecture

Glorious Technicolor, Breathtaking Cinemascope and Stereophonic Sound

The Robe, premiered at the London Pavillion

One of my earliest childhood memories is of a scene in a motion picture: a ragged, mad, bearded beachcomber finds a chest of treasure washed up on the beach, together with a beautiful, unconscious blonde. I can remember being deeply impressed by the sight of him slobbering over the combined loot – running his hands through the pearls and over her lovely extended neck. I was certainly less than four at the time and it affected me like something seen in the woodshed. At about this time also there is another memory of an evening when my parents went out leaving me in the care of my brother and sister. To placate me I was given the use of a crystal set that I wasn't normally allowed to touch. The headphones were put on my pillow, the cat's-whisker was twiddled and I listened enraptured to the strange noises; it became dark and I fell asleep with the sounds still scratching out of the flat circular boxes. A few years later, at about the age of eight, my father took me to see The Singing Fool – of this I remember only the moment when the sound of a voice from a gramophone coincided with the opening and closing of Al Jolson's mouth in a moving photograph.

These, my earliest experiences of primitive entertainment machines, could, I'm sure, be matched by any of us. We must all have found that contact with the fantasy world is made all the more memorable when the bridge is a newly experienced technological marvel. We are not more convinced by a new process but the first acquaintance with it will leave a most convincing impression – for there is tremendous entertainment in simply experiencing a device which is new to us however banal the matter being presented by it. It was because of this fascination in process that, in the late forties, we went to see colour films for preference. Given a choice between three unexceptional films I would go to the one in Technicolor even if, as was likely, it was called Son of Sinbad. At that time also, my most used record was The Shanghai Sailor played by the band of the Coldstream Guards because it contained a remarkably well-recorded flute passage which made my home-made Hi Fi equipment sound as good as it was. There was, I think, a general interest in equipment as such among the electronic amateurs produced by the war pushing at the inertia of productive resources. For many years there had been a serious resistance to

technical innovation in the cinema and gramophone companies. They found it pretty hard to realise that there could be economic advantage in the introduction of any technique which affected their production and presentation methods. EMI, the largest producers of records in this country, were using presses manufactured before the 1914 war in the same building that had always housed them. They pressed virtually the same raw materials into discs with the same groove form in 1950 as they had for 40 years – and they were still minting money. The 35 mm stock used by the film industry hadn't changed all that much either. Chemists had improved the emulsions, optical advances in lenses had been introduced and sound engineers had developed recording techniques – but no basic change, one which affected projection methods, would be tolerated. Technicolor, and all the other colour processes, had arrived unimpeded because they affected only emulsion and processing.

And it wasn't for the lack of ideas. In 1929 Fox Films released a 70 mm picture called Grandeur – this was shown only at the Gaiety Cinema, New York. In 1937 Henri Chretien had developed an anamorphic lens: Paramount claims to have made a test picture with Chretien anamorphs in the '30s and to have rejected the system as unsatisfactory. Also in 1937 Fred Waller, the inventor of 'Cinerama', had built equipment to project a film inside a sphere, a process he called 'Vitarama'. But it wasn't until after the war that the film industry felt impelled to force the introduction of techniques known to them for many years. Ideas from the '20s, like Fox's 70 mm projection, had been swallowed up in the depression in the USA – by the time things levelled out the 1939 war was approaching. Since 1950 there have been notable changes at the exhibition end of the industry. The time was ripe, we were ready to go – and not only to the cinema. Wartime advances in fundamental electronic thinking opened up a new set of possibilities in radio engineering; TV in nearly every home had changed the pattern of the entertainment industries. Above all, the tremendous post-war production potential had to be deflected to satisfy a new public demand – 'now make me happy'. A large part of industrial production, in capitalist countries anyway, is now geared to the task of amusing the public. Some of

Bibliography: 11

This talk to the students, though thoroughly researched, now appears inadequate in the matter of bibliographic references. While I have most of the lecture slides, the textual sources are lost.

this production and capital investment is provided as equipment for piping an entertainment service to cinema theatres or to home TV receivers – much of it comes as personal equipment by means of which the owner can create his own amusement; still-photography, home cine, tape recorders and so on. Both public and private play equipment have been subjected to a surge of activity in the last ten years.

Technical change has been most obvious in the cinema – perhaps the rate of change has been too slow for its salvation – but who knows? When Life *magazine reviewed entertainment in the USA in a bumper issue of 1959 I found it difficult to sort out what was happening. An editorial headed 'The Structure of Entertainment' took a dim view of Hollywood's position in stating categorically that 'half the US movie audience disappeared in the last ten years'. But Ernest Havemann, on another page headed 'The Business of Show Business', says just as emphatically 'There are still as many movie theatres in the US as ever, close on 19,000. They sell about 45 million theatre tickets a week at the highest average price in motion picture history'. For 30 years 'going to the cinema' has been the major pastime of the western world. There has been a decrease in cinema attendance during the last few years but there is still no certainty about TV's ability to hold the audience it has gained. However, if the habit of cinema-going is revived it will only be partly because entertaining films are made – it will also be because the pleasures of being surrounded by a large, well projected, fine-grained image accompanied by undistorted reproduction of well-recorded multi-channelled sound at high output levels are unmatched by any entertainment available in the home.*

In 1951 film producers were already feeling the draught in America – they realised that changes in exhibition technique were the most effective reply to the challenge of TV. 20th Century Fox worked fast. Earl Sponable, their research director, went to Paris on Spyros P Skouras' instructions and bought rights to Chretien's anamorphic lens; within two years, in September '53, The Robe was shown at the Roxy Cinema, New York. The great advantage of the anamorph lens was its simplicity. A modifying lens in front of existing cameras compressed a wide-angle view onto standard stock and a similar lens

in front of a standard projector threw a wide image onto the screen. The only other essential was the installation of larger screens in every picture theatre using the system, to permit a proportion of 2.5 to 1 instead of 1.5 to 1. But even this was hard enough to persuade exhibitors to adopt in spite of the known advantages. Waller had demonstrated in his moves towards Cinerama that secondary but important clues to space perception are derived from an image which fills the whole of one's vision. Adelbert Ames of Princeton had confirmed the theory. The larger the screen the more convincing the impression of three-dimensional space; the more profound the engagement of the spectator within the action. TV could not compete in this region of experience and the principle was rightly judged. All other technological developments in cinema presentation stem from the assumption that screen size must be maximal. When introducing VistaVision Paramount urged every exhibitor to 'instal the largest feasible seamless screen both as to height and width'. In following this initial dictum exhibitors have been lead along from one advance to another.

The virtues of CinemaScope's optical system, from the exhibitor's point of view, were simplicity and economy. But Spyros P Skouras was not content to stop at the big image; stereophonic sound could also be incorporated to extend the acoustic system similarly. The sound track used for cinema presentation is normally carried on an optical track – variations in a transparent strip at the side of the film allow more or less light to strike a photo-electric cell which generates the signal to, eventually, animate the loudspeakers. Stereophonic sound requires more than one track – 20th Century Fox decided that four would give them the required advantages – one operating a speaker in the centre behind the screen, one at either side of the screen and a further track operating effects speakers within the auditorium. Four optical tracks would take up far too much space on the film and there are severe limitations to the size to which optical sound heads could be reduced. The optical system had the advantage that the sound could be printed photographically together with the picture but another sound system was available – one which utilised magnetic variations in an iron coating applied to the film – and it was possible to squeeze

The Robe, squeezed CinemaScope projection print

20th Century Fox trademark, squeezed

CinemaScope ad

Marilyn Monroe, Betty Grable, Lauren Bacall

Betty Grable spread wide

in four of such tracks – one on each side of the sprocket holes at the sides of the film. A few minor adjustments had to be made to get these on 35 mm film – the sprocket hole size had to be reduced (the new size is known in the trade as 'Foxholes') and this meant changes to the projectors. It meant separate processing of the film to add the sound to the release prints by electrical recording and special sound heads had to be fitted to projectors. But it was considered worth the trouble if the exhibitors could be persuaded to co-operate.

The first showing of The Robe, with its stereophonic sound and new aspect ratio, was a great success – the first week's gross at the Roxy was 264,428 dollars, a world record exceeding by 100,000 dollars any previous show anywhere. Two other 20th Century Fox productions followed quickly – How to Marry a Millionaire and Beneath the Twelve Mile Reef. MGM adopted the CinemaScope process for its production Knights of the Round Table. These three films were top grossers in 1954 when a special Academy Award was given to 20th Century Fox for CinemaScope. In that year 7,643 theatres in North America had been equipped for projection of CinemaScope films. In that year also 815 cinemas outside North America were equipped. Spyros P Skouras was making a big effort that year to sell CinemaScope to exhibitors throughout the world. Skouras insisted, at that time, that the whole system be bought, including stereo – anyone wishing to show CinemaScope films, and these were the biggest moneymakers of the day, would have to install all the equipment needed to present CinemaScope in as near to ideal conditions as the size of the cinema would permit. In England the Essoldo circuit bought CinemaScope lock, stock and barrel; Granada came in too. Rank, with the largest circuit available, stuck out against stereo. The major part of the cost of re-equipment was in the sound system and Rank said he would be glad to have CinemaScope films but only with an optical track. A few top-grade Rank theatres were adapted for stereo but Rank refused to back the system for his circuit as a whole. Skouras held out for a while but had to give in eventually. I can't but think of this as Rank's basest act – worse even than making Tommy Steele pictures. His refusal has led to a great deal of

confusion in the public about what they were hearing and seeing – for a cinema advertising a CinemaScope film may or may not be showing a stereo print and it is even possible for the image area to be smaller than when squarer pictures were projected.

Apart from stereo there were other financial commitments which worried the exhibitors. The large image size advocated by CinemaScope originated from existing projectors – this meant that a given amount of light was spread over a larger area with a corresponding decrease in illumination. To make the maximum use of the available light a screen of high reflectance, called 'Miracle Mirror', was introduced. The screen is embossed with a pattern which reflects light back only to those parts of the auditorium occupied by seats.

Any improvement has to be paid for not only in cost of re-equipment but also of maintenance. We were wonderfully impressed by CinemaScope when it was first introduced – we were getting big screen plus high reflectance from newly-fitted specially coated screens. As these screens became dirty over the years we may have seen less light than we got before CinemaScope. The new sound also has its problems: dust was the bugbear of the optical tracks – dust is still a nuisance, but magnetic sound requires extreme electrical cleanliness as well. Magnetism induced in any part of the projector or splicers or film handling equipment that comes into contact with the film can cause clicks and noise in the track. Regular careful demagnetisation is necessary every two weeks. Every advance in exhibition technique demands an increase in the skill of projectionists and their equipment must be maintained at peak efficiency if the care and skill of film production technicians is not to be wasted.

Paramount realized the difficulties that 20th Century Fox were up against and stepped in with their proposals. These were mainly changes in production technique. In a pamphlet to exhibitors explaining VistaVision they offered only what they knew exhibitors were prepared to accept: 'Paramount makes no demand on any theatre, but there is one thing on which there is complete agreement among all studios and all exhibitors, big screens are here to stay'. Apart from the large screen it was stressed that everything they offered could be exhibited on good standard equipment. VistaVision was claimed to be 'a new simple, compatible and flexible overall system'. The distinctive feature of VistaVision was the technique of making a large negative image in the camera and reducing this onto the standard 35 mm release print. The Paramount cameras were adapted to take 35 mm film horizontally giving a frame three times the area of the standard negative image. A larger negative size has the disadvantage that depth of field for a given lens aperture decreases proportionately to the increase in negative size. This tendency is combated by the use of wide-angle lenses; the wider the angle the closer the lens is to the film plane and the greater the depth of field and, fortunately, large screen films demand a greater use of wide-angle lenses. Throughout the new cinema processes there is this problem of finding a balance between gain and loss in respect of grain size, depth of focus, light losses, perspective distortion in extreme wide-angle lenses, grain distortion and the physical dimensions required to carry increased amounts of information. Since the chain reaction started there has been an eager juggling with possibilities and solutions to establish an acceptable standard for production and projection. The search for that standard is still going on.

VistaVision took the line of least resistance. 'Compatibility', for Paramount, equalled compromise – particularly at the exhibition end. Unlike CinemaScope, VistaVision had no new aspect ratio. They accepted the fact that cinema prosceniums are of different shapes and sizes and refused to lay down fixed recommendations applicable to all theatres. In very large theatres they suggested that an aspect ratio of 1.85 to 1 should be aimed at. This could be increased, if the theatre architecture demanded it, to a maximum of 2 to 1 but they were willing to accept an aspect ratio of 1.66 to 1 in small theatres. Paramount film producers were asked to frame their pictures in such a way that it wouldn't matter too much if bits were cut off from either the sides or the top of the ideal ratio. The same attitude of compatible compromise was taken with the sound for VistaVision, selecting 'Perspect-A', cinemas were equipped with multiple loudspeakers to create some of the effects of stereo without the accompanying difficulties in production and exhibition. Magnetic

multi-track requires separate microphone and recording channels for each track to be used on the set. Apart from the problems of positioning the microphones for satisfactory acoustic results additional microphones also give lighting engineers headaches in preventing shadows from them being cast on the set. Perspect-A records in the normal way with one microphone, the recording being optically printed with the picture. A low-frequency modulated control signal is added to the track which directs sound at varying volume levels to the different speakers. This direction signal is added in by a man sitting at a consol watching a playback of the scene: he routes the sound manually to a position he judges most appropriate to the action on the screen. A comparatively inexpensive control unit in the theatre, operated automatically by the low-frequency modulation superimposed on the track, separates sound to the multiple speakers. Paramount, they said, would have no magnetic sound release: 'It is our opinion that this move will give greater dramatic effectiveness, greater simplicity and greater flexibility at a lower cost and with less service trouble than any other multi-horn system'.

CinemaScope had certainly had trouble with its stereo. As a film fan I have been aware of changes over the years – changes that I regret; it seemed that stereo wasn't what it was in the young days of CinemaScope – so different and unemphatic that I suspected that stereo prints were not being used generally even by cinemas that I knew to be equipped for them. The explanation, I discovered recently, is that audiences complained that, in some parts of the theatre, one or other of the loudspeakers was inaudible. It was also said that stereo gave too much effect of movement for the front seats and was of little use for the rear seats. The cure was to arrange for all main speakers to be given all of the signals at fixed levels of output and the separation to occur only above this norm. This reduced very considerably the pronounced stereo effect of early CinemaScope showings. The effects track was also disliked by some members of the audience – they didn't like the sound of horses galloping along the side aisles or the swish of arrows across the theatre – it was distracting, they said. The effects track, therefore, has not been as much used in the last few years. This

Superwide aspect ratio

Paramount trade mark

doesn't mean that stereo is a failure in cinemas, only that the public quickly became irritated by the deficencies of crude sound installations in theatres that were not designed for the acoustic subtleties of stereo. If big screens are here to stay stereo is here to stay with them – though the slogan 'In the Wonder of 4-track High Fidelity, Magnetic Stereophonic Sound' may lure us less often. However, the Journal of the Society of Motion Picture Theatre Engineers, May 1959, reports that 20th Century Fox has restored the emphasis on stereophonic sound and has announced an improved method of recording.

When CinemaScope was first introduced, 20th Century Fox also made much of the arguable three-dimensional aspect of CinemaScope. The other great slogan: 'You see it without the use of special glasses' was perfectly true – but it didn't say that, with or without glasses, there was any very strong three-dimensional experience. VistaVision also made some attempt to get on the 3-D bandwagon relying not on its screen size but on its improved image quality claiming, rather lamely, 'This will give new depth perception in exhibition'.

An acceptable, true 3-D was one of the failed objectives of the fifties. The major factor of depth perception in human vision is the different viewpoint that each eye contributes to our appreciation of a scene, true cinema stereography would present each with a difference of scene equivalent to normal biopic vision. Great difficulties arise in attempting to present the whole of a cinema audience with a different image for each eye.

Two systems without the use of filters have been reported. One of them makes use of two projectors, displaced from one another, which form an image on a grid of vertical wires. Parallax introduced by the projection causes each eye to select only the image intended for it. This method involves considerable light losses and is prohibitively expensive – one such experimental installation had a grid of 100 miles of copper wire weighing 6 tons. Another method is to use a system of tiny mirrors which black out in synchronism with the sequence of projection of the images – this requires fantastically complex machinery to operate the mirrors. Both of these systems impose an almost complete fixation of the head – the tolerance of

movement being less than an inch. At present there is no doubt that spectacles offer a more practical solution. Prior to the war some trick stereo films were made by MGM using the anaglyph principle by separating the two images with colour. A red image and a green image were projected simultaneously, each member of the audience had cardboard spectacles holding coloured gelatines which presented only one of the images to each eye, the other being filtered out. Dr Edwin Land, one of the undisputed geniuses of our era, in 1930 invented the first practical mass produced filters for polarising light. These Polaroid filters opened up new possibilities of three-dimensional viewing, without irritating colour effects from the filters, by separating the two images through different states of polarization of the light.

It wasn't until after the war that Warner Brothers took the process up in a big way and made some important Polaroid productions. At first, they exploited the frightening sensory effects in some black and white horror films which had as their climax the alarming emergence of the monster into the audience. This trend concluded a year or so ago with the application of a new treatment which Warners called 'Emergo' when a stuffed monster was actually hurled through the auditorium on cables. It is possible to make colour films also with polaroid filters and some first-rate films were made: Warner's The Charge at Feather River with Guy Madison was a fine western; MGM's Kiss Me Kate, a musical, was also brilliantly done in 3-D colour, as was the best of the horror films Warner's House of Wax. The success of these few films can be measured by Edwin Land's fabulous financial affairs. In 1952 gross sales of the Polaroid Corporation, which he founded to exploit his inventions, were 13 million dollars; in 1953 they were 26 million dollars; in 1954, 23 million. The demand for 3-D glasses accounted for the jump in sales in 1953.

Warner Brothers have not continued production of their 3-D movies – the need to use spectacles proved too much of an obstacle and the visual effects were very tiring for prolonged viewing. Lately a means of using polaroid filters without light losses has been put forward and it may be that there will be a revival of this approach.

Binocular vision was thought at one time to be basic to

House of Wax, Polaroid left eye frame

House of Wax, Polaroid right eye frame

House of Wax, distributor's exploitation leaflet

the three-dimensional sensation of space in motion pictures. Other clues have been noticed and these are now being exploited. There is known to be a subjective effect of stereoscopy associated with camera movement. The effect is more apparent if the indices by which an audience reads the image as flat are eliminated. Several factors contribute to the effect of flatness in the cinema: softness of focus, film grain, sheen from the screen and also the rectangular picture mask. Improvements in these directions have been more durable in their increased involvement of the audience in the picture space.

The curved screen shape is an image very dear to the fifties. It has become the generalized symbol for cinema entertainment: as the rounded-off barrel shape has come to mean TV so the wide screen proportion, curving inwards along its length, has come to mean its competitor, the cinema. It implies 3-D but, in so far as CinemaScope is concerned anyway, its effectiveness in this respect is not very remarkable. It does have other advantages: when projecting very wide pictures the light beam strikes the sides of the screen at a seriously oblique angle causing a loss of image brightness at the ends. With a curve of equal radius to the projection throw the reflection angle remains the same for every part of the screen. The curve introduces distortion of horizontals so severely, under certain conditions, that the curvature has to be compromised. So essential has the curved screen become to the cinema that when VistaVision, in its true spirit of compromise, made a 50mm release print of the same dimensions as the VistaVision negative they advocated keeping the screen flat but using curved masks at top and bottom to give the impression of curvature.

Real curvature not only presents problems of distortion but it also makes difficulties of focus at the edges of the screen. Camera lenses are strictly planar. An ideal lens focusses evenly and without distortion in a plane. If a camera is pointed at right angles to a straight wall the focus is determined by the distance between the camera and a point at the centre of the wall; the distance between the lens and the wall increases on either side of the central point but the focus should be even right out to the edges. A projection lens is similarly planar. It is this characteristic of normal lenses that makes the extreme curvature of the Cinerama screen so complex optically.

Some idea of the difficulty can be gained from the financial history of Fred Waller research. Waller worked for several years as head of Paramount's trick film department. In 1937 he devised Vitarama to project a moving picture inside a sphere for display purposes – the scheme used 11 cameras and 11 projectors. A company was formed to adapt the idea to cinema presentation, obtaining financial and laboratory support from Lawrence Rockefeller. The principle was applied to an aerial gunnery trainer during the war and in 1946, since more money was needed, Time Inc. joined Rockefeller to form the Cinerama Corporation. By 1950 Rockefeller and Time had spent 350,000 dollars and declined to spend more for the end was still not in sight – although the system had been reduced to one camera with three lenses a good deal of work remained to be done. A new company was formed, Cinerama Inc., which, in collaboration with another new organisation, the Cinerama Productions Company, brought the system to the point of commercial exploitation with the first showing of This is Cinerama in September 1952.

Cinerama can involve the spectator more effectively than any other cinema presentation. The first reports of audience reaction to this new process told of screaming, fainting women, ducking men and sick children – no wonder we were a little apprehensive when it arrived at the London Casino. The theatre publicity and lobby displays made no attempt to inform about the subject-matter of the film – audience participation was what they were selling and what we got was a physical, almost visceral, sensation. As the postcards available in the foyer said: 'I was in Cinerama'.

Projection of Cinerama is a difficult business – the installation is costly and running expenses are high. The semi-circular screen is attacked by three projectors from points on the periphery of an extension of the screen curve – the beams intersecting at the centre of the circle formed by screen and projectors. Cross-reflection of light from one side of the curve to the other caused trouble but was cured with the development of a louvred screen made up of thin

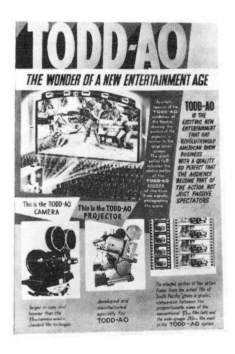

Cinerama projection system

Charles Eames, multi-visual Moscow World Fair presentation

Mike Todd with O'Brien's bugs-eye lens

Philips projector

vertical strips. Each projector is manned by an operator but, once the film is running, control is relinquished to a master projectionist whose main job is to control the projector arc lamps to maintain even illumination over the whole screen. The seven-track sound recorded on separate 35mm tape is controlled by a sound engineer in another booth. This elaborate organisation of each performance makes it nearer to a live theatre show. In fact, the extra large screen processes are known to the trade as 'roadshows'. Indeed, it was thought at first that the most exciting possibilities for future productions would be in filming original performances of great Broadway musicals and to tour this record around the country instead of the usual shop-worn live roadshow. Matching of the light sources was not the only problem with multiple projection. Every projector has a certain amount of judder and this cannot be tolerated in Cinerama – miraculously efficient film transport devices are required to maintain synchronisation and even movement. It was obvious that someone would try to reduce complexity of recording and presentation without losing too many of the advantages.

Mike Todd had been introduced to Cinerama. He had no financial interest in the company but it was thought that his talents as a showman would be useful. He very soon disagreed with the other members of the team and backed out while still holding onto a tremendous charge of enthusiasm for the potentialities of the system. Todd, with remarkable persistence, persuaded Brian O'Brien, the foremost lens expert in America (Todd described him as 'the Einstein of the optical dodge'), to develop a system which would iron out the bugs in Cinerama.

With the American Optical Company, and four million dollars found by Todd, O'Brien reduced the three cameras of Cinerama to one with a phenomenal 9 inch lens that photographed an angle of 128 degrees. The four 35 mm strips of Cinerama (three carrying pictures and one sound) became one 70 mm film taking a large size picture and the six-track sound as well. The process was called Todd-AO – Todd American Optics. But a system, however good, wasn't enough – one of Cineramas main difficulties had been in getting something to show with the new media – Todd managed to raise sufficient money to make Oklahoma, the first film in Todd-AO. He then sold all his holdings in the process itself to make Around the World in Eighty Days and his last film South Pacific.

Cinemiracle came next, with a process using three cameras but projecting from a single booth. Four years in the laboratory and 6,5 million dollars went into the production of Windjammer first shown in 1958. At the same time a Russian process called Panoramic, which used Cinerama principles, was unveiled in Moscow. It showed, aptly enough, a travelogue entitled How Broad is my Country. The Russians went several feet and decibels better than the Americans with a screen 38 ft. high and 102 ft. wide, combined with 120 loudspeakers.

Waller's Vitarama idea still exists in the form of a process owned by Walt Disney called 'Circarama', using eleven 16 mm cameras and eleven projectors showing one movie on a completely circular screen. This was used in the United States pavilion at the Brussels exhibition to show scenes of American life.

Another presentation technique was used by Charles Eames in the recent United States exhibition in Moscow. Its direct source of inspiration was an educational project known as 'the Georgia experiment', an attempt by George Nelson, Charles Eames and Alexander Girard to introduce new lecturing techniques into visual education. This used five still slide projectors simultaneously, several 16 mm film projectors and a batch of tape recorders. It took eight people to operate the equipment to lecture to about as many students. The Moscow exhibit consisted of seven screens and seven separately phased projectors. Less directly, I think, the idea stems from a general preoccupation with multiple visual experiences in our culture. The TV monitoring booth through which the producer selects the transmitted image from a set of small screens supplied by different cameras in the studio is one manifestation. This interest in multiple images has also found its way to the big screen itself. In A Star is Born[1], you may remember, there was the remarkable scene in which the wide screen contained two subsidiary moving images. An intense conversation was taking place in front of a television set broadcasting a prizefight and its excited commentary. Another room of the same open plan set was occupied by guests at a party watching the

[1] The Judy Garland/James Mason version.

CINERAMA

This is Cinerama, triple frame, roller coaster section

cine-projection of a film. This is just one example of many that could be quoted. Certainly we can expect not only an increasing spectator involvement through higher quality but also new kinds of experience altogether from new assemblages of moving imagery.

As more and more processes and modifications become available there is greater difficulty in any film product in a new medium earning its cost. Production costs increase, subjects get bigger and more spectacular, release prints cost more, additional tracks for stereophony are expensive. Yet the possibility of showing any such production becomes more restricted and it takes longer to earn costs with roadshow exhibition. The concept of compatibility, a system which permits showing a wide range of product in different exhibition conditions, the notion that obsessed Paramount when developing VistaVision, is becoming a generally accepted principle. But with this difference; compatibility is no longer a technique of compromise: it is admitted that exhibition facilities must continue to vary in differently sized communities. Production costs can only be returned with the maximum earning power achieved by the very widest distribution. The latest systems have boiled down into an amalgamation of VistaVision, CinemaScope and Todd-AO. There are several of these all having similar characteristics:

'Technirama', developed by Technicolor, provides an overall service to producers which incorporates the advantages of most other systems. It recognises the value of a large size VistaVision negative and films horizontally on 35 mm stock with a frame covering eight perforations. A slight squeeze was introduced to the negative which has an anamorphic factor of 1.5 using an anamorph derived from reflection through prisms rather than reflection through a lens as in CinemaScope. This negative can then be processed by Technicolor and release prints provided to suit any kind of exhibition equipment: a double frame print for projection in VistaVision-type horizontal projectors; a CinemaScope-type print on 35 mm film with an anamorphic factor increased to 2; a 16 mm squeezed print can be obtained and also normal unsqueezed 35 mm and 16 mm optical prints. Technirama Super 70 was introduced later – it unsqueezes the same negative onto a 70 mm print with six-track stereophonic sound. United

Artists used Technirama for Solomon and Sheba now being projected from a 70 mm print at the Astoria. Metro-Goldwyn-Mayer, in conjunction with Panavision Inc., are also using a large film negative which they call 'Camera 65'. Another process named 'Superscope' does a somewhat duller job of squeezing normally photographed negatives to make prints for anamorphic projection.

The reason for the recent emphasis on increased size of negative and print is that grain and sharpness had suffered so much deterioration in comparison with old black and white films that complaints were rife. The blame was put on 'undue magnification (anamorphic or otherwise), bad processing, shocking degradation of colour, definition, gradation, grain etc.' With their large screen, large negatives and large prints these latest systems seem to differ from Todd-AO only in that they don't claim incredibly wide-angle lenses. 66° is the widest angle for Technirama as compared with the 128° of Todd's bugs-eye lens.

Two general standards seem likely to become stable. A 70 mm six track print for exhibition in fancy-priced luxury cinemas. And the other, a CinemaScope print with an aspect ratio of 2.35 to I, which carries four magnetic tracks plus an additional optical track of half the normal width – this is known as a 'MagOptical' print and it can be played by theatres equipped with either sound system. New projectors have also been designed which can cope with this variety, such as the Phillips Multi-Purpose Todd-AO projector which can project anything from Todd-AO to standard 35 mm film.

Magnetic sound recording hasn't only made stereophonic recording on release prints possible. It had come into general use by sound engineers in the early fifties. Before the war magnetic recording on steel tape had been developed. It wasn't until after the war that the allies discovered that the Germans had devised a method of recording on a microscopically thin iron oxide coating on plastic tape. It has had great value in the cinema industry – it gave good quality, the signal to noise ratio was good, it could be played back immediately (optically recorded sound has to be photographically developed before it can be played back), and it could be re-used while unwanted optical track was scrap. But elsewhere the invention of magnetic tape has been of far-reaching significance. It has unequalled value as an information storer. It is the memory of computers. And in the last ten years it has become the major vehicle for storing picture information in television. Photography and the electronic techniques of the television industry have never mixed well. Filming is slow and it passes on any degradation of the image through film grain to the transmitters. The mechanical systems for moving film through shutters have to be mated to quite different modes of extracting moving picture information through scanning. The TV technique is essentially linear and magnetic tape recording of the linear electric signals has now been perfected so that performances for TV can now be recorded and stored on a tape six inches wide, using an electronic marvel – the Ampex machine. There is every prospect of new developments in this direction. As the size of these vision recording devices is reduced to the point where they become portable it may be that TV news will be as fast and as flexible as that of radio broadcasts.

The slowness of photography has also been attacked elsewhere – within the photo-chemical process itself. Edwin Land, the inventor of the polaroid filter, was dissatisfied with the delays of photography as it affects that other side of the entertainment industry – the gratification of personal creative needs. After the negative has been exposed on light sensitive film inside the camera the film has to be developed by wet processing inside a darkroom. When the negative is dry it has to be put into another piece of apparatus to project the tone-reversed image onto light sensitive paper, and a further series of wet development and fixing operations begins. Land devised a system by which the exposure was developed and printed onto paper, by the camera itself, sixty seconds after the original exposure. During the last ten years Polaroid Land cameras have become the top sellers in the USA. The special films produced by Land's company sell in incredible quantities and are of equally incredible quality. Popular Photography, reviewing a newly issued film in 1958, went into superlatives: 'only the most technically proficient darkroom workers are able to match the brilliance and gradation of prints that are being torn from Polaroid Land cameras by even the rankest of beginners'. Land has now introduced a new film which, with the phenomenal speed of 3000 ASA, is the fastest film material in the world. To make this usable under normal light conditions an automatic photo-electric shutter has been produced with a minute aperture of f54. Polaroid Land have also issued a material which makes it possible to project a black and white transparency 2 minutes after initial exposure.

There is nothing to match this kind of development coming from the old established photographic manufacturers. Some great new photographic lenses have been produced; films have been improved, particularly colour film which has become the principle medium for amateur use. The convenience of colour film in 35 mm form has helped to increase the popularity of the 35 mm camera. Two main design trends have emerged in the fifties. First, a version of the single lens reflex camera, which enables the photographer to see the subject through the same lens that is going to expose the picture, is now being marketed by most manufacturers. Second, high-priced cameras are being simplified so that, although the elaboration of setting combinations is still available, the operation is automatic wherever possible. The camera now has very wide amateur use, not only for the pleasure that it provides in enabling people to record faces and places that they like – it has become a symbol for vacation, worn like a chain of office. A neighbour of mine in Newcastle, a middle-aged dypsomaniac lorry driver whose wife left him many years ago, is known to be on holiday when seen wearing his cheap camera round his neck – he doesn't go away, but he's on holiday.

The glamour of a camera is very hard to resist and I feel that the same kind of fascination draws one to desire many exquisite but basically useless objects such as pocket radios, pocket gramophones, miniature tape recorders and that unlikely object, the Japanese combined transistor-radio/camera. There is perhaps some further gratification to be gained from using, rather than merely owning, some of the other equipment that mid-century man likes to surround himself with.

Hi Fi, until 1950, was something appreciated only by radio enthusiasts – now it has become big business.

The distinguishing characteristic of Hi-Fi is less its ability to reproduce high fidelity sound than the idea of unit assembly. It was natural for the radio technician and home constructor to think of his equipment in terms of units; each part of his system could be independently modified and he wasn't a cabinet designer anyway. The snob appeal of Hi-Fi is very much in this tradition. In the '30s, people who wanted to equip their homes to play records would probably buy a piece of furniture called a 'Radiogram'. This is now a pretty obsolete machine. Homes, as a rule, have a TV set – there may also be an old radio about somewhere but it isn't likely to be used very much. The youngsters will probably have a portable electric gramophone to play the pops. Those seriously interested in the reproduction of music will have Hi-Fi equipment made up from a combination of units from different manufacturers. Turntable, pickup, preamplifier, amplifier, loudspeaker. If he wishes to add radio to this set-up two types of tuners are available – AM and FM. Amplitude Modulation, the pre-war broadcasting system, had become impossibly clogged even before 1939. A limited number of broadcasting wavelengths are available and so many stations were emitting signals so close to one another that selection of any single transmission could only be done at the expense of frequency range.

Shortly after the war the BBC began broadcasts of ultra short wavelengths using a different signal-carrying method, known as Frequency Modulation. This, like TV, can only be received over short distances, but by installing small transmitting stations all over the country general coverage is now obtained. The enthusiast will probably have an FM tuner but he may also wish to receive foreign broadcasts so he will have a superhet Amplitude Modulation receiver as well. A magnetic tape deck can be added to the system if desired. Equipment of this kind is capable of very high standards in its electrical components. Flaws are most likely to occur at either end of the chain: at the pickup, where physical movement of a point is involved and at the speaker, where movement of the cone has to move air. The limitations at the air movement end involve sheer size of the loudspeaker and its housing and the acoustics of the room itself. It has probably reached the stage where improvement can only be effected by acoustic

architecture on a domestic scale. The same standards of Hi-Fi also apply to home stereo; this is just a multiplication of the same type of units fed from a special kind of record and pickup. A number of composite stereo machines have come onto the market in the fifties. They resemble radiograms, not only because they look like them but also because they are likely to have as short a life. The virtues of stereo are negated as soon as the two speakers are put so close together that they are indistinguishable as two separate sound sources.

Home cinema, TV and stereo may well have reached a point where the improvement of facilities can best be introduced by architects with a thorough understanding of home entertainment appliances. They should cater for these special needs as they now provide sensible kitchens and plumbing.

It would be a pity to leave out of this account of entertainment technology in the '50s at least some passing reference to the great advances in printing techniques. The most important introduction in the '50s has been the varied attempts to set type photographically. Photo-litho, whereby an image is transferred to the paper from a photographically treated thin metal plate, has been increasingly used. It seems unfortunate that one is often forced to mould metal into letter shapes and print from them by normal means before one is able to obtain a satisfactory original to photograph – photo-typesetting cuts out the metal stage and enables settings of text to be made from a master alphabet negative. Colour printing techniques have also been gaining ground; so much has colour technique advanced that we can expect newspapers to use full colour for illustrations. This has already been achieved at an experimental level and has, in fact, been cautiously introduced by a few newspaper proprietors.

TV is another field in which colour will play an increasingly important role. Even when the TV buying boom in England was in full swing it was common to hear, from those who weren't buying, 'I'm waiting for colour' – even five years ago it seemed imminent. We didn't get it. The Americans who have got it don't find it all that easy to control. A stable black and white picture is quite a miracle and to bring under control the many

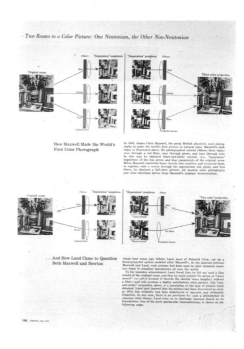

Hi-Fi ad

Land colour theory explained in *Fortune* magazine

Early demonstration of webb offset

TV and the wide screen

variables of a three-colour system may be possible in the lab but it's asking a lot to balance these out in domestic conditions.[2]

Extraordinarily enough, here also it is Edwin Land who has made the breakthrough. In an article in Scientific America, May 1959, he announced the most fantastic of his findings. In this short paper he reverses every assumption about colour vision that has been made since Isaac Newton formulated a theory of colour. Scientific America gave it top billing but its editorial note puts the facts mildly in describing the work as 'suggesting that classical theories of colour vision are inadequate'.

John Campbell Junior, editor of Astounding Science Fiction, was less cautious. He says, in a literally astounding editorial, 'As an off-hand estimate, I'd say that the electronics industry in the United States has just had the plug pulled out on a 200 megabuck investment – their entire colour TV program just went down the drain. Finished – kaput – wiped out'. Dr Land, as a first step in investigating colour with the object of producing colour film for his sixty-second camera, set up a lab for the examination of light-colour phenomena as described by Newton. During one experiment, using colour filters from different light sources, colours were seen that had no right to be there, according to classical theory. At first they were attributed to eye fatigue effects, an explanation that had been accepted by earlier observers of the same phenomena, but the results could be controlled so perfectly that a completely new theory had to be given to explain their persistence.[3]

This is Land's experiment: he takes two black and white photographs of a coloured subject, both from the same viewpoint. In front of one exposure there is a red filter, in front of the other he puts a green filter – these provide two black and white transparencies. The only difference in these two images is that of tone between one area and another caused by the colour selective effect of the filters. These two black and white transparencies are put into two projectors and the two images are superimposed on a screen to make one picture. In front of the beam of light from one of the projectors a red filter is placed – the other is left with white light. The image on

the screen is visible in a full range of colours – all the reds, blues, yellows, greens, blacks and white of the original subject. According to classical theory this is impossible – if the eye sees colour it was supposed to be because the eye is responding to different wavelengths – reds for specific longer wavelengths and blues for specific shorter wavelengths. It was unbelievable that the result of Land's experiment could produce any other effect than a dilution of red light by white light, which could only result in pinks. Surprisingly enough, practically any filters are said to produce similar results; the only essentials are that two filtered records (the two black and white transparencies) are separated by some colour interval, though this can be exceedingly small (two different filters in the yellow range will do) as long as there is a measurable difference of wavelength. A photograph through the longer wavelength filter is termed the long record and a photograph through the shorter wavelength is termed the short record. When the two records are projected it is essential that a filter of long wavelength (though not necessarily the same as that used to make the record) is put over the long record and a filter of shorter wavelength over the short record – though here again the wavelength is not critical – it can even be white light, as long as the shorter waves are present. A fully coloured image will result. If a spectrograph, an instrument which measures wavelengths, is used to examine the light on the screen it will register only the wavelengths of the filters, for other wavelengths cannot possibly be reflected from the screen under these conditions.

Land has, by these means, sought to establish that the human eye doesn't react to different wavelengths of light to register colour but deduces colour from quite different kinds of information. Strangely enough it is reported that when a colour photograph is taken of the projected image the full range of colour is visible on the colour slide. This suggests that, as far as light is concerned anyway, colour technicians have been trying to give too much information. Maintaining the balance of overspecified colour systems has created one snag after another. The third channel may not be informing about the colour of the object but about the light source illuminating the object. This has demanded a precise

[2] I too find it astonishing to encounter these comments on colour TV. It doesn't seem possible that a present-day commonplace could be discussed as a chimera little more than twenty years ago.

[3] We haven't heard much about the Land colour theory of late so I suspect that Newton continues to win out over Goethe. Land has, in the meantime, given us an extraordinary (and still improving) 'instant' colour film and that masterpiece of apparatus design, the SX camera.

matching of the light source illuminating the image. Does this great problem no longer exist? A reduction of colour information to a two-channel system would have tremendous repercussions. If anything, John Campbell's comment was an understatement.

This work by Land is most rewarding, I feel, not simply because it gives the promise of new technical solutions, new luxuries for us to enjoy. It also reveals something more important: it shows that technicians, empirical scientists of Land's kind, are not simply manipulating the knowledge given to us by classical science. At any time, if we look hard enough, some new experience will provide more knowledge about the subtleties of the human machine, which can, in turn, establish new relationships of that organism to its environment.

Polaroid of lecture audience at the ICA, 1960

Audience at Cambridge University, 1960

Audience at Newcastle University, 1960

Audience at Royal College of Art, 1960

Design

Look magazine's fabulous fifties

Persuading image

The fifties have seen many changes in the human situation; not least among them are the new attitudes towards those commodities which affect most directly the individual way of life – consumer goods. It is now accepted that saucepans, refrigerators, cars, vacuum cleaners, suitcases, radios, washing machines – all the paraphernalia of mid-century existence – should be designed by a specialist in the look of things. This is a more novel state of affairs than one at first suspects. It is surprising to realize how recently Industrial Design has established itself as a profession; how new are the schools throughout the world that offer training in this field. A high proportion of them have come into being within the last ten years. A new professional class, whose task it is to fashion the appearance of objects in everyday use, is here. Not merely *here,* its activities are found to be of overwhelming importance to the total world population. America's last recession, with all its side effects, was due largely to the diminution in sales of automobiles in the USA – a situation in which one of the key factors was the failure of car designers to strike the selling image. Siler Freeman, *Look* Business Editor, said: 'The way America reacts to the 1959 models will determine to a large degree how much prosperity America will enjoy. If auto sales jump the chain reaction can be miraculous.'

Design is a sales weapon – goods that sell to consumers must show the hand of the stylist. Not only can design stimulate sales but the designer himself has become a marketing aid. In a recent copy of the *New Yorker* three corner spaces on consecutive pages were devoted to the advertising of a range of dictaphones. The designed object took second place to the presentation of the personalities involved. The first of these ads told of the specialist colour consultant who had chosen the colours of the range – the second was devoted to the design consultant – the third to the executive genius who welded these talents into the manufacturing organisation. The fact that someone had thought hard about what colour was to be applied to the housing of the units was considered a more valuable sales point than the technical specification of the equipment itself. Of course, the high power virtuoso industrial designer is not a new phenomenon – Raymond Loewy and Walter Dorwin Teague have been at it for a good many years. William Morris and Walter Gropius realized the potential. What is new is the increased number of

Orginally a lecture given in Newcastle and at the ICA in London, 1959, called 'The designed image of the fifties'. *Design* magazine requested a shortened version (Bibliography: 12) which it titled 'Persuading Image'. The above replaces some of the cut material.

exponents and their power and influence upon our economic and cultural life. Design is established and training for the profession is widespread.

Few of the great designers can have been trained as such – there was no-one to train them. They dropped into it – some were trained as architects or sculptors or painters, many were journalists – men who were able to talk their way round a problem, with a quick grasp of technical affairs and a flair for selling good form and themselves. Now there are people, a few thousand more every year, who are emerging into industry as trained designers and they will be faced with the something that will not have been included in the training of many – marketing. The student designer is taught to respect his job, to be interested in the form of the object for its own sake as a solution to given engineering and design problems – but he must soon learn that in the wider context of an industrial economy this is a reversal of the real values of present-day society. Arthur Drexler has said of the automobile 'Not only is its appearance and its usefulness unimportant . . . What is important is to sustain production and consumption'. The conclusion that he draws from this is that 'if an industrialised economy values the process by which things are made more than it values the thing, the designer ought to have the training and inclinations of a psycho-analyst. Failing this he ought, at least, to have the instincts of a reporter, or, more useful, of an editor.'[1]

The image of the fifties shown here is the image familiar to readers of the glossy magazines – 'America entering the age of everyday elegance'; the image of *Life* and *Look, Esquire* and the *New Yorker*; the image of the fifties as it was known and moulded by the most successful editors and publicists of the era, and the ad-men who sustained them – 'the fabulous fifties' as *Look* has named them. Being 'plush at popular prices' is a prerogative that awaits us all. Whether we like it or not, the designed image of our present society is being realized now in the pages of the American glossies by people who can do it best – those who have the skill and imagination to create the image that sells and the wit to respond humanly to their own achievements.

The present situation has not arrived without some pangs of conscience. Many designers have fought against the values which are the only ones that seem to work to the economic good of the American population. There is still a

Cadillac, El Camino, 1954

Pontiac, front end detail

[1] Foreword to *Problems of Design,* George Nelson, Whitney Publications.

hangover from the fortyish regret that things do not measure up to the aesthetic standards of pure design; the kind of attitude expressed in 1947 by George Nelson when he wrote: 'I marvel at the extent of the knowledge needed to design, say, the *Buick* or the new *Hudson* – but I am also struck by my inability to get the slightest pleasure out of the result'.[2] There has since been a change of heart on both sides; on the part of the designers, the men who establish the visual criteria, towards a new respect for the ability of big business to raise living standards – and an appreciation, by big business, of the part that design has to play in sales promotion. What was new and unique about the fifties was a willingness to accept a new situation and to custom-build the standards for it.

There is not, of course, a general acceptance of this point of view. Some designers, especially on this side of the Atlantic, hold on to their old values and are prepared to walk backwards to do so. Misha Black goes so far as to suggest that advanced design is incompatible with quantity production when he says: 'If the designer's inclination is to produce forward-looking designs, ahead of their acceptability by large numbers of people, then he must be content to work for those manufacturers whose economic production quantities are relatively small'.[3]

While Professor Black was consoling the rearguard for being too advanced Lawrence Alloway was stressing the fact that 'Every person who works for the public in a creative manner is face to face with the problem of a mass society'.[4] It is just this coming to terms with a mass society which has been the aim and the achievement of industrial design in America. The task of orientation towards a mass society required a rethink of what was, so convincingly, an ideal formula. Function is a rational yardstick and when it was realized in the twenties that all designed objects could be measured by it, everyone felt not only artistic but right and good. Max Bill wrote in 1952: 'the aesthetics impulse which stimulates the emergence of good practical forms is always a basically moral one'. The trouble is that consumer goods function in many ways; looked at from the point of view of the business man, design has one function – to increase sales. If a design for industry does not sell in the quantities for which it was designed to be manufactured then it is not functioning properly.

The element in the American attitude to production which

Dream kitchen

[2] A lecture at The Chicago Institute of Design, reprinted in *Problems of Design.*

[3] *The Honest Designer,* the Percy Wells Memorial Lecture given by Misha Black to the Technical College for the Furnishing Trades, Shoreditch, 1958.

[4] *Architectural Design,* February 1958, page 84.

worries the European most is the cheerful acceptance of obsolescence; American society is committed to a rapid quest for mass mechanized luxury because this way of life satisfies the needs of American industrial economy. By the early fifties it had become clear in America that production was no problem. The difficulty lay in consuming at the rate which suited production and this rate is not only high – it must accelerate. The philosophy of obsolescence, involving as it does the creation of short-term solutions, designs that do not last, has had its drawbacks for the designer – the moralities of the craftsman just do not fit when the product's greatest virtue is impermanence. But some designers have been able to see in obsolescence a useful tool for raising living standards. George Nelson in his book *Problems of Design,* states the case very forcibly: 'Obsolescence as a process is wealth-producing, not wasteful. It leads to constant renewal of the industrial establishment at higher and higher levels, and it provides a way of getting a maximum of good to a maximum of people'. His conclusion is: 'What we need is more obsolescence not less'. Mr Nelson's forward-looking attitude squarely faced the fact that design must function in industry to assist rapid technological development; we know that this can be done by designing for high production rates of goods that will require to be renewed at frequent intervals.

The responsibility of maintaining the desire to consume, which alone permits high production rates, is a heavy one and industry has been cross-checking. With a view to the logical operation of design, American business utilized techniques which were intended to secure the stability of its production. In the late forties and early fifties an effort was made, through market research, to ensure that sales expected of a given product would, in fact, be available to it. Months of interrogation by an army of researchers formed the basis for the design of the Edsel, a project which involved the largest investment of capital made by American business in post-war years. This was not prompted by a spirit of adventure – rather it was an example of the extreme conservatism of American business at the time. It was not looking to the designer for inspiration but to the public, seeking for a composite image in the hope that this would mean pre-acceptance in gratitude for wish-fulfilment. American business simply wanted the dead cert. It came as something of a shock when

This is the **EDSEL**

"A remarkable new automobile

joins the Ford family of fine cars"

Edsel ad

Cadillac ad

the dead cert came home last. The Edsel proved that it took so long to plan and produce an automobile that it was no good asking the customer what he wanted – the customer was not the same person by the time the car was available. Also the market had changed: the Edsel was designed for the medium price bracket but in the course of its production the medium price market was attacked from below – all the low price cars were being steadily elevated into the medium price field so that there is virtually a two-class system in operation in America now. And in any case, by that time it had been pretty well established with other commodities that consumers didn't buy what they said they wanted. Customers don't know what they want – they purchase things.

Peter Drucker, in *Harpers Bazaar* April 55, in a piece on 'The Promise of the next 20 years' said: 'Automation requires continuous production of set levels of output for great lengths of time – it is essential therefore to establish a stable, predictable and expanding market'. Industry needed something more than a promise of purchase – it needed an accurate prophecy about purchasers of the future. Motivation research, by a deeper probe into the sub-conscious of possible consumers, prepared itself to give the answers.

It had been realized that the dynamic of industrial production was creating an equal dynamic in the consumer, for there is no ideal in design, no pre-determined consumer, only a market in a constant state of flux. Every new product and every new marketing technique affects the continually modifying situation. The rapid modulations in a product's ability to provide status satisfaction are typical of the rate of transition. Status symbols are essentially an instrument of social change. For example, it has long been understood that the status aspect of car purchasing is of fundamental importance to production. A Cadillac will work as a status symbol for anyone who can purchase it, but only for a limited period – as long as it is new and fairly rare.

Maintaining status requires constant renewal of the goods that bestow it. As *Industrial Design* has said: 'post-war values were made manifest in chrome and steel'.[5] But the widespread realisation of aspirations has meant that gratification through automobile ownership has become less effective. Apart from superficial changes of body

[5] *Industrial Design*, February 1959, page 79.

Plymouth – 'A rich man's car at a poor man's price'

treatment, automobiles had become very much alike. Models in all price groups had reached the same size – the maximum. They all held a reserve of usable power and provided pretty much the same comfort and utility value, The process of upgrading the lower price cars operated in two ways. Styling narrowed the gap – Plymouth, the low price car of the Chrysler group, is closer stylistically to the Imperial, the most expensive, than the Dodge. Chrysler or de Soto from the same stable. Plymouth is the rich man's car at the price that most Americans can afford. The second kind of elevation is through optional extras – any of the low price models can have all the refinements of the higher grades for an appropriate additional payment. There is now a fair degree of confusion about the status of the owner of any vehicle. Other outlets, home ownership and the greater differentiation possible through furnishing and domestic appliances, have taken on more significance. Company policy has to take many such factors into account. Decisions about the relationship of a company to society as a whole often do more to form the image than the creative talent of the individual designer. Each of the big manufacturers has a design staff capable of turning out hundreds of designs every year covering many possible solutions. Design is now a selective process, the goods that go into production being those that motivation research suggests the consumer will want.

Motivation research has had a big effect on design. It created a new automobile type in the hard-top when Dichter formulated the Mistress versus Wife theory of car purchase. It also put forward general principles which have affected overall styling attitudes. *Chicago Tribune's* study of automobiles indicated that one significant function of the automobile is to express aggression – a dominant concept of the mid-fifties and one which designers have successfully translated into form.

Most of the major producers in America now find it necessary to employ a motivation staff and many employ outside consultants in addition. Chevrolet has a panel of psychologically-oriented experts who evaluate the psychological overtones of the sounds and smells of their various models. The sound of a door slam is regarded as especially significant. Chevrolet's general manager said in 1957 'We've got the finest door-slam this year we've ever had – a big car sound.' The design consultants of America have also had to comply with the trend to

SYLVANIA
Thunderbird
7-TRANSISTOR

with Flying Colors!

Thunderbird transistor radio

Oldsmobile ad

motivation research, and *Industrial Design* reports[6] that most now have their own research staffs. This direction of design by consumer research has led many designers to complain of the limitation of their contribution. The designer cannot see himself just as a cog in the machine which turns consumer motivations into form – he feels that he is a creative artist. Aaron Fleischmann last year, in the same *Industial Design* article, expressed these doubts: 'In the final analysis, however, the designer has to fall back on his own creative insights in order to create products that work best for the consumer; for it is an axiom of professional experience that the consumer cannot design – he can only accept or reject'. His attitude underrates the creative power of the yes/no decision. It pre-supposes the need to reserve the formative binary response to a single individual instead of to a corporate society. But certainly it is worthwhile to consider the possibility that the individual and trained response may be the speediest and most efficent technique.

Consumer feed-back and creative impulse are two of the ingredients for the designer – there are others. Engineering skill has always been necessary and knowledge of communications technique is becoming essential. It is increasingly necessary to convey usage information on products. One of the more taxing demands on a designer is to develop symbols which will simplify control of domestic appliances.

Design in the fifties has been dominated by consumer research. A decade of mass psycho-analysis has shown that, while society as a whole displays many of the symptoms of individual case histories, analysis of which makes it possible to make shrewd deductions about the response of large groups of people to an image, the researcher is no more capable of creating the image than the consumer. The mass arts, or pop arts, are not popular arts in the old sense of art arising from the masses. They stem from a professional group with a highly developed cultural sensibility. As in any art, the most valued products will be those which emerge from a strong personal conviction and these are often the products which succeed in a competitive market. During the last ten years market and motivation research have been the most vital influence on leading industrialists' approach to design. They have gone to research for the answers rather than to the designer – his role, in this period, has been a submissive

[6] *Industrial Design,* February 1958, page 34–43.

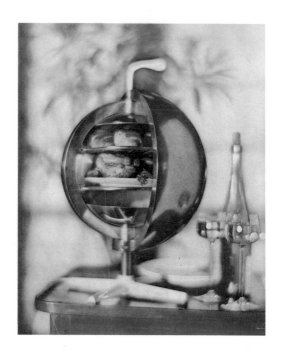

Alcoa table oven

one, obscuring the creative contribution which he can best make. He has, of course, gained benefits from this research into the consumers' response to images – in package design particularly techniques of perception study are of fundamental importance. But a more efficient collaboration between design and research is necessary. The most important function of motivation studies may be in aiding *control* of motivations – to use the discoveries of motivation research to promote acceptance of a product when the principles and sentiments have been developed by the designer. Industry needs greater control of the consumer – a capitalist society needs this as much as a Marxist society. The emphasis of the last ten years on giving the consumer what he thinks he wants is a ludicrous exaggeration of democracy; propaganda techniques could be exploited more systematically by industry to mould the consumer to its own needs.

This is not a new concept. Consumer requirements and desires – the consumer's image of himself – are being modified continually now; the machinery of motivation control is already established. At present this control operates through the intuitions of advertising men, editors of opinion and taste-forming mass circulation magazines, and the journalists who feed them. But these techniques are too haphazard, too uncertain – fashion is subject to whims and divergencies, to personal eccentricities which squander the means of control. As monopolistic tendencies increase we can expect a more systematic application of control techniques with greater power to instil the craving to consume. It will take longer to breed desire for possession when the objects to be possessed have sprung, not directly from the subconscious of the consumer himself, but from the creative consciousness of an artistic sensibility – but the time-lag will have distinct advantages for industry.

An industry programmed five years and more ahead of production has to think big and far-out. Product design, probing into future and unknown markets, must be venturesome and, to be certain of success, stylistically and technically valid. As the situation stands at the moment it is anybody's guess (some guessers shrewder than others), which images and symbols will mean most to the public in 1965. It is like someone in 1945 trying to forecast a specific description of Marilyn Monroe. New solutions in product design need to be as inherently likeable and efficient as

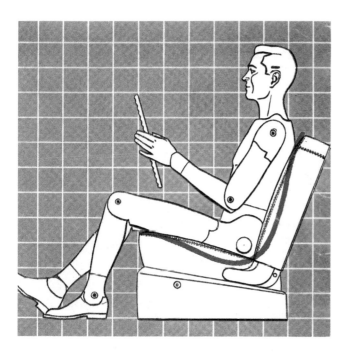

Ford's model man

M M and be as capably presented to the public by star propagandists. Many successful products attain high sales after several years of low production rates. The market is made by the virtues of the object: the Eames chair and the Volkswagen, best-sellers in recent years, are concepts which date back to the thirties. Detroit cannot wait that long and this impatience is a clue to what we can expect in all the consumer industries. New products need market preparation to close the gap. Industry, and with it the designer, will have to rely increasingly on the media which modify the mass audience – the publicists who not only understand public motivations but who play a large part in directing public response to imagery. They should be the designers' closest allies, perhaps more important in the team than researchers or sales managers. Ad man, copywriter and feature editor need to be working together with the designer at the initiation of a programme instead of as a separated group with the task of finding the market for a completed product. The time-lag can be used to design a consumer to the product and he can be 'manufactured' during the production span. Then producers should not feel inhibited, need not be disturbed by doubts about the reception their products may have by an audience they do not trust, the consumer can come from the same drawing board.

Within this framework the designer can maintain a respect for the job and himself while satisfying a mass audience; his responsibility to that amorphous body is more important than his estimation of the intrinsic value of the product itself – design has learned this lesson in the fifties. The next phase should consolidate that understanding of the essential service he is providing for industry and consumer, and extend the use of new psychological techniques as part of the designer's equipment in finding more precise solutions to the needs of society.

Addendum

While it is gratifying to find so much comment evoked by my article I am less happy to see that their sense of outrage has blinded its critics to the general tenets propounded. The phrase that caused the alarm – 'designing the consumer to the product' – is a redefinition of a well-known process; for the ultimate political evil it was called fascism, when directed at purely commercial objectives it is called salesmanship, without the moral overtones it is known as education. We are all concerned, in one way or another, with the conversion of others to a point of view.

Put briefly the article said this: 1, increased productive capacity is a basic social good; 2, any means of achieving increased productive capacity, even the production of goods of dubious value, is, in the long term, likely to benefit society; 3, is it possible to have accelerating productive capacity without short term ills, i.e., manufacture of meretricious goods? Yes; by fully appreciating and utilising current communications and consumer manipulation techniques we can devise methods of gaining increasing productive capacity through the production of socially beneficial goods, i.e., goods well-designed for their purpose, with all that that implies today.

Stated in this form most of the objections to my thesis would vanish with the exception of Dr Banham's (whose reading was as slipshod as any since he repeats much of what I said in a tone of contradiction) but he is so much a democrat that he equates 'controlled' with 'being pushed around'. If his conception of democracy is carried much further there is a danger of his becoming conservative.

Design magazine, June 1960, followed up the publication of *Persuading Image* with a 'symposium' for which it 'asked a number of designers, critics and manufacturers in Europe and America to comment on the issues raised'. I was given 'the last word.'

Artificial obsolescence

Obsolescence can result from so many factors so interwoven that what is artificial and what is natural cannot readily be identified. Very high obsolescence rates are found in the aircraft industry and also in women's dresses. In the aircraft industry design obsolescence is caused by a continuous effort towards higher and higher standards of performance. This, I take it, is not 'artificial obsolescence'. Women's clothes become obsolete according to a cycle determined by the whim and genius of Paris fashion houses. I suppose this is 'artificial'. One is more artificial than the other because there may be thought to be a greater need for increased performance of aeroplanes than for adornment of women, though one can see that such values are relative to the technical sophistication of the society in question.

A healthy economy, in western capitalist terms, must effectively maintain a desire to consume after the physical needs of a population have been satisfied. The current solution of frequent styling changes is well proved. However wasteful, the techniques of redefining the object through style, and redefining the consumer through the kind of advertising which seeks to persuade him that he has changed – and thus his needs are different – have permitted expansion of productive potential.

Induced obsolescence is sometimes accused of damaging design standards. I don't know that this is fair, for high style – the American label for what we term good design – has been a valued ingredient in the change cycle. There will always be designs which combat the tendency towards change. The Volkswagen, Citröen, the Eames chairs, the Pither stove and Cona coffee maker have virtues which keep production at a balanced level for long periods without the stimulus of changed designs. Change is most likely to occur in those objects that least deserve to live. Promoted obsolescence does also provide other pleasures; newness, for its own sake, gives a joyful bonus.

All too often real advances are prevented by a reluctance in industry to change the production system. Artificial obsolescence can be caused by inflexible production plants which inhibit fundamental change

NEW CARS

A FULL COLOR GUIDE TO THE 1958 AMERICAN AND FOREIGN MODELS

and encourage superficial modifications. An investigation into the needs for making large-scale production units more flexible would be valuable in this context. Until Detroit can switch from making cars to making houses – and back – according to social need, we must expect it to preserve its empire as best it can.

Volkswagen ad

Inquest on the Festival of Britain

Question 1: The term 'Festival style' has often been used. Was there, in fact a single Festival style, and if so, what was it?

In so far as industrial design is concerned it cannot be said that there was a *Festival* style. Style is the projection into form of a well-defined attitude – aesthetic, social or philosophical. Style, any kind of style, emerges with the attainment of desired objectives. There was no stylistic unity of purpose in the consumer goods exhibited at the *Festival of Britain.*

The objects that I now regard as characteristic of the *Festival* were all, I think, commissioned by the *Festival* authorities. They hung together because the designer had a precise specification both at the material level and in relation to the mood of the occasion: Ernest Race's outdoor chairs; balustrades and barriers; some of the display detailing; thin rod structures often with balls at the terminations (a sympathetic echo of the current delight in molecular models); an eager use of expanded metal as an infilling material; decorative perforations in metal; printed spots – these are the characteristics which made *Festival* a style. Perhaps it is unfair to include this photograph of an umbrella stand recently purchased by the Senior Common Room at King's College, Durham University, but it is an exaggeration which vividly demonstrates the disastrous perpetuation of the style in furnishing.

The most successful objects in the *Festival,* stylistically, were the buildings – but here the style was borrowed, not indigenous. I doubt if the normal visitor to the South Bank exhibition now recalls a single item among the goods displayed there, but there is a good chance that he will remember with pleasure the total environmental experience.

The *Festival* was an elegantly prepared platform from which to jump into a newly designed future – unfortunately the leap found us just where we were.

Question 2: Has the style made an important contribution to subsequent developments in design?
How did it relate to contemporary developments overseas?

You will have gathered that my response to *Festival* style is negative. It was, and is, a subclassification of 'contemporary', a term sanctioned and frequently used by

Bibliography: 17. A questionaire put by *Design* Magazine to review the Festival ten years after the event.

Festival inspired umbrella stand

the Council of Industrial Design prior to the *Festival,* and which has doubtful value.

Other styling characteristics of the *Festival* have also left an onerous heritage. The treatment of type on buildings has suffered badly. Most architects during the last 10 years have succumbed to the use of hideously distorted Egyptian types to label quite presentable buildings. The official *Festival* choice gave a bad lead to architects, whose addiction has since been nourished by the *Architectural Review.*

I regret also the hangover of the *Festival* delight in pageantry. This is coupled with an idea that our industrialists cherish – that an aura of tradition, some scent of our royal heritage, is what makes our goods attractive to overseas markets. However true this may be, it is a dangerous belief to rely on when markets can change overnight. The inversion of this attitude affects our present design position too, for the orientation of design to specific overseas markets can only be a short-term solution – copying current American styles is the best way to stay a year or two out-of-date in America.

The success of German, Italian and American design during the past 10 years has derived from products which create a national character simply through their consistent excellence, because sufficient brilliant designers have been available and have been given the generous backing of leaders of industry to exploit their flair. Braun, Olivetti, IBM achieved their standing largely through their design policy. It seems that British industrialists have yet to be convinced that a dedicated approach to design is the primary factor in the establishment of brand character.

Question 3: What do you consider were the main pace-setting industries that were represented at the Festival? Has the pace been maintained?

When looking through *Design in the Festival* (an illustrated publication produced by the CoID in 1951) one is struck by the good impression that the transport section makes. The Rolls, the Morris Minor and the Jaguar XK 120 all have great distinction, achieved through consciously different styling approaches, and all have sold phenomenally. The success of the Morris Minor owes a lot to the executive decision which gave Alec Issigonis his

Bridges drill

Braun turntable and tuner

Morris Minor

Richard Huw's fountain

head. But it took another 10 years before BMC let him come up with the Mini-Minor – they were too busy flirting with Farina.

Both domestic appliances and kitchen equipment had reached a very high standard during the post-war surge but, although the standards of 1951 may have been maintained, little development of the position has been made. Machine tools showed a promise which has not been fulfilled – the market which then assured sale for a machine which could do its job properly has now been tempered by a demand for machines which also *look* as though they are capable of producing the elegance and precision of modern consumer goods. But very few English manufacturers pay much attention to the way machines are labelled – dials and operational symbols are often badly detailed in comparison with German machines, for example. Operators' handbooks sadly ill-considered. The clarity of design and finish in the Bridges micro-precision drill shown at the *Festival* has yet to gain full acceptance as a standard for larger industrial machines.

Question 4: If you agree that some industries reveal weak design standards do you think they have improved?

Among the weaker industries, from the design standpoint, were the furniture manufacturers exhibited at the *Festival*. Perhaps because their design is dominated by furnishing ideas, television and radio cabinets also made a poor showing. TV and radio are pulling out from under the drab weight of the woodworkers' crafts now, but the notion seems to have got about that if the cabinets need not match the furniture today then they will have to match the curtains. Once again I must say that it is the conservatism of manufacturers that holds back progress in design. Every manufacturer seems content merely to match his competitors' ranges. There is too little stress laid on product design research in the consumer goods industries, too little initiation of product programmes at the design level, not enough probing of markets and too many curbs on imagination; production programming is all too often restricted by backward-looking sales executives. This string of complaints is prompted by the thought that if we were to repeat the *Festival* in 1961 we would not be able to put on a much better show than 10 years ago, in spite of the increased efforts of the CoID. And perhaps some of the

fault lies with the CoID, for it has been slow in finding standards for itself. The CoID's publications at the time of the *Festival* were miserably designed and wantonly inconsistent in design theory. No clear lead had been given by the CoID, only vague well-meaning generalisations. We can only hope that the change in the CoID's own policy in recent years will have an effect and will lead to a firmer realization of its responsibilities.

Question 5: What contribution did the Festival make to exhibit design techniques?

Display technique, the contribution of the professional exhibition designers, was lamentable. Most of the great exhibitions since 1851 have produced some display feature of historic importance; a manipulation of interior space which commands respect to this day. The work of Frederick Kiesler and le Corbusier in the *Paris Exhibition,* 1925; that of Persico and Nizzoli in Milan, 1933-34; the Spanish Pavilion and the Temps Nouveaux Pavilion in Paris, 1937; Ruscone's exhibition of studies in proportion and Ernesto Roger's *Architecture, the measure of man,* both from the Milan *Triennale,* 1951; the contribution of Charles Eames and Alexander Girard in the fifties – the list is as long as your arm, but why go on? The *Festival of Britain* was singularly lacking in authority in its confined spaces and it was the display technique which failed. The Dome of Discovery provided a space of rare and vital proportions, yet it was wrecked by the display-men who converted it into a warehouse full of clobber. In general, one trailed through corridor after corridor of frilly whimsy, glad to escape into the open and to the prospect of exhilarating exhibition architecture – and Richard Huws' fountain, one of the few exhibition details of international class.

Popular Culture and Personal Responsibility

NEW PRODUCTS ARE THE BY-PRODUCT
of a society undergoing change. They reflect the needs of unaccustomed leisure time, the fading boundaries between work and play, between gracious living and easy living — and present unfettered challenges to the product designer.

It might be supposed that a speaker on Art and Design in a conference on Popular Culture and Personal Responsibility would have some pretensions to intellectual status beyond the average or normal. As an artist who teaches and practises design (mainly because of the unpopularity of his paintings), I have often been called long-haired. My wife's remark that I am a long-haired artist who is fast becoming an egg-head emphasises the general position I occupy in society as a person with some claims to intellectual standards above the norm.

But a few years ago I began to doubt that, in a twentieth century urban culture, such distinctions have the kind of meaning that they had in sixteenth century Italy or eighteenth century England. In 1949 I went to the cinema about three times a week, a compulsion which had little to do with the merits of the films I saw; Rank cinemas, at that time, showed a healthy profit. In the late fifties, as my attendance at the cinema declined, I became aware that my thoughtless change of habit had created a crisis in the film industry, not only was Rank losing money but I had even caused severe cuts in production at major Hollywood studios. A few weeks after I purchased a camera I read of the fantastic increase in sales of amateur photographic equipment. If I buy paperbacks instead of cloth-bound books the publishing industry makes a fuss about paperbacks taking over. When I bought just one car we had a national traffic problem. Only a few weeks ago I read in a newspaper that fruit-growers in England are very worried about the drop in sales of cooking apples. They attribute their difficulties to the modern housewife who cannot be bothered to cook an apple pie like mother used to make; the point struck home, my wife has never made an apple pie, I only get my favourite dessert when my mother-in-law comes to stay.

It is not surprising that in the face of these and countless other facts I have come to feel in myself an overwhelming normality. Preston Sturges made a film some years back about a young man who was discovered to be a statistically average individual; this being was worth his weight in gold to the advertising agencies and politicians because he had only to give his opinion on any subject and the pulse of the whole culture was measured; market research and public

Bibliography: 14

opinion polls became redundant. Perhaps I do not come up to this high ideal, but I do feel my consumer reactions are typical.

It seems to me that the artist, the intellectual, is not the alien that he was and his consumption of popular culture is due, in some measure, to his new role as a creator of popular culture. Popular art, as distinct from fine art, art created by the people, anonymously, crudely and with a healthy vigour, does not exist today. Its present-day equivalent, pop art, is now a consumer product absorbed by the total population but created for it by the mass entertainment machine, which uses the intellectual as an essential part of its technique. The results are highly personalised and sophisticated, but also have a healthy vigour.

Although the intellectual participates in the production and consumption of popular culture he is apart from it in one important sense; he is more aware of the entire circumstances of the phenomenon as a social situation than is the normal consumer. This awareness is most important in that he understands that he is adopting standards oriented to mass tastes and it is this new catholicism which has caused alarm among the critics of popular culture. They feel that he has sold his soul to the devil.

My own view is that there is less to regret than one might suppose. An ideal culture, in my terms, is one in which awareness of its condition is universal. A culture in which each of its members accepts the convenience of different values for different groups and different occasions, one in which the artist holds tight to his own standards for himself and gives the best he can to whom he can without priggishness and with good humour, whilst facing his historical situation with honesty.

It is usual to include within the scope of the term 'mass media' such modes of communication as the cinema, TV, magazines, newspapers, radio, advertising and so on. Other fields, less obviously concerned with transmitting a message, are addressing their audience in the same language and I was glad to find that art and design were included in the terms of reference for this conference. Marketing techniques do not stop at presenting a product; a product can be moulded to a market and sometimes vice versa. Product design itself can even start in the advertising agency. In the case of a commodity like toothpaste or cosmetics the package is of greater importance than its contents in influencing the purchaser. Many products, in which efficiency of operation is the only real essential, are dependant on the design of the shell as the factor ultimately determining sales. In its efforts to gain and hold the affection of the mass audience a product must aim to project an image of desirability as strong as that of any Hollywood star. It must have gloss and glamour, and evoke a yearning for possession.

Advocates of good design have deplored the trend towards the treatment of consumer products in terms of fashion styling. But it is necessary to consider the historic background which has led to this situation. The main force which determines the changing attitude to all manufactured goods is the need for any production plant to produce, and for its ancillary departments to find markets and dispose of products. A manufacturing plant comes into being only when a need for an object exists. It is viable only as long as a demand for its product continues. A healthy and efficient manufacturing unit must grow and improve its resources, yet the fact that its sole function is to satisfy a need means that the nearer it comes to achieving its aim the closer it comes to suicide. An ideal product, a design par excellence, might be a product which was perfectly adapted to its function; it would have a useful life stretched to the limits of available raw materials and its appearance would satisfy aesthetic considerations in such a way that it would have a permanent claim to value. But a culture which accepted only these three criteria would have to face a gradual constriction of its technological development. The interesting fact is that technology thrives best on short-term products and rapid turnover. The fastest rate of technological advance yet known has been in the aircraft industry. Since Wilbur Wright took to the air in a powered bi-plane at the beginning of this century technical development has been fantastically rapid, but it has only been achieved by means of the fastest obsolescence rate in history. Every advance puts millions of pounds and production hours on the scrap heap. But the aircraft industry has never had to regret the losses and governments have rarely felt it wise to cut the costs, for in this field high obsolescence rate is rightly regarded as a function of technological advance. The consumer appliance industries are similarly placed in this respect, though with some interesting differences. The force which applies the pressure on the aircraft industry is that of performance. No one has yet reached a stage where more miles per hour or higher altitude or improved control is not an immediate and essential objective. But in car design there are so few areas where increased efficiency of operation could encourage the high obsolescence rate necessary to keep production resources operating that artificial stimulants for rapid turnover have been found. The main method for promoting change is body styling, so the automobile coach-building industry uses the technique of haute couture. The same attitude is to be found in the major appliance industries now; some small engineering advances occur in refrigerator design, but the main effort at promoting regular change is made in restyling the box at regular intervals to stimulate the idea in prospective purchasers that the fridge they have at home is out-of-date and they themselves will be out-of-date if they do not change it.

This is the situation that has come about and it has occurred in the face of many doom prophecies from some very eminent diagnosticians of cultural ills. In the design world the warnings have recurred since the early days of the Industrial Revolution, but it seems to me that the philosophers and designers who laid the basis for the machine age aesthetic need, today, to have their tenets questioned. They may have been wrong, and I am not sure that they were not morally wrong, at least when they reached such extremes as in this comparatively recent quotation from Lewis Mumford's *Art and Technics*:

'Once we have achieved the right form for a type-object, it should keep that form for the next generation, or for the next thousand years. Indeed, we should be ready to accept further variations only when some radical advance in scientific knowledge, or some radical change in the conditions of life has come about – changes that have nothing to do with the self-indulgent caprices of men or the pressures of the market.

Then, and only then, does a modification of the type become imperative. Otherwise the ideal goal for machine production is that of static perfection, a world of immobile platonic forms, as it were a world of crystalline fixity, rather than continual change and flux.'

This cold expression of the death-wish poses some difficult problems. How can we decide that the right form for a type-object has been achieved? I would say that Sir Herbert Read is as good a judge as anyone, but if we take a look at some of the illustrated examples in *Art and Industry,* we might well be glad that the pressures of markets and the self-indulgent caprices of men have since brought a hundred variants of each type-object shown. Some of these, moreover, regardless of whether or not they satisfy the platonic yardstick, are a good deal easier to use and pleasanter to look at than the classic objects of the thirties. The moralists did, however, do a good job because they established some regulating ideas and they put forward an attitude, Form and Function, which has become the dominant and most elevated style in most industrialised societies. I find it necessary to say most rather than all, because Soviet Russia is, surprisingly, an exception. It was successful because the formal approach was accepted and became a style, but the moral philosophising was rejected. Perhaps one reason that they did not stem the tide of mechanised profusion was that the philosophy contended that the machine had a life of its own that was not an extension of human personality, that human fantasy, human irrationality and human love had no place in the machine world. Lewis Mumford went so far as to say, 'If you fall in love with a machine there is something wrong with your love life'. But have we not now reached a stage in the industrial era when appreciation, gratitude and even affection are not out of place in our feelings for the products of the machine age? For underlying the philosophy of impermanence, the continual change and flux, is a permanent endeavour to raise living standards, emotional as well as material, and we should not underrate its value to every member of industrialised society.

The moralists' high style, usually labelled 'good design' is one of the most remarkable success stories of recent years. Good design sells more products, and what

U S Air Force graveyard

Harley Earl's Alcoa chair

could be better than good design but more good design? The good designers are as capable as anyone else of coming up with a new solution. Charles Eames did not sit back in his classic chair of 1934 and hope it would last a thousand years, he has since produced four new models of the type-object chair. Modern technology offers a chance to proliferate and the human race is finding a way to control and channelize the spate of new forms and ideas. It does so by exploiting the techniques of the mass media to communicate a sense of style. The mass media cannot project a moral philosophy of form, but they can, and do, go some way to set examples of what is smart, enviable and worth attaining. *Vogue, Harpers Bazaar, Life* and *Look* put across the imagery of good design because it is good copy. Mies van der Rohe, Frank Lloyd Wright, Corbusier, Eames, Saarinen, Buckminster-Fuller, all the big-name designers and architects, and the best works of anonymous designers, get a more than fair showing in the glossy magazines with the biggest circulations. Hollywood sets are well-designed when the occasion calls for it. If the standards of the design moralists become the visual standards of the masses it will be because the mass media have succeeded in presenting the imagery, if not the ideas, persuasively to the mass audience. Where the mass media depart from the moralists is in their refusal to accept the dogma of permanent values and in their efforts to welcome and promote the machine age with humour and affection. If some object survives from the past it does so because someone loves and respects the qualities embodied in it rather than because it attains some remote platonic standards. The automobile is assimilated so completely into our culture now that its idiosyncratic reflections of human whims and subconscious desires occur as fluently as changes in women's fashions, or book design or magazine layout, and it says much for the ingenuity of man that metal is bent to his whim as easily as cloth or paper.

This Candidian view of the best of worlds needs, of course, to be tempered with some reservations. The techniques of the mass media are powerful and it is fortunate for society that the mechanics of the mass media do breed people with visual taste and discrimination. It is important, too, that they should be of open mind and also that they should respect the audience they feed for what it is: an inquisitive, acquisitive, basically good-natured and essentially receptive swarm. The mass media afford advantages to society when they are most tolerant, cordial and self-respecting, conscious of their own high standards and the need to uphold them.

The mass media have to work within the sphere of play and are constantly widening the boundaries of this sphere. The machine, in its closest contacts with the mass audience, falls also within that area of human activity and often affords the kind gratification that we associate with toys: typewriters, telephones, kitchen gadgets, washing-machines, cars, garden tools all have their serious value, but the sensual and visual functioning that is increasingly the designer's main concern provide the pleasure of games. This is not suggesting that the activity is of a lower order, the classification has its uses, for this is the way that the mass media are playing the game and playing it well. If, as seems the case, the only alternatives for maintaining high productive potential are war or totalitarianism I would say that the mass media are reasonably harmless and inherently beneficial. The danger in the efficiency of the mass media seems to me to be in their ability to influence public opinion in spheres other than play, for instance in political affairs. The showmanship of McCarthy, who ruthlessly employed the techniques of the mass media, was good business for newspapers, for the glossies and for TV regulated by audience statistics. It is for us as teachers to promote in the youth we teach a healthy suspicion of all dogma, whether it is politically oriented or aimed at fixing the pattern of our culture. What is needed for the youth of today is that they should be educated in a positive sense towards a complete understanding of the techniques of the mass media, whose products they already know and appreciate. Freedom of choice for the individual is the most precious of his democratic rights and it can only be properly exercised if he or she is in possession of all of the facts; his or her freedom should allow everyone to be what they want to be, but with cognizance.

Natural selection operates as effectively in the domain

How luxurious can an Austin Seven get?

Austin ad

of man's mechanical extensions as in his biological processes; survival of those elements best fitted for survival occurs within the great mutation rates of our mechanical productions. If we were to try, and I think we should, to work consciously with the system and not against it, then our efforts should be directed at finding synthetic aids to this process of natural selection and this is our problem now. Such synthetic aids do exist, the Council of Industrial Design is one. Exhibitions, store displays, good window-dressing also work to modify public taste, and they function best when they realise their position as part of the mass media and use its gloss and glamour and professionalism, the very qualities which have evoked suspicious comment. The analysts of popular culture in recent years have been negative in their approach. Whyte, Packard and Hoggart, whose ideas as we know have been given full rein in the mass media, are unanimous in their condemnation. The story is the same: the end of the world is upon us unless we purge ourselves of the evils of soft living and reject the drive for social and economic advantages. The effect of this criticism of our culture, coloured as it is by the hysterical overtones of its re-interpretation within the mass media, has been to create an atmosphere of unrest, which can itself be dangerous.

The mistake that critics of the mass media are making is to complain that pop art, as fed by the mass media to the mass audience, is not like fine art. But of course it is not. Fine art is assessable in terms of value judgments and its qualities are not transient, whereas pop art's values establish themselves by virtue of mass acceptance and will be expendable. What we might begin to worry about today is why current fine art is coming to assume all of the characteristics of pop art. If we were to list the essentials of pop art we might include these characteristics as fundamental to it: glamour, overt sincerity, wit, direct appeal, professionalism, novelty, an ability to co-exist within an existing pattern of style, and lastly, expendability. Only one of these properties, expendability, seems to be incompatible with the concept of fine art. Glamour, the lush emanation that the Hollywood star system employs, is something we are quite familiar with in art; French court painting and even Italian religious art

exude the same magic for the populace. Is Dickens
much the worse for a sincerity that outdoes Liberace's?
Wit is common to Sterne, Erik Satie and Paul Klee.
Much painting has direct appeal, every work of
Michelangelo was acclaimed from the moment of
unveiling. Professionalism – look at Rubens. Novelty
– the essential newness of his preoccupation is an
almost basic criterion for the artist. Artists working
within the framework of an overall style produced the
Gothic cathedrals. But expendability and fine art are
not concomitant. A work of fine art emerges only from
a consciousness of personal satisfaction which must be
shattered if the conception included the knowledge
that its value would be transitory. Yet, today, there is
increasingly a tendency for fine art to bear the stamp of
an expendable product. Art currently sanctioned by
American museums and Government Information
Services is more and more expendable (the American
situation is beginning to apply in Britain also). Art is
replaced from year to year with as little regret for the
loss of last year's star as there is for the inevitable
demotion of last month's pop record from the Top Ten.

The fine artist, the intellectual, can and should work
within the dual terms of the title of this conference:
when contributing to popular culture through the mass
media he must feel a sense of personal responsibility as
part of that culture and recognise that his act is
directed towards an audience and their needs. The
responsibility that he owes to himself is to ensure that
he also produces art objects which give him maximum
private gratification – unless the artist feels that he can
create values only for himself and regards the joy of
others only as a gratuitous intensification of his own
satisfactions he is less than an artist. This is his
personal responsibility and I suggest that it is
something that must be preserved as outside the
province of the mass media. I said earlier that the artist
must hold on to his own, and this sense of personal, yet
impersonally timeless, value is what I feel to be his.

Ulm

In 1948 Inge Aicher-Scholl, Otl Aicher and Max Bill conceived the idea of establishing an 'institute for promoting the principles of the Bauhaus'. The municipality of Ulm, having already created a people's university of some distinction, was approached and in 1953 a site was donated by the town, and the design and construction of a new school building was undertaken. The inauguration of the Hochschule für Gestaltung by Walter Gropius took place in 1955.

Among the staff invited by Max Bill to develop the curriculum was the Argentinian painter Tomás Maldonado. Maldonado joined Bill as his deputy in 1955 and a period of intense polemic ensued. Until 1956 Max Bill's word was law, then a faculty board of five members was established with Maldonado as chairman. In 1957 the board was reduced to four and during that year Max Bill's resignation from all the school's activities brought it to three, its present number. This brief outline of changes in the administration points to a dramatic and vital discussion of the pedagogical objectives.

The controversy centred upon a re-assessment of the fundamental conception of the school as a new Bauhaus. What was the role of a new Bauhaus against the technological background of the 1950s? The Bauhaus had promoted an ambiance of freedom for *self expression;* it advocated *learning by doing* and *re-education of the senses;* it demanded that this activity should have a *practical application* in human affairs and that *art* was the prime motivation. These five principles were the rocks on which the Hochschule für Gestaltung had been built and these are the rocks which subsequently have been painstakingly dug out and discarded from the foundations. The major difference between the HfG and any other school of design in the world is precisely in the rejection of those principles which gave the Bauhaus its meaning and which colour the attitudes of almost every school now available for the design student.

Examination of the syllabuses of other schools will show homage to the preparatory course developed in the Bauhaus in the 1920s and its major contribution to pedagogy. For example, in the article *Training Product Designers* (*Design* April 1958 pages 27–45) it can be seen that the first year course of the industrial design department at the Central School of Arts and Crafts lists

Bibliography: 9

Max Bill's Hochschule buildings at Ulm

several subjects in which the emphasis is on creative expression, typical of the Bauhaus influence:

'Basic design: experimental exercises to explore the possibilities of line, shape, mass, colour, tone and texture in a variety of materials.

Creative photography: experimental use of photographic processes as a new field of expression.

Creative machine setting.

Modelling and sculpture.'

But a reaction is already in evidence. Although the Royal College of Art Department of Industrial Design (Engineering) has a first year heavily loaded with basic design of the free creative kind, F C Ashford, head of the department, added this note on the course in the article *Training Product Designers,* previously mentioned: 'the lectures on mathematics, temporarily discontinued through financial stringency, are to be re-introduced, and will be closely integrated with geometry, trigonometry, applied mechanics and numerical methods of analysis'. In *Design* (April pages 49–52) an article describes how some of the disciplines of Ulm have been introduced into a course at the Regional College of Art, Manchester. These moves are symptomatic of a trend – the HfG has pioneered a comprehensive philosophy of design education fitted to the fifties and its influence will be increasingly felt throughout the world.

Max Bill's status and the Bauhaus myth attracted to Ulm a world-wide recruitment of students and teachers. Students are mature in comparison with most schools – last year the average age was 28. Many of the teachers are young. The narrowed age differential has helped to produce an atmosphere of interrogation – every pedagogical proposition is systematically examined by everyone from the faculty board down to the first year student undergoing the ardours of the foundation course. In Maldonado's words 'The school of the future must be a "school in situation" capable of being changed whenever circumstances make it necessary, whether this be 5 or 50 years.' The machinery now established at Ulm to permit this consists of a senate (all lecturers employed for more than five hours per week, two student representatives and one workshop instructor) which elects, each year, three of its members to a faculty board. The faculty board

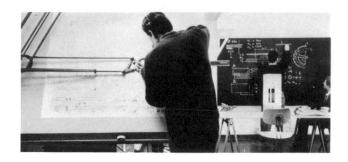

Designing at Ulm

elects its own chairman who assumes responsibility for the direction of the school to its sponsors, the Geschwister-Scholl Foundation.

Every student spends the first of his four years at Ulm in the foundation course. He then enters either of the two main divisions of production or communication, where he remains until the termination of his studies. Production is further divided into product design and building construction. Communication breaks down into the visual and verbal departments. Workshops for wood, metal and plaster, a photographic studio and a letterpress printing-shop serve all departments. Research institutes are being established in which graduates may continue research or work as salaried employees on product development commissions from German industry. In the communications institute, not yet completed, research and employment in the communications industries of film, radio, television, advertising copywriting, visual design, book production, etc., will be conducted at a post-graduate level as well as pure research in such subjects as perception.

The foundation course is directed by Maldonado and has been his major concern since his arrival at the school. It has four purposes: it introduces the students to the work of the departments, above all establishing an appreciation of the analytical method applied to all design problems at Ulm; it seeks to make the student conversant with the most important questions of technological civilisation; it trains students to work together in various disciplines and prepares them for work in teams of specialists; it also adjusts differences of level in previous education. Work in the foundation course is rigidly organised and a good deal of time is devoted to practical training; students are taught to use instruments with absolute precision. The success or failure of a student may be measured with a pair of callipers and a ruler. Drawings are required to be perfectly explicit, clean and to regulation sizes.

The theoretical side of the course is equally unambiguous with the emphasis on scientific, mathematical and geometric methods. When the student has completed his first year he has a sufficient control of his hand and knowledge of drawing techniques and conventions to represent fairly complex formal ideas. He has been trained to use hand tools (cameras and photographic processing

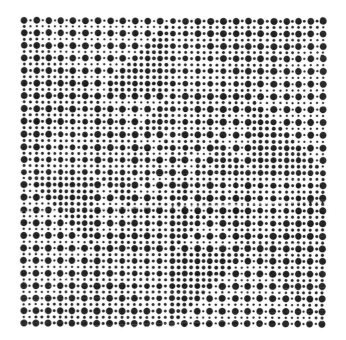

Foundation year study

equipment among them) and has handled machine tools; he also knows that this training must be related to the wider sphere of automatic machining and assembly of machine products to the theory of which he has been introduced. Mathematical, statistical and analytical methods will have been offered him as further tools. He will have learned a little about fashionable ideas in topology, cybernetics, information theory, theory of games, ergonomics and semiotics; social history will have taught him the importance of these ideas. The moral issues of his future work will have been put to him and a clear sociological framework will bind it all into a point of view; somewhat puritanical, at times a little self-righteous, but certainly a coherent base for any branch of research at the Hochschule für Gestaltung.

Industrial design is in many ways the least novel of the four departments. Its products do not strike one as remarkably different from those of the leading industrial design schools here or in America. Many of the published examples of work have been consultancy jobs by lecturers, sometimes assisted by students. One is more aware of the differences when the *methods* of designing are compared. Many problems will be approached statistically before forms are sought. Lighting research, for example, will first examine every known lighting product – these are then catalogued under type groups. These given solutions are then broken down into constituent elements and the documentation is charted according to characteristics. A pattern, analogous to the periodic tables of elements in chemistry, locates areas of new possibilities. Permutations of the analysed functions give deduced types, and practical experiments can be conducted with the derived elements to establish new forms. These methods are, of course, slow – it will be some years before their value in terms of evolved products, and evolved designers, can be assessed.

The formulation of principles has been the first task of the faculty. It is upon the validity of its objectives and the methods created for their achievement that the school must be judged. No new forms or new product solutions should be demanded from Ulm at this early stage; what might emerge is a new type of design specialist with a brain tuned to the technological background in which he will work – subject to pedagogical disciplines as severe and reasoned as those of his partners in industry, technicians trained in scientific and philosophic modes of thought.

The dangers in such training when applied to the designer lie in those sectors where a freedom of choice exists. Sooner or later one or more solutions in a complex of decisions must be adopted simply as 'preferred'. As soon as freedom of choice becomes a factor, style is involved. The crisis at Ulm will occur in the margins – its general theory is irrefutable – its attitude historically right. Style: what is it? How is it disciplined and rationalised? These are already key questions at Ulm; when Ulm has answered them, or refused with sufficient clarity to accept them as real issues, a new style will have arrived.

Petrol pump designs

U-L-M spells H.f.G.

A visit to Ulm means only one thing in our circle. *Hochschule für Gestaltung* doesn't roll off the tongue like Bauhaus – 'Ulm', however badly pronounced, is easier than 'college for the untranslatable'.

One's first impression of the building, or rather buildings for the school consists of a string of loosely attached structures, is pleasant enough. Their coherence is more apparent in the aerial photographs which decorate the prospectus than when confronted with them. The site, a hill-top some way out of town, and the rambling distribution of mainly low buildings makes it difficult to get more than a fragmentary view. On one side the VWs, Morris Minors and Fiats line up on the parking lot – on the other an ox-drawn plough is at work in an immediately adjacent field. The scene is so improbable that Inge Scholl's (she founded the school) achievement seems all the more incredible. The unfinish of the buildings is fetching, but this 'Brutalist' (P & A Smithson thought it wasn't at all bad) treatment is often due more to lack of funds than intent. Money is still required to complete the main hall and some wall and ceiling surfaces are awaiting cladding. The austere furniture, and this is uniform for both students and resident teachers, adds up to a standard of convenience that many an English university hostel might envy.

The comfortable though not comfy accommodation put at our disposal consisted of a two-level apartment, one of a series of eight designed for the use of bachelor instructors. The two levels were separated by a bed one side of which was raised six inches from its floor, the other side eight feet from the other floor. There are no reports of anyone getting out on the wrong side of the bed but one lecturer is reported to have fallen through it to the lower level when a fracture occurred in the slotted plywood spring. Ulm sleeping, as so much found there, gives the impression of having been created by Max Bill as his immediate response to clear-cut social and economic needs. The value of his solutions may vary, but no one (except perhaps Bill himself) would question the triumph of his most successful coup, the importation of Tomàs Maldonado (its present Rector) to the school.

The severe pedagogical method, administered by a

youngish staff to a student population with the high average age of 28, must present some problems. The school is ambitious and the pressures, internal and external, place a great strain on everyone connected with it. The concrete achievements, and the building is concrete enough for anyone, are formidable. The support it has been given by the West German Government, the municipal authorities and by German industry, not to mention $ 250,000 from America, is well merited. This is an international school, its allegiance is only to its own high objectives; it should be supported internationally and given an opportunity to make its contribution in a field that can stand fresh ideas – the education of the designer.

Bibliography: 7. The flippant, 'hip' style was supposed appropriate for 'Not quite architecture', *The Architects' Journal*'s gossip column. I confess I am ashamed of it now.

Reviews

The visual arts today
Editor, Gyorgy Kepes, Wesleyan University Press

The trouble with symposia is that they rarely seem to justify the time and effort taken to prepare them. This book contains 22 short articles by eminent authorities in the fields of art and science and about as many snippets of published statements by artists. All the contributors are of great distinction and each of the articles would gratify the editor of any magazine lucky enough to print it. But collected into an immaculately printed, elegantly bound culture book their merits inevitably fade, and the conflict between the topical expendability of much of the matter and the permanence of the substance of the publication provokes irritation. It is a weighty book with much lightweight reading – a symptom of the tendency in American academic life to bolster scholarly repute with publication for its own sake, with trophies which look better in a report by the dean of studies than they do in the hands of the student.

Gyorgy Kepes, the editor, is Professor of Visual Design at MIT. He has had excellent opportunities to associate with some of the best scientific and technical minds of our time and he has taken full advantage of these. His exhibition *The New Landscape,* later published as a book, revealed the extent of his infatuation with the visual by-products of scientific thought, and his continuing efforts at a synthesis of the arts through scientific affiliation seem always laudable but somehow ineffectual. In this, his latest attempt, he puts forward the views of 'more than 50 outstanding minds' on today's art and its relations to the complexities of modern life. Unfortunately, the 50-odd nibbles at the problems, in spite of their pre-digested character, leave a certain amount of dyspepsia.

Two of the articles are very much to the point. John Burchard conducts a well-timed *post mortem* on the withered partnership of architecture and the other visual arts under the title *Alienated Affections in the Arts;* and James S Ackerman reveals, in a penetrating survey, the divorce of art history and art criticism. These giants of the humanities stand up well against such scientist contributors as Paul Weiss, a biologist, and Andreas Speiser, a mathematician, who exemplify in their articles the shallowness of present relationships between art and science.

Design, October 1961

Rudolf Wittkower, as ever, is absorbing on proportion. There are odd moments throughout the book when the reader begins to sit up and take notice, but not often with such alacrity as when he meets the article by James J Gibson on *Pictures, Perspective, and Perception,* an essay which sparkles with ideas as the author forges before your eyes the terminology of his creative thinking. Mr Gibson is unique, a throwback to another age of empirical science, who seems oddly out of place in this era of methodology. While being naïve in the extreme in his understanding of contemporary art, his studies on the nature of vision abound with notions of great importance for the artist today.

Introduction to twentieth century design
Arthur Drexler and Greta Daniel, Museum of Modern Art

The Museum of Modern Art in New York is the only institution of its kind which includes design among its terms of reference. Its Department of Architecture and Design not only promotes regular exhibitions of consumer goods but has also established a design collection to preserve important examples of 'the arts of manufacture'. Some of this material has now been published by the museum in a book called an *Introduction to Twentieth Century Design.*

In its *Good Design* exhibitions, held annually from 1950–55, the museum performed a valuable service for designers and manufacturers in presenting the best of their work to the public with a seal of merit from the most powerful arbiters of taste in the USA. It differs from The Design Centre in Britain in that it underlines historical aspects of design and it functions as a custodian of relics as well as a propaganda machine. The task of curatorship in this field has demanded a search for criteria; Arthur Drexler, director of the museum's Department of Architecture and Design, discusses the postulates which have determined the collection in his introduction.

We are told that the criteria for selection of objects to be included in the permanent collection are *quality* and *historical significance.* 'An object is chosen for its quality because it is thought to have achieved, or to have originated, those formal ideas of beauty which have become the major stylistic concepts of our time.' 'Significance . . . applies to objects not necessarily works of art but which nevertheless have contributed importantly to the development of design.' Value, within these terms, is assessed by a committee of trustees of the museum (sprinkled with such illustrious names as Ford, Rockefeller and Guggenheim) from recommendations made by the staff of the Design Department.

Any short list of design masterpieces is bound to be inadequate. This seems, at times, unduly biased. The earnest wish of the sponsors that the collection will provide a record of 'the most beautiful artifacts of our time' may be fulfilled in respect of the 38 chairs included, but what about those light fittings? Of the six shown only one by Gerrit Rietveld has any beauty or historical significance, though certainly the other five endorse the catalogue note

Design, December 1959

'the well designed individual lighting fixture remains a relatively rare object'; and I should have thought that the designs illustrated on page 77 are likely to prove less valuable to posterity than a page from Sears Roebuck. Shaky, too, is the taste which collects random-looking electrical control gear because it resembles a Jackson Pollock. The collection is very conscious of its art auspices, and its foibles derive from this slant. The trustees are clearly susceptible to the cleaned-up craft approach – only about a third of the objects illustrated could be classed as industrial products. Arthur Drexler is fairly smug about this characteristic: he finds it easy to accept the fact that the definition 'major stylistic concepts of our time' excludes, in practice, those styling concepts which have dominated consumer goods in 'our time'; he is no less assured when, in announcing that 'the collection, as yet, includes no television set, no refrigerator, no telephone and only a relatively few mechanical appliances', he lays the blame on 'commercial factors irrelevant, or even harmful, to aesthetic quality'. Yet this can hardly explain the fact that *Twentieth Century Design* does not present a single example of production equipment –not one hand tool.

But it is from the conventionality of its attitudes that it acquires some strength; for the collection only scores heavily with the big guns: Aalto, Breuer, Mies, le Corbusier, Rietveld, Saarinen, Eames – a list which stems from the museum's predilection for functionalism and the conviction that 'every one of the major innovations of modern furniture design has been the work of an architect'. In aligning its taste with the Modern Movement in architecture it has, perforce, aligned itself with arts and crafts techniques. Drexler himself reveals the fly in the functional ointment when he points out that geometrical form and the precise finish of much Bauhaus design is the result of hand finishing in prototype workshops and that adjustment to mass production 'usually deprived a design of just that kind of detail which had given the hand-made prototype its machine-made look'.

Drexler, throughout this short text, stands clear of the mass produced article –there is a tacit admission that consumer goods lie beyond the province of the craftsman designer. He seems embarrassed by the boycott, but so heartfelt is his withdrawal that he concludes with the first published statement I have seen of an attitude that could well become important for the next design era.

Briefly, his thesis is that consumer goods are now designed
for comparatively short periods of usefulness – so short
that aesthetic value is virtually inappropriate. Current
production techniques require forced consumption, and
forced consumption is, in his opinion, often 'antisocial'.
Responsibility for these social disorders is put squarely on
the inhuman production systems which can only produce
economically in large quantities. He suggests that the
solution may be that the designer should take a hand in
designing systems of greater flexibility – by recomposing
the aesthetics of production rather than styling to the tune
of consumption: 'The designer's creative effort might shift
away from static absolute values . . . towards the design of
process – the machines themselves.' It may be that the
moralist will retreat to an ivory factory thus tackling his
problem at the other end. In the design of machine tools
and productions systems the craft ethos can again
predominate, functionalism can operate at its narrowest
extremes: the philosopher-aesthete-engineer-designer may
well find a place there, if that is where society needs him.
Only, one wonders, what is the pay-off for the Museum of
Modern Art? The most beautiful collection of blueprints
from the second half of the century?

Theory and design in first machine age
Reyner Banham, The Architectural Press

Over the past few years the pages of *The Architectural Review* have been distinguished, from time to time, by articles on the Modern Movement in architecture from the pen of Reyner Banham, its then literary editor. These articles kept our tabs on his work in progress towards a major documentation of the formative years of the International Style in architecture. The field was wide open and Dr Banham has had a ball – his book makes available for the first time in English a great deal of information and textual quotation. But the historians are snapping so impatiently at the heels of the pioneers and at each others' that Dr Banham is already parrying, in certain chapters, rebuttals of his propositions. For this is no cold analysis; in spite of his fingerwagging admonition to Giedion on the dangers of plugging a line, Banham also has a theory. Oddly enough his theory is as uncontroversial as the substance of his book is polemical. The gist of his thesis is that 'modern architecture' is not functional – that buildings in the International Style are a symbolic fantasy, and pretty inadequate at that. The controversy lies less in the thesis than in the mechanism of his argument, which is to tie every possible movement and master back into Futurist thought, however tenuous the contact with the Futurist dream of the machine age.

It would be presumptuous of me to attempt to discuss in detail the subject matter of this book. As much time would be needed to examine it thoroughly as Dr Banham himself has spent in finding out who said what and when. His research has been extensive and deep – a mind as encyclopaedic as his would be required to review it more than superficially. Having admitted this one feels free to say that any specialist on the movements he covers is likely to be infuriated beyond measure, as much by his acrobatic use of quotation as by the conclusions drawn from them – for Banham makes his authorities work very hard for Banham. He manages the formidable task of organising his material and integrating his quotations into a continuously readable text with a skill that only a journalist of great ability could command, and however difficult a problem of translation he rarely leaves us monolingual readers baffled.

Unfortunately journalism colours his language, so that when we have submitted to Marinettian, Corbusian,

Wrightian, Lippsian, Muthesian, Scheerbartian and even Dannunzian (in the manner of d'Annunzio), we are confounded by an 'anonymous Lethabist', and are required to assess the merits of an 'unLethabetic' statement and a 'superficial Boccionism'. A 'Schinkelist' can produce the 'Schinkelesque' when 'Schinkelism' is abroad. *Mensch!* Good gimmicky shorthand, but dubious art historical terminology.

A pity, too, that an important work on modern design theory is so badly designed. It was inevitable that many of the illustrations, surviving through several generations of reproduction, should be a little degraded – we are grateful for the exquisitely apt and rare collection – but there is no good reason for the incredibly casual setting and distribution of captions.

There is no need to exhort designers to purchase this book –its obvious merits and the wealth of vital material make it essential reading for students of the period. As for the dilettantes – having read it we are well placed in a ringside seat to enjoy the rich vituperation that such grand, rhetorical, big man criticism of near history is bound to evoke.

Design, October 1960

Teaching

Diagrammar

The tasks I set my first year students are designed to allow only a reasoned result. Rarely is a problem presented in terms which permit free expression or even aesthetic decision. The student is prompted to think of his work as diagrams of thought processes – equipment which will enable him to derive further conclusions. Artistic personality or manipulative charm is coincidental to the result.

1 is the result of taking a small piece of lino, cutting successive marks and making adjacent prints after each additional cut. This cinematic realisation of time element registers in a clear way the growth of ideas and the sequential aspect of each act.

In 2 the student is required to position several forms on a sheet of paper. There is then assumed to be a flow from one side to the other – small pieces of paper are stuck on to indicate the response of the flow to the forms. The process of revealing the currents and vortices, the high and low pressure areas, requires no aesthetic decision: the position of each mosaic particle is determined only by a logical estimation of the energies developed as a result of the conflict between the even flow and the fixed forms fairly arbitrarily established in the first instance.

Students are shown two micro-photographs of sea-urchin eggs. One illustrates the first stage of cell division in which the single cell is divided by its own internal forces. The second shows a similar cell being divided under the influence of external forces in a centrifuge. The difference is clearly projected by the image itself. 3 is an attempt to create forms implying a similar difference of generating forces.

Forces may also be suggested by signs. Representing a kinetic situation or a stage in an event is the objective of 4.

5 is a space-filling exercise. Immersing a drop of cholesterol in water causes a great increase in the surface area of the drop while the bulk remains constant. The need to extend surface results in a protrudence of tendrils which continue to occupy any available space as long as the drop remains immersed. The student is invited to fill space as eagerly as the cholesterol complying with the same limitations. The

Bibliography: 10

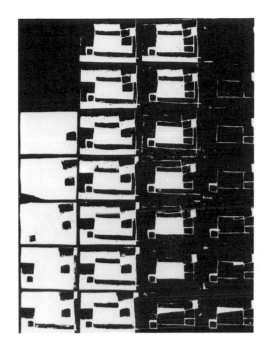

1

2

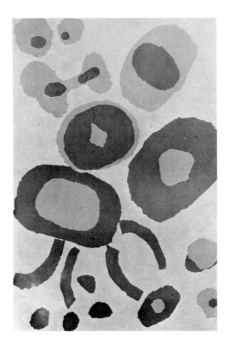

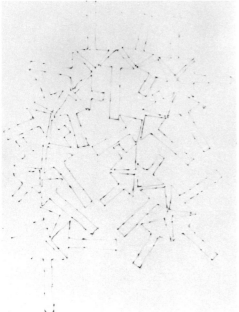

trick is to oppose the natural tendencies of the human hand to repeat configurations – and to defeat calligraphy specific to a personality. Conscious effort is required if restrictive repetition is to be avoided.

Most images have dominant forms which, for one reason or another, demand precedence over others. Certain classical optical illusions suggest that some visual situations present a balance of forces which permit the spectator a freedom of choice. 6 is an example of an exercise in which the objective is to produce such an ambiguous image. It should be possible to read it as black forms on a white ground or vice versa with equal ease.

7 shows simple juxtapositions of forms from which conclusions can be drawn about the phenomena of space perception. Clues for space perception are discussed and the student is asked to make a written statement to accompany each drawing he produces.

3

4

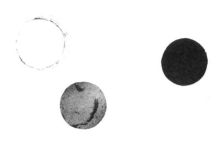

5

7

6

First year studies at Newcastle

Foundation year life class

Since Walter Gropius introduced the idea of a foundation course into the curriculum of the Bauhaus at Weimar in 1919 there has been an increasing application of Bauhaus methods of first year teaching in the major schools of design throughout the world. One aspect of that training, the notion that artists should join with craftsmen in the design of goods for mass production, has for many years, been applied by William Johnstone, Principal of the Central School of Arts and Crafts in London. A most distinguished list of painters has served under him as a bridge between the everyday crafts and the visual sensibilities that some artists develop under the traditional disciplines of fine art education. Another attitude to the Bauhaus first year is apparent at the Hochschule für Gestaltung at Ulm, where the emphasis is on technical training and research into problems of form which are required to be solved without recourse to artistic considerations. Between these two poles, both stemming from Bauhaus ideology, there are many attempts to train designers towards a sensitive understanding of form so that now every municipal college of art and design at least pays lip service to Gropius's principles. Design education has changed with a changing world – indeed it has been partly instrumental in that change – but fine art education has stuck in a deeply worn groove.

Fine art education in England has, from the foundation of the Royal Academy in 1768, been dominated by the classical Beaux Arts techniques of pedagogy. Study of the antique, in which the student cowers beneath the theatrical gestures of an over life-size plaster cast; still-life, requiring the manipulation, and subsequent rendering in paint, of a collection of junk no self-respecting secondhand dealer would bother to bid for; finally and above all, the nude, a suburban housewife with a yen for romance comes into the life class to earn herself a new dress – posing for art students whose main ambition is to dribble paint like Jackson Pollock or to cut holes into building board as neatly as Ben Nicholson. There is no doubt that the concept of the fine art academy can do with a rethink: it is surprising how little has been done to shed the bric-à-brac and to offer art students some intellectual disciplines to replace the picture-making paraphernalia. The work of the Department of Fine Art at King's College, Durham University, should be viewed in this light – as an exploration of the possibility of giving new form to the training of students of fine art.

Bibliography: 15

Victor Pasmore at crit.

In schools of craft and design there are procedures and skills to be taught. It has never been possible to teach fine art students much. The process of art teaching is that of encouraging an atmosphere conducive to self-education. This is particularly true now when even the evaluation of technique no longer grants a teacher real assurance. In this century, at all events, there are no techniques more valid than others. Finger-painting in chicken fat is as plausible an approach as best quality oil paint applied with hog bristle, filbert-shaped brushes. Nor can a picture be judged on its success at communicating an anecdote. If the traditional art school props are discarded some new disciplines are required to fill the gap.

At Newcastle we have concentrated on the establishment of a rigidly defined programme of work in the first year. This course is aimed at developing modes of thinking which will induce a self-critical attitude in the student. He must learn to question the significance of every mark he makes. What are the meaningful differences between one succession of proportional relationships and another? What distinguishes this curved line from that curved line? Into what category of form does this shape fall? Why is the negative of this area less dominant than its positive? Other exercises are concerned with relating this introspective consideration of abstract elements through analytical drawings of objects to the visual world surrounding the student. The problem is made more demanding, not by an increased elaboration of the subject matter, but by extending the scope of considerations from two into three dimensions. Every fortnight a review of the latest phase of activity is made, with contributions from all the instructors engaged in the teaching of first year students – Victor Pasmore, Geoffrey Dudley, Roy Ascott and myself. Professor Kenneth Rowntree also joins the dicussion. This is found to be most valuable in maintaining the aggressively critical attitudes which are found to be essential at this, somewhat distilled, level of visual experience. The student also engages in normal academic studies in art history, and essays are required so that written language becomes a natural tool of expression for the artist.

During later years direction is gradually relinquished and the student finds his own needs and satisfactions. The vindication of the first year of the degree course at Durham University is in the great variety of styles and attitudes to be found in the work of final year students. Some gravitate

Crit. preparation

Richard Smith and R H at crit.

towards the classic art school studies and spend much of
the later years in the life-painting rooms which are freely
available to them: when they do so it is with a true sense of
conviction and personal need. Other students pass through
the four-year course without ever having painted a nude
figure. No one approach is preferentially graded. Many of
the graduates of the department take a further year of art
Teacher Training and go on to teach in secondary schools
where some will try to apply the principles of their
undergraduate training to children. My own experience is
that this approach to art teaching is more fruitful when the
maturity of the student is such as to permit an intellectual
gratification. The created products of the first year are
necessarily narrowly repetitive and the normal
satisfactions of artistic production are considerably limited
on this account. It may well be that the ABC of art can only
be taught after the preliminary release through
self-expression in primary art education has given a
student sufficient awareness for him to respect the value of
an alphabet.

About art teaching, basically

Basic Design at Newcastle

Any kind of teaching has two objectives. First, the development of practical disciplines which will promote orderly and logical modes of thought – the ability to analyse action already taken, to make deductions about a future course of action and to draw conclusions from the final product which will project a further series of self-directed acts. Secondly, it provides given knowledge, established facts about the state of the world, the existing theories and methods, tools and techniques by which evidence of thoughtful action is fabricated.

Teaching of the arts must also engender creative sensibility – an intangible quality which arises out of a careful nurturing of the two prime pedagogic weapons, a demand for solutions to specific problems and training in the presentation of solutions.

The classical Art Academy has always placed its emphasis on the second of these divisions of pedagogy, the teaching of method. The student was set before an object – most often a nude woman – and by prolonged practice, together with the acquisition of knowledge about the physical configurations involved, a personal recording of the subject was achieved. Since art is so evasive and unwilling to subject itself to logical analysis it had become accepted that art teaching, too, must be cautious in suggesting that intellectually disciplined procedures can produce artists. So an inductive approach has been preferred. With the relaxation of technical disciplines, which has been forced upon the academies by the changed structure of art in the twentieth century, we have been left with a void and a few tentative proposals for filling it with substitute disciplines to replace the well-tried practice of learning by doing.

It has, for some time, been felt that a change of orientation is necessary which places emphasis on the first of the teaching objectives I mentioned. It should be possible to establish a programme of systematic study of fundamental elements which will provide a coherent grounding for any young artist who will be assimilated into the current art scene. Malevich, Klee, Maholy Nagy, Albers, Max Bill and many other artists who have considered the problem of art pedagogy have initiated sequenced courses of exercises designed to isolate the many separate factors which contributed to a work of art. Point, line, plane, perspective, proportion, mechanical articulation, kinetic effects, colour and so on, all the ingredients for a codified theory of

Bibliography: 21

deductive art pedagogy, which one might suppose could form the basis for a new art academy, have been postulated; but no art academy exists which has accepted the need for the application of an overall programme. That approach so far has found its main expression in training for designers of textiles, furniture, industrial products and advertisements – but what is thought fit for the graphic designer or architect is viewed with suspicion for Fine Art students.

Certainly one must accept that there are difficulties. Basic design requires more teaching effort per student. It demands not only more time but also the quality of the teaching must be higher than that needed for the still-life or antique room. Basic form studies are lamentably unrewarding for the student unless he is prodded, provoked, fed with ideas and stimulated into an awareness of the validity of his own solutions. But perhaps the major obstacle to successful adoption of basic design as an art school discipline is the danger of its acceptance by students as a stylistic formula – once a student has been fired with enthusiasm, a thick vein of easily achieved end products is opened up and a vogue is established for specific pleasing forms which can be as drearily repetitive as the adopted mannerisms of earlier methods of art training.

The studies now known in Britain as Basic Design are gradually gaining a measure of support. Art teacher training establishments produce graduates who have felt the influence of the ideas in their own art training and they are carrying this over into their art teaching in primary and secondary schools. However, revaluation is needed at the present time for there is a danger that the methods will be misapplied and the attitudes distorted; the major distortion, to my mind, being the implication that basic design can teach art students to become Modern Artists, that Abstract Art is the objective of basic design studies. This leads to an unnecessary confinement of vocabulary for which the only cure is a widening of the basis of the language. In art school training, at least, it seems to be imperative to bridge the gap between the disciplines of the life room and the rigours of basic design. The links now being attempted are usually of two kinds, those designed to stimulate observation: analytical drawing, visual assessments of construction, etc., and those which seek correspondence between abstraction and visual appearance: deriving rhythms, point relationships, linear organizations and so on from a given scene. The base could be widened too in another direction, through exploitation of imagery as such – the study of material which is dependent on psychological and sociological overtones for its effect.

Any one-man teaching effort in the field of basic studies is likely to be limiting for the students; the force-feeding approach that is required for this kind of teaching is not only too exhausting for a teacher working in isolation, but his contribution is also coloured by his own personality and interest – it should be a team effort and it must be a team which is willing and able to press regular modifications into the course. This is necessary for the student and as much for the teacher, for continuous repetition over the years can induce a boredom in him which will communicate itself to the student. Although there is need for a clearly programmed and comprehensive course the programme needs frequent renewal.

One is reluctant to place too high a value on individual products of a basic design course. A student is expected to make a great many marks on a great many pieces of paper. Many of the examples have little intrinsic merit, their interest lies in the contribution they make to a series of considerations. They are often intended only to establish the large range of possibilities rather than to narrow down on an optimum. The value of each lies in the directness of the visual statement – the assistance it gives in clarifying a situation, the way in which it presents the situation for analysis. The student is prompted always to think of his work first as diagrams of thought processes – equipment which will enable him to derive further conclusions. On the other hand, it is also necessary to avoid the implication that the work is valueless once the analysis is made. The tool does not become redundant so it is essential to engender in the student a respect for the sometimes unprepossessing aid – his diagram. While they are not art, they have considerable value as a record of study and can form, as a collective whole, a coherent survey of his development. Individually the products tend to be depersonalized – as a portfolio they express a clear personality. Ultimately it must be recognized that a basic course for art students is successful or not in the degree to which it is capable of stimulating in students a plastic sensibility. An ability to recognize the plastic values of the

products of his investigation into visual phenomena is important, given that this is hedged with warnings and reservations.

These are personal reflections on my own experience as a teacher of basic design, first at the Central School of Arts and Crafts and, since 1953, in the Department of Fine Art, King's College, Newcastle-upon-Tyne. An exhibition, 'The Developing Process', held at the Institute of Contemporary Arts in 1959, brought together the teaching work of the staff at King's College and Leeds College of Art and the views of the teacher contributors to this exhibition were published in an illustrated catalogue published by the Department of Fine Art, King's College.

What kind of art education?

Richard Hamilton The first aim of our course is a clearing of the slate. Removing preconceptions. People come to art school with ready-made ideas of what art is. We have to do some erasure. Then we have to build up a new sense of values. We try to put across the idea that any activity should be the outcome of thinking. That is one of the common preconceptions – that art is not something you think about but something you feel. What we do is to introduce problems which can be solved intellectually; the graphic quality is not so important.

Victor Willing Distinguishing between induction and deduction in problem solving, you have said elsewhere that you are concerned with deduction. Shouldn't students do both?

R.H. Yes, they have to sooner or later, but analysis is the major part of their work. I think this is a reasonable approach in the beginning. Once they have a subjective notion it is put through an analytic process until they discover what its constituents are and the way in which these can be used to make a work of art.

V.W. The teacher is defining the rules of the game?

R.H. I would not like to think so. It's really staking out an area of interest and letting the student find his own rules and solutions.

V.W. Do some students go on to become interested in solving practical problems by going into industrial design?

R.H. No. If they did they would be somewhere else. At Newcastle University they are working for a degreee in Fine Art and usually persist until they get it.

V.W. What can they do with it?

R.H. They can teach and that's about all.

V.W. Is giving a degree a way of making art education acceptable to the grants authorities? Shouldn't one aim at persuading the educational establishment that they should leave it to the school to decide whether a student is using his time usefully, without the charade of a degree?

R.H. Well, at Newcastle we award our own degree. The system works. What we are saying is that a person has attended a four-year course, taken learning about art fairly seriously, and has managed to do this without getting into any difficulty in respect to social behaviour which has

Bibliography: 34

upset the University authorities. I suppose students have a right to a statement to that effect. When we also have to say that one student has done this with more talent and enthusiasm than another there are dangers.

V.W. Do art schools receive more neurotics than the rest of higher education?

R.H. The universities as a whole probably have a high proportion of neurotics. Perhaps a few more find their way into art schools than into other departments. You see at once when an art student is under mental stress because it's immediately apparent in the work being done. Whereas someone in a physics department might not reveal it.

V.W. 'Self-expression', which has been for so long the avowed aim of art classes from infant to secondary education, has often been most apparent alongside traditional teaching – perhaps thought of as a valuable release. I wonder if a high proportion of the casualties of traditional education find their way into art schools? Art schools are not equipped for therapy, are they?

R.H. Tomás Maldonado's main thesis about Ulm's pedagogical line is that it differs from the Bauhaus by rejecting self-expression. He regards self-expression as a main tenet of the Bauhaus and a misapplication of Montessori in adult education. If Ulm has any interest for me it is in this exclusion of self-expression from the education of someone who is beyond the need of it. At Newcastle the things we teach in the first year have this much in common with Ulm; we try to prevent enjoyment in the act of making marks for its own sake. I feel that a good deal of effort should go into considering whether art at the level we are talking about does overlap too much with therapy.

V.W. If you were doing a basic course at a school of 'environmental design' do you think it would be the same?

R.H. Similar; it would work perfectly well because it is a training of the mind and not a training in styles and techniques. What puzzles me about Ulm, though, is that it was initiated by artists – Maldonado, Bill, and others, who were founders, came from the world of modern abstraction, and then the principle was adopted that fine art would have no place in their school of environmental design. They denied that style was an important aspect of the production of consumer goods but the school evolved

coincidentally one of the strongest consumer goods styles that has emerged in recent years. I would have accepted this as one of the inevitable outcomes that one might have looked forward to with some interest. Yet Maldonado thinks of this as a disaster that has befallen Ulm.

V.W. The 'products' of an environmental design school, builders and industrial designers, are involved in design for the community. The Fine Art School does not have traditionally a sense of responsibility to the community in this way.

R.H. There is going to be a need to filter off people from production. There are three possible solutions to the problems that automation will bring. You can reduce the number of working hours per man (this is happening now). You can shorten the working life of each individual by prolonging education and lengthening the retirement span – with a short productive period in the middle. There are limits to these means because a point of inefficiency is soon reached (and retired people aren't all that happy.) You can also reduce the number of people engaged in productive pursuits and stimulate guilt-free non-productivity. One meaningful way of diverting productive activity is to encourage people to work in useless pursuits such as art and to make it possible for them to contribute to the productive members of society some enrichment of their leisure time. The art school is a very good centre for thinking about this. We can distinguish between productive and non-productive units and let them marry at some later stage than the pedagogic one.

V.W. That implies an art education which covers the whole cultural development of the student.

R.H. Yes, his whole cultural development and the way he relates to society. At the moment art schools don't understand what they are doing – what their product is. Whether it is to produce artists, or designers, or teachers. What I am concerned with is producing people with good minds, who are capable of seeing society as a whole, trained to think constructively though not necessarily productively.

Marcel Duchamp

Towards a typographical rendering of the Green Box

Marcel Duchamp's *Green Box,* published in an edition limited to 300 copies in October 1934 by Rrose Sélavy (a pseudonym used by Duchamp on occasion), contains '93 documents (photographs, drawings and manuscript notes of the years 1911–1915) as well as a plate in colour'[1]. These are the documents which surround Duchamp's masterpiece, the *Large Glass,* entitled *La Mariée mise à nu par ses célibataires même*[2]. The box supplements the Glass and is so fully integrated into its development that a complete appreciation of the painting is impossible without some knowledge of its contents. Fifteen of the papers are reproductions of drawings and paintings or photographs of glass paintings; the other seventy-nine are fascimile reproductions of hand-written notes which range from a ten-page folded sheet to a six-word fragment on a scrap of squared paper. The ninety-four items are loose in the box and no indication of a preferred sequence is given. Each of the notes is reproduced with a fanatical exactitude on a wide variety of papers torn around templates to the shape of the original. Some of them are entirely textual, others are combined with sketches of details of the Glass, in several the drawing dominates a descriptive notation. Some flicker like a momentary thought; some have been returned to again and again: erasures, underlinings, stresses and amendments abound – modulations of an idea are sometimes revealed by a calligraphic sign – subtle inflexions may be apparent only in a difference of writing instrument.

The box is a work of art in its own right, a literary masterpiece having a unique form. Its stature among the documents of modern art is immense – yet it is probably the least known. Its comparative neglect is due to the rarity of the original edition and the fact that so little has been done to assist a clear understanding of what the notes say. There is no typeset version, even in French –the language in which the notes were written – and few have been translated into English. The work must be made more accessible and the essential first step is a full English version, a full version for there is no doubt that anything far short of a complete publication of all ninety-four documents can be only marginally informative. Not only a translation of language is required, if the quality of the original manuscripts is not to be diminished too severely typographical equivalents for the calligraphic complexities must be found. Duchamp's gesture, an outrageously lavish publication of as precise a reproduction of the manuscripts as could be devised – including every blot and tear – was not a perversity but a perfectly estimated answer to the needs of the situation. The truth is that anything other than the facsimiles themselves cannot fully convey the extraordinary quality of the box as an art object. However, some fairly satisfactory typographical representation of the documents is possible and should be attempted. It is the purpose of this article to examine the problem and indicate a possible approach.

To date, there have been only four published translations into English of any appreciable portions of the documents:

J Bronowski:
This Quarter, Surrealist issue, September 1932, pp. 189-192. Four notes translated:
'Preface'
'Progress (improvement) of the lighting gas up to the levels of flow'
'Superscription'
'to separate the ready-made'

Humphrey Jennings:
London Bulletin, 4-5, July 1938, pp. 17-19
'Some passages from "The Lighthouse of the Bride" by André Breton'. Translated from the Breton article in *Minotaur No 6,* 1935.
Contains part of the note headed 'La Mariée mise à nu par ses célibataires'.

Roditi:
View,
Series V, No 1, March 1945,
Marcel Duchamp issue.
Complete translation of Breton's 'The Lighthouse of the Bride' from *Minotaur No 6.*
Contains part of the note headed 'La Mariée mise à nu par ses célibataires même'.

George Heard Hamilton:
Marcel Duchamp from the Green Box,
Readymade Press, 1957.
Edition limited to 400.
Translation of twenty-five notes.

Bibliography: 8

[1] This is Duchamp's description. I suspect that he declined to state simply "94 documents' because 93 (3 × 3 and 3) honoured his 'refrain', the triple rhythm of the Glass.

[2] A typographic problem arises in all the following Duchamp texts. Titles of works are, as elsewhere, given in italics. *The Bride stripped bare by her bachelors, even,* is the title (in English) of the work we often call the

Large Glass. 'Glass' is hardly a title so it is not italicized, but it is capitalized to distinguish it from glass, the substance that supports the image. The *Green Box* is similarly a title through usage though its actual title is the same as that of the *Large Glass.* There is a painting called *Bride,* but the Bride is also a component of the Glass. Titles of specific separate works are italicized but names of parts of the Glass are not.

The translations by Jennings and Roditi need not concern us – they are included here since a considerable portion of the longest note, Duchamp's ten-page essay on the two principle elements of the Glass, Bride and Bachelors, is translated with the article – their main importance is that they introduced the English-speaking public to André Breton's revealing article.

In 'The Lighthouse of the Bride' Breton stayed close to the Glass, and his brilliant analysis of this 'mechanistic and cynical interpretation of the phenomenon of love' is the first key to it. It was possible to conceive that here in the Glass 'where the rigorously logical and expected are married to the arbitrary and gratuitous' an epic saga, abstruse but comprehensible, was enacted. The value of Breton's advocation of Duchamp's work, his affection for and complete knowledge of it, cannot be overstressed. The diagram with its references, which appears later, owes much to him.

Professor Hamilton's reading has the benefit of Marcel Duchamp's collaboration – indeed, it is difficult to imagine a useful translation without the author's help in deciphering parts of the manuscript. This is the most recent work on the *Green Box* and the largest single body of translation; the book contains twenty-five 'jottings', approximately one third of the notes, but the majority of them are brief and they represent much less than a third of the text. The format immediately reveals a crucial issue: in a bound volume the order in which the items appear is fixed and a decision must be made to determine what this order shall be. The solution of *from the Green Box,* though Duchampian in spirit, is a negative solution: 'Since the documents in each copy of the *Green Box* are arranged in no order, the sequence of our selection has been determined by chance.' Henry Steiner's layout reduces the disadvantages of defined succession by giving a double spread to each item so that no two notes are seen together – thus every fragment is allowed to retain its own identity. Having adopted the principle of random distribution this is very necessary; misleading relationships would have occurred with any less ingenious approach. An unhappy consequence is that so much white space surrounds the shorter notes that an appearance of pretentiousness arises – a 'poetic' look which is alien to

Duchamp. To build the box itself into an intelligible account of the Glass one inevitably begins to sort and order the material into some meaningful sequence. Some of the notes have clear affinities and are susceptible to grouping – notes concerned with the development of particular elements or areas of the Glass, general notes, notes in which the relationship to the Glass is very tenuous. While it would be in some measure restricting to have an order imposed, a fixed disorder would be equally restricting without being as informative. The notes in *from the Green Box* are very much on the fringe of the Glass – twenty of them do not relate specifically to the Glass at all. George Hamilton has filtered off those notes which can best be isolated, but the treatment for the main body has yet to be found. The notes included in this volume are from unillustrated originals, with only one exception – this has an unimportant marginal sketch in the facsimile, omitted from the book. The selection, which carefully avoids the monstrous publishing difficulties of the more elaborate texts, can only hint at the detailed interrelationships enclosed within the box. But we are at least a step closer and the preface, stressing the literary importance of the documents, is a valuable contribution to Duchamp studies.

The earliest translations, published in Paris, appeared in *This Quarter.* J Bronowski was asked to make English versions of a few of the notes. These were described by André Breton (guest editor for this issue) as 'an extract from a large, unpublished collection of notes by Marcel Duchamp which were intended to accompany and explain (as might an ideal exhibition catalogue) the *verre* known as 'The Bride Stripped Bare by her Own Bachelors' [3]. Bronowski was invited to undertake the translation since the matter of the documents was regarded by the editors as 'in part technical' [4]. *This Quarter* gives translations of four separate notes though the layout does not make this clear. The translator has been at some pains to transpose the visual complication of the manuscript: he uses footnotes to describe those passages for which a simple translation would be inadequate. Among the group of notes is one headed 'Preface'; a reproduction of the facsimile appears on pages 187 and 188. This is one of the major documents of the box and one in which the problems of

---

[3] An early translation of the title. Duchamp preferred *The Bride stripped bare by her bachelors, even*. 'even' retains the ungrammatical illogicality of his *'même'*.

[4] Bronowski trained and worked as a scientist, but his wide interests were revealed early by the publication of a monograph on William Blake.

sequence [of a set] of small happenings appearing to necessitate one another under causal laws, *in order to extract the sign of relationship between,* on the one hand, this *position of Rest* (capable of all eccentricities), on the other, a *choice of Possibilities* available under these laws and at the same time determining them.

Or :

we shall determine the conditions under which may best be demonstrated [the] super-rapid position of Rest [the snapshot exposure] (= allegorical appearance) of a set ... & c.

Or :

Given, in the dark, (1) the waterfall
(2) the lighting gas,

we shall determine [2] (the conditions for) the super-rapid exposure (= allegorical appearance [3] of several collisions [acts of violence] appearing strictly to succeed one another—in accordance with certain causal laws [4]—*in order* to extract the *sign of relationship* between this snapshot exposure (capable of all eccentricities) *on the one hand* and the choice of the possibilities available under these laws *on the other.*

Algebraic Comparison :

a   *a* being the demonstration
b   *b*   ,,   ,,   possibilities

the ratio $\dfrac{a}{b}$ — is in no way given by a number *c*

[2] This has " *we shall consider* " written over it.

[3] This has " *allegorical reproduction* " written over it.

[4] There is a ring round these six words, and the note, " *unnecessary.* "

PREFACE [1]

Given (1) the waterfall
(2) the lighting gas
we shall determine the conditions for an instantaneous position of Rest (or allegorical appearance) of a

[1] This word in the manuscript is ringed in red, and has the note, " *perhaps nothing,* " written against it.

The Bronowski version of *Preface,* from *This Quarter,* Surrealist issue, September 1932, pp 189–191.

$[\frac{a}{b} = c$, but by the sign written between *a* and *b*.

As soon as *a* and *b* are " *knowns*," they become new [5] units and lose (their relative [6] numerical or extensive) values; there remaining only the sign "—" written between them (*sign of relationship* or better of . . ? *think this out*).

Given the lighting gas

typographical interpretation are immediately apparent. The Bronowski version is reproduced here in a slightly smaller size. When compared with the manuscript it becomes obvious that heavy demands have been made of the translator. Bronowski's extract, since it works within the normal limitations of printed text, must be selective; Duchamp's many alternatives and additions could not all be given. Perhaps it is more selective than it need be: one passage *'Par repos instantané = faire entrer l'expression extrarapide'* has been lost; there are also some additions – the word *or* used twice to distinguish the three sections, does not appear in the original. The six footnotes used for 'Preface' cannot inform completely about the ringed words, the additions, corrections and alternatives. They imply the complexity of the original but they cannot go far in conveying it. The pity is that their presence suggests completeness and accuracy. In fact, footnote number 1 is untrue – *rien Peut-être* is not written against the word 'Preface'; it occurs on side 2 of the note beside the word *avertissement* which has been omitted from the version anyway. There are many ringed words and variants not footnoted. Some words and phrases are printed in italics; these passages are underlined in the original – the change results in a different kind of stress. No doubt the translator underlined the appropriate words in his typescript and this was, understandably, read by the printer as an instruction to set the words in italics. Bronowski did not see proofs and was unable to ensure the accuracy of his interpretation. The heading of the last note has been placed in such a way that its first line, written above the heading, is appended to 'Preface' – which has the unfortunate consequence of altering completely the tone of query that ends it. This criticism of the first attempt to make a portion of the documents available in English seems ungrateful; it is intended only to indicate the difficulties and emphasise the need for careful typographical interpretation.

'Preface' has been used again to demonstrate a third approach, one which provides an analogy and seeks to arrive at an equivalent which does not limit the multiplicity of readings. The translation for this version has been made by George Heard Hamilton and corrected by Marcel Duchamp; the type specification is my contribution – the proofs were read by Duchamp and

Préface.   1

Étant donnés 1°. la chute d'eau
2°. le gaz d'éclairage,

on nous déterminerons les conditions
du Repos instantané (ou apparence allégorique)
d'une succession [d'un ensemble] de faits divers
semblant se nécessiter l'un l'autre
par des lois, pour isoler le signe
de la concordance entre, d'une part,
ce Repos (capable de toutes les excentricités innombrables (2)
et, d'autre part, un choix de Possibilités
légitimées par ces lois et aussi les
occasionnant.

Par repos instantané faire entrer
l'expression extra rapide

// On déterminera les conditions de [la] meilleure
exposition du Repos extra rapide [de la
pose extra rapide (= apparence allégorique)
d'un ensemble ..... etc

'Preface', facsimile, published 1932

2

...un l'ait être.

Avertissement.

[dans l'obscurité]

Étant donnés * 1° la chute d'eau
Soit, donnés * 2° le gaz d'éclairage, dans l'obscurité

? ?

on determinera (les conditions de) l'exposition
extra rapide (= Reproduction allégorique
apparence allégorique) de plusieurs
collisions semblant se succéder rigoureusement
[attentats]
chacune à chacune suivant des lois, pour
isoler le signe de la concordance entre cette
exposition extra-rapide (capable de toutes les
excentricités) d'une part et le choix des possibilités legitimées par ces lois d'autre part.

─ comparaison algébrique
$$\frac{a}{b}$$ a étant l'exposition
       b " les possibilités

le rapport $\frac{a}{b}$ est tout entier non pas dans un
nombre c $\frac{a}{b} = c$ mais dans le signe (─) qui sépare
a et b ; a et b dès que sont connus, ils deviennent
des unités nouvelles et perdent leur valeur numérique relatives (ou de durée
; reste le signe ─ qui les séparait (signe de la
concordance ou plutôt de ?... chercher)

Obverse of facsimile

it aims at being a definitive typographical version. American rather than English usage and spelling have been adopted since Duchamp's second language derives from his long residence in New York.

Setting Duchamp in type has not only its semantic pressures – one must be careful not to be at variance with the Duchamp stylistic timbre. After all, some of the most exquisite and personal typographic achievements of the twentieth century are his; the magazines published by Duchamp in collaboration with Man Ray and Picabia are models of the Dada typographic style. Less known and perhaps more remarkable treatments of letter forms are found on the lid of the *Green Box* and in the cover designs credited to him on several catalogues, magasines and books. It is obvious that a smart use of grots[5] with precisely organised margins is not going to mean very much in this context; on the other hand, the 'literary' faces would present an alien elegance. A mixture of type has been used here in an attempt to show the changes of hand. It is necessary to lead heavily to permit insertion of added words. Plantin has a large size on its body, it is a dark face and nowadays it has a slightly jobbing look. It is an easy face to contrast. These properties made it acceptable for the main setting. Modern and Bembo were used to indicate changes of hand or writing instrument whenever appropriate. No doubt an even wider variation of type style would be necessary for other notes. The text-book quality of the setting is intended; when it appears, the complete typographical translation with its accompanying diagrams, should have very much the appearance of a primer to the Glass.

This obsessive attitude towards the setting may seem ludicrous in face of the increased obscurity of the result. In isolation 'Preface', though a self-contained statement, does not relate intelligibly to the total organisation of the *Large Glass.* It is packed with clues but these clues must be patched together with those from other papers in the box to build the overall concept. There are often restatements, modifications and developments of the same idea on different sheets. Indeed, 'Preface' gives several versions of its theme within itself; they are not alternatives but mutually dependent variations. One continually senses, when handling the documents of the box, a desire to be

perfectly explicit simultaneously with an indifference as to the result. The expression of the urge, rather than its conclusions, is important – one variant is as valuable as another and the idea gets a bonus from this multiplicity of expression – the system is synergetic. It is this attitude that makes it essential to reproduce every mark if the philosophic impact of the original is not to be lost.

The function of the *Green Box* is to construct a terminology for the Glass. If 'Preface' is placed in its context and its relationship to the Glass is illustrated it will become apparent how indispensable is the box to a complete experience of the painting. This particular note deals with events in the lower part of the Glass; the elements grouped there are a kind of production line. For the line to operate, the mechanism must be powered (by the waterfall) and raw material (the illuminating gas) must be fed in. Duchamp is very concerned here, as in all his work, with process – with operations demanding an appreciation of a cycle of events. In the case of the *Large Glass* the image is conceived as a static recording – a fast exposure capturing the operation in a 'State of Rest'. 'Preface' is, in a way, a justification for the absence of actual movement in the work: it explains that the Glass is a narrative description of a subject under guise of another suggestively similar, an emblem of the event described. It is near to a still in the cinematographic sense but the connotations of that word are too direct. In another note Duchamp invents the term 'delay':

Kind of subtitle
Delay in Glass
Use 'delay' instead of 'picture'
or 'painting'

Duchamp's machine demands the minimal requirements of all production plants – a source of power and a substance to modify. These must be 'given' and Duchamp welcomes this basic premise. The activity contained within the lower half of the Glass depends on these two quantities. The positions of sources of activity are indicated in the diagram which appears later by a black disc. All the terms used in the diagram are taken directly from the notes of the Green Box. The elements are shown approximately in the positions that they occupy in the Glass – broken lines indicate

[5] The type family known as 'grotesque' belies its name in being the simplest kind of sans-serif.

elements which, though projected, do not actually appear in the Glass at the stage of completion it had achieved when smashed in 1923. Arrowheads show the path of activity from the source points. There is a well-defined progression from left to right in the Bachelor Machine, then a vertical ascent towards the barrier which separates Bride from Bachelors. The Bride's 'terms' are also transmitted from left to right, then descend to join the mirrored effects of the splash. In spite of the severe isolation of the Bachelors from the Bride a degree of communication is permitted – an electric process transmits commands to the Bride above.

The waterfall energises the mechanism of the Bachelor Machine via the waterwheel – the waterwheel, by means of a chain and sprocket, raises a weight of variable density (in the form of a bottle of Benedictine) – the fall of the bottle operates the sledge which in turn opens the scissors spindled on the bayonet of the chocolate machine, thus controlling the splash of liquid scattered suspension from the chute. The liquid emerging from the chute is the final form of the lighting gas after it has been moulded by malic moulds, solidified in the capillary tubes and extruded as spangles of solidified gas which rise (they are lighter than air and are assisted in their ascent by the suction from the pump) into the sieves. The combined operations of the Bachelor Machine terminate in the splash (explosion). Thus the energy of the waterfall has been converted into mechanical operation and the lighting gas, in its progress, has been involved in changes of chemical state.

The upper half, since there is no possibility of direct contact between the two halves of the Glass, requires its own supply sources. The only 'given' substance of the Bride machine, that which is not inherent within its own chemical and mechanical functions, is the dew which undergoes chemical change at the core of the Bride's processing plant. The Bride is conceived as an engine with its own self-contained activity. She emanates commands from a store of alphabetic units, the terms of her commands being controlled by the triple grill in their passage towards the area of the pulls. This synopsis gives some idea of the scope of the text. 'Preface' has revealed its complexities in some detail.

The *plan* and *elevation*[6] are stages in the elaboration of the precise visual method of the Glass, which is as intensely realised as the verbal documentation. The Glass itself, shown here as it existed prior to its completion by smashing[7], makes its own impact. Its plastic qualities are gloriously self-sufficient but its unique historical position makes essential the wider dissemination of its literary concomitant.

[6] *Plan* and *elevation* appear on page 223

[7] An accidental finality.

191

Preface   1

Given 1. the waterfall

       2. the illuminating gas,

~~one will determine~~
we shall (determine) the conditions
                                                    ?
for the instantaneous State of Rest (or allegorical appearance)

of a (succession) [of a group] of (various facts)

seeming to necessitate each other

under certain laws, in order to isolate the (sign)
    the
of accordance between, on the one hand,
                              all the   (?)
this State of Rest (capable of (innumerable eccentricities)

and, on the other, a choice of Possibilities

authorized by these laws and also

(determining them)

For the instantaneous state of rest = bring in

the term: extra-rapid

We shall determine the conditions of [the] best

exposé of the extra-rapid State of Rest [of the

extra-rapid exposure (= allegorical appearance).

of a group . . . . . . etc.

'Preface' typographic version, published 1960

nothing perhaps

(Notice.)   [in the dark] ←   2

Given: 1. the waterfall

If, given   2. the illuminating gas, (in the dark,)

consider   **?** ←→ **?**   considerations

we shall (determine (the conditions for) the extra-rapid

organization   allegorical Reproduction

exposition (= allegorical appearance) of several

collisions seeming strictly to succeed

[assaults]   unnecessary

each other (according) to certain laws, in order to

the

isolate the (Sign) of accordance between this

extra-rapid exposition (capable of all the

eccentricities) on the one hand and the choice of the possi-

bilities authorized by these laws on the other.

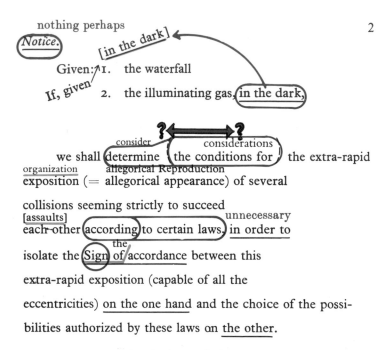

Algebraic comparison

a   a being the exposition

$\dfrac{}{b}$ b   „   the possibilities

the ratio $\dfrac{a}{b}$ is in no way given by a

(-)

number c $\dfrac{a}{b}$ =c but by the sign which separates

as soon as   are

a and b;   a and b   being " known,, they become

new   relative

units and lose their numerical value (or in duration);

of ratio

; the sign $\bar{z}$/which separated them remains (sign of the

?

accordance or rather of . . . . . . look for it)

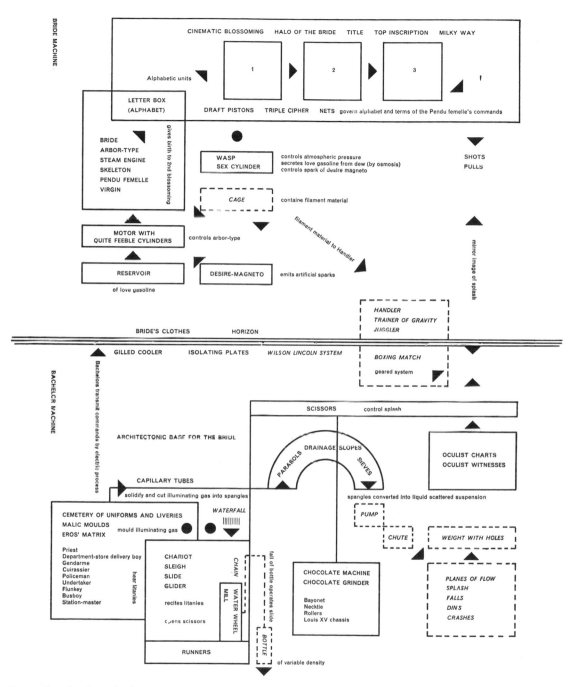

BRIDE MACHINE

CINEMATIC BLOSSOMING   HALO OF THE BRIDE   TITLE   TOP INSCRIPTION   MILKY WAY

Alphabetic units

1   2   3

LETTER BOX
(ALPHABET)

DRAFT PISTONS   TRIPLE CIPHER   NETS govern alphabet and terms of the Pendu femelle's commands

gives birth to 2nd blossoming

BRIDE
ARBOR-TYPE
STEAM ENGINE
SKELETON
PENDU FEMELLE
VIRGIN

WASP
SEX CYLINDER

controls atmospheric pressure
secretes love gasoline from dew (by osmosis)
controls spark of desire magneto

SHOTS
PULLS

CAGE   contains filament material

MOTOR WITH
QUITE FEEBLE CYLINDERS

controls arbor-type

filament material to Handler

mirror image of splash

RESERVOIR

of love gasoline

DESIRE-MAGNETO   emits artificial sparks

HANDLER
TRAINER OF GRAVITY
JUGGLER

BRIDE'S CLOTHES   HORIZON

BOXING MATCH

geared system

BACHELOR MACHINE

GILLED COOLER   ISOLATING PLATES   WILSON LINCOLN SYSTEM

Bachelors transmit commands by electric process

ARCHITECTONIC BASE FOR THE BRIDE

SCISSORS   control splash

PARASOLS   DRAINAGE SLOPES

SIEVES

OCULIST CHARTS
OCULIST WITNESSES

CAPILLARY TUBES

solidify and cut illuminating gas into spangles

spangles converted into liquid scattered suspension

CEMETERY OF UNIFORMS AND LIVERIES
MALIC MOULDS
EROS' MATRIX

mould illuminating gas

WATERFALL

PUMP

CHUTE   WEIGHT WITH HOLES

Priest
Department-store delivery boy
Gendarme
Cuirassier
Policeman
Undertaker
Flunkey
Busboy
Station-master

hear litanies

CHARIOT
SLEIGH
SLIDE
GLIDER

recites litanies

opens scissors

CHAIN

WATER WHEEL MILL

fall of bottle operates slide

CHOCOLATE MACHINE
CHOCOLATE GRINDER

Bayonet
Necktie
Rollers
Louis XV chassis

PLANES OF FLOW
SPLASH
FALLS
DINS
CRASHES

BOTTLE

RUNNERS

of variable density

Diagram from the *Green Book*

Notes from the *Green Box*

The Green Book

When Marcel Duchamp produced the work called *The Bride Stripped Bare by Her Bachelors, Even* he contrived an art form without parallel, a unique marriage of visual and linguistic concepts. It was his intention that the *Large Glass* should embody the realization of a written text which had assisted the generation of plastic ideas and which also carried layers of meaning beyond the scope of pictorial expression. The text exists beside the glass as a commentary and within it as a literary component of its structure. Without the notes the painting loses some of its significance and without the monumental presence of the glass the notes have an air of random irrelevance.

Duchamp proposed to publish the writings so that his complete endeavour of the years 1912–23 should stand as a total work of art. But a period of eleven years passed before they were printed and then the documents emerged characteristically enigmatic – as a flat case containing ninety-four loose items; each handwritten note reproduced in exact facsimile including torn edges, blots, erasures and occasional illegibility: the *Green Box,* as it appears in the photograph opposite, published by Rrose Sélavy in an edition of three hundred numbered copies in 1934.

No sooner has one begun to consider the advantages of a typeset version of the text than one appreciates the logic of Rrose Sélavy's decision to reproduce the notes in facsimile; for the actual meaning seems to suffer when calligraphy is converted to hard metal. This reaction is not the result of the strong affection that one inevitably feels for the hand of the artist – it is simply due to a realization of the impossibility of conveying the elaboration of information contained in the text by normal typographic means. What the facsimiles present, above all else, is the evidence of a prolonged meditation on art – a conscious probing of the limits of aesthetic creation. They convey the doubts, the rethinks and doubletakes, the flat bewilderment and the moments of assurance; the pauses and reaffirmations are there, the winces, private sniggers and nervous ticks. So loaded are these marks with the effort of their production that one soon sees that the permanence and clarity of type offer too overtly the arcane subtleties of Duchamp's thinking. A solution to the problem of a typographic rendering of the notes is to make a

Bibliography: 16

straightforward setting and then add a mass of footnotes to list the changes, insertions, stresses and other indications less susceptible to treatment in type. This results in such a complex of references that it can only make more laborious a contact with ideas already difficult to reach. Given the possibility of editorial description of calligraphic oddities it remains impossible to project the sporadic nature of much of the writing which is often implied only by a change in the character of the hand itself or a change in the writing medium. To demand that such niceties of appreciation of the original documents should be communicated may seem pedantic to the point of fanaticism, yet that has been our aim in this book, for all the oddities of phrasing, punctuation, layout and typesetting are considered attempts to render as closely as possible the form of the original documents.

In the treatment of individual notes there was always a clear objective – the attainment of a direct equivalence between the facsimile and the typeset translation. But, of course, many factors intervene which make a complete analogy impossible. We tried to provide all the words and all the marks which convey the ideas and as much as possible the variation of visual quality of the notes which gives clues to the way in which ideas developed and were modified. The one departure from this principle was in the treatment of erasures and obliterations – wherever there seemed to be a deliberate intention to make indecipherable a word, or group of words, it has been omitted but if a word or paragraph was crossed out but left clearly legible it has been so treated here. In our typeset version there is to be found a good deal of variation in the lengths of lines. This is due partly to the natural difference of line length determined by French and English grammar and spelling, and partly to the removal of obliterated portions of the text. This uneven line length has given a poetic appearance to the page which should be regarded as a coincidental product of the principle of trying to match each line of French with a line of English. English grammar also made it necessary occasionally to transpose words from one line to another – this has been done with the minimum distortion of line values.

In general we have tried to maintain the individuality of the notes by giving each separate page of the original a separate page in the book. Here again, departures from principle were necessary. The five text pages of the folded insert in this book consist, in the original, of a single sheet of paper concertina-folded to give ten closely written numbered pages. In a few cases two or more separate notes have been put on one page when the differences of type and position can adequately convey the distinctive character of each.

For the purposes of production in book form it was necessary to make decisions for which there was no model to guide the choice. Duchamp had no preference as to the order in which the notes appeared, so the sequence was determined by the typographer. Some of the documents are dated and some offer clues of chronology. Others are susceptible to grouping according to their theme or subject and within these groups the relationship of components to the major functions of the glass, and a progressive assurance in the author's grasp of a theme, suggested a suitable order. Three major factors were considered in establishing the sequence: *(a)* subject, *(b)* the relationship of the subject to the cycle of activity, *(c)* chronology, and in that order of importance. For example, the Bride comes first because she seems to have reached a degree of completeness in her realization before the Bachelors have hardened into form, and the dating of certain pages confirms that precedence. On the other hand, the earliest document in the *Green Box* is a reproduction of the *Coffee Mill,* dated 1911, which doesn't appear in this book until quite late in the sequence; it is placed opposite a drawing which sketches an idea for a butterfly pump to appear under the last of the cones and to the *chute.* There are strong affinities between the form of the butterfly pump and the lower view of the grinder in the coffee mill, a connection which Duchamp himself would be loth to press, but since the *Coffee Mill* marries less happily with previous material it is permitted to make contact if and when it can.

By 1914 most of the ideas had reached an advanced stage of elaboration and many of the components had been executed as separate studies. The extraordinary detailing of Duchamp's imagined subject, before he began work on the *Large Glass,* is revealed by the *plan* and *elevation* (1913) which show the elements of the lower part of the glass positioned to fine degrees of accuracy. This, almost physical, control of location in space is essential to the *trompe l'œil* treatment of these objects – a hallucinating effect of reality which can best be understood by an appreciation of the overall dimensions of the glass. It stands nearly nine feet high so that the junction, slightly above centre between top and bottom, comes roughly at eye level and coincides with the horizon at which the perspective is aimed. The perspective, so meticulously elaborated, manipulates human vision as consciously as a seventeenth century peepshow. The drawings which concern themselves with this organization of the perspective are like an engineer's plans in their disciplined execution. They have been redrawn for this edition. The decision to rework them was a calculated risk of restoration suggested by two needs. Three of them had become so smudged and dirty that all subsequent reproductions have borne less information than the original and the translation of words had to be substituted as inconspicuously as possible. The renewing process has used photographic techniques and a hand that has striven to remain as anonymous as that of a process engraver. Other drawings have received less reverent attention, but here also the departure from Duchamp's own hand can be justified by a claim to greater clarity in the transmitted signal and to a new unity between diagram and text which balances that of drawn note and handwritten description in the original. The sketches of components of the Bride are much more fluid than those of the Bachelors and depend for their quality on the Duchamp touch – so the Bride drawings keep his hand. As Duchamp informs in a telling note: 'The principal forms of the Bachelor Machine are imperfect: rectangle, circle, parallelepiped, symmetrical handle, demi-sphere i.e. they are measurable'. The bachelor apparatus is so explicit that nothing is lost in making it more so. Most of the smaller sketches in the latter sections have therefore been remade with an increased precision.

Some twenty of the notes included in the *Green Box* do not deal directly with the subject matter of the *Large Glass*. The anticlimax which occurs as a result placing them together at the end of the book is accepted as an unavoidable consequence of my attempt to hold the continuity of the rest: the key to a full appreciation of Duchamp's masterpiece lies in an awareness of the sequential interrelationship of its component themes.

The notes describe the processes through which each element makes its contribution to the ultimate union of the Bride and her Bachelors – the erotic climax of their activities. In the *Large Glass* itself the function of apparatus can only be inferred from its construction. Some simple mechanical principles are not beyond the scope of pictorial expression: a drawing of an axle held free in bearings implies the possibility of rotation. But what picture can adequately convey the concept of love gasoline being distilled from dew? The *Green Box* informs at this non-pictorial level of experience. Water falls, the mill wheel begins to spin and starts the slow reciprocations of the chariot, we overhear its chanted litanies relieving the still silence of the cemetery of uniforms and liveries where the given gas is cast into malic forms. We become aware of the moulded gas seeping towards the elaborate conditioning which will prepare it for its final orgastic splashing and observe with wonder the beauty of its auras. The juices flow in the Bride, messages are transmitted from pools of random possibilities, the throbbing energy of a robotic world strains to create. *The Bride stripped bare by her Bachelors, even* rumbles into its fantastic splendour.

The Pasadena retrospective

Duchamp (right) playing chess in the Pasadena Museum, 1963

The Marcel Duchamp exhibit at the Pasadena Museum is the first major retrospective. It may be the last, though the dream of assembling the entire output some day is irresistible. It is a unique opportunity to see and respond to the whole artist. With Duchamp we have relied on second-hand acquaintance – there is the hoard at Philadelphia, otherwise the distribution of the small output is sparse. Duchamp has busied himself for many years in the propagation of his achievements through the media of printed reproductions and certified copies, so that now we begin to accept the substitute as the work. I certainly fell into the well-laid trap so thoroughly that I boasted of knowing what he had done without ever having seen more than a few things in the flesh – justifying my claim by asserting the cerebal nature of his achievement. A contrived diffidence in Duchamp's public statements confirmed this attitude, for the ground was cut from under the artefacts while inches were added to the pedestal beneath his personality.

But recently the work did seem somehow more accessible. Robert Lebel's book, published by the Trianon Press is comprehensive: it illustrates 122 of the 208 items listed in the catalogue raisonné. Both the notes for the *Large Glass* (in an English translation) and the complete writings in French under the title *Marchand du Sel* were published in legible form a few years ago. The man seemed presented, the mind pinned bare for the probes. The wisely humorous French-American intellectual who is said to have ripped art to shreds, then taken up chess, whom Harriet and Sidney Janis in an issue of *View* paying homage to him labelled 'Anti-Artist', has been cosily accepted, then adored. Suddenly the image is destroyed; 'Marcel Duchamp Anti-Artist' is revealed as a fake and it only took his work to do it. What makes nonsense of the myth is Walter Hopps' painstaking accumulation of a great artistic œuvre. Duchamp didn't leave history to winnow the chaff, he did it himself. The brilliance of his invention was rigorously restrained to produce a total output of wonderfully consistent distinction. It is a shock to find that the assembled work reveals a hand of fine sensitivity, an eye of acutely personal taste, and a mind capable of taking key thoughts of our time and translating them into subtle plastic expression. So many superlatives, but the exhibit demands them. Anti-Artist my fanny.

The first room contains a selection of paintings dated

Bibliography: 26

1902-11. It is labelled 'Early Work', and that it certainly is when one considers that 1902 represents the precocious artist at the age of 15. It has always seemed to me that the Lebel book suffers distinctly from pretentiousness in illustrating the pre-1911 paintings so liberally. There is a great deal of biographic illustration in the book. Marcel at the age of 9, Marcel dressed as a lady, Marcel undressed, Marcel playing chess with any number of people. The small black and white reproductions of the early paintings reinforce the note of deification and it is easy to accept them as student work included by an over-indulgent biographer. In the exhibition they serve Duchamp better by displaying more than a youthful talent. Several paintings are of major importance. Duchamp emerges as a distinguished Fauve, a colourist of originality and daring. When colour and the sophisticated handling of paint are drained out of the pictures in black and white reproductions we are left with what seems like coarse drawing and somewhat off-hand composition. The *Portrait en Buste de Chauvel* and the *Portrait de M. Duchamp Père, Assis* (both of 1910) are marvellously painted. The quality of the portraits and the nudes of 1910 causes regret that some works of early 1911 might not have appeared at Pasadena. Perhaps more surprises are in store – the Derainesque figure compositions of that year have yet to be seen and their role assessed in leading up to the lonely leap that Duchamp made about the end of 1911 and through 1912.

Two remarkable paintings of late 1911 are shown, *Portrait of Chess Players* and *Portrait*. Cubism is the stimulus for these paintings and it would be reasonable to suppose that without Cubism they might never have existed. The release which Cubism offered from a fixed viewpoint of the subject gave Duchamp his impetus; the debt ends there. The stylistic devices of Analytical Cubism affected him less than most other painters who came under its spell. Duchamp is always involved much more with subject than language. His syntax is perfectly adjusted to a concept. People, at this stage, were defined with great precision as personalities. The great Cubist painters are concerned with generalities, subjects are interchangeable between Braque, Picasso and Gris; humans in Cubist paintings are deprived of individuality and except in rare cases such as Picasso's Kahnweiler and Vollard portraits they become robots. Duchamp is specific. His chess players are his brothers

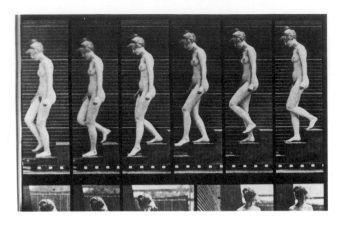

Portrait (Dulcinea), 1911

Nude descending a staircase from Muybridge's *Human Figure in Motion*

Nude Descending a Staircase, 1912

Duchamp-Villon and Jacques Villon. Every drawing among the studies which contribute to the painting shows the family features; the freedom used in relating the elements never hinders the projection of a time, a place, an occasion, the opposition of real minds in the course of a game.

Similarly the picture called *Portrait (Dulcinea)* is of a person psychologically and physiologically manifested. While the novelty lay in his assumption that movement in the subject was as important as the mobility of the artist, the idea was extended so that the subject was also demonstrably various in mood. Change of posture was not the only change of state – a young man in a train could be sad and this must temper the image. The departure which Duchamp makes from Cubist premises is elegantly displayed in a most moving presentation at Pasadena. *Portrait* is followed by the *Nude Descending a Staircase No. 2,* the *King and Queen Surrounded by Swift Nudes,* the *Passage of the Virgin to the Bride* and the *Bride* painting. It's quite an experience – one that could almost be gained in Philadelphia for all but one of these pictures belong to the Arensberg Collection. Yet, without the *Passage of the Virgin to the Bride* (from the Museum of Modern Art, New York) the group is infinitely reduced in its significance. Succession is important. No one modulates more purposefully than Duchamp from one work to another. Intelligently communicative as they are in isolation, each gives immeasurably to our understanding of the next. The pace at which his mind progresses during 1912 is perhaps the greatest marvel of that year of aesthetic miracles in Europe – a year of masterpieces by many painters, vintage in every way, none more exciting than Duchamp's.

The step from *Portrait* to the *Nude Descending* can be recognized as a move away from the particular to the general. In *Portrait* we see a girl from five viewpoints, or a girl seen five times from the same viewpoint. She is like a model promenading from left to right then back again. Each view is distinct and separate, odd only in being combined on the same canvas. We get to know the character of the girl, the masculine head, her lanky figure and its quirky posture, her hair style, the severe cut of her clothes – at this point we notice that in her re-appearance she becomes nude and in so doing she assumes anonymity. When the nude goes on to descend a staircase she is stripped of personality entirely. In this picture another decision has been made, another programme written.

As a scientific study, chronophotography, the technique of investigating a moving subject with the camera, was then some 20 years old: it had been around long enough to have influenced Degas' paintings of dancers. The two masters of the research were the American, Muybridge and the Frenchman, Marey. The difference between the approach of these two to the exploration of motion, tells us something about Duchamp's descending nude. Muybridge developed a technique of serial photography by which a rapid sequence of still shots made it possible to examine motion as a chain of changing relationships. His photographs are presented as strips of separate frames showing a breakdown of stages of the total image of the event, man jumping, men wrestling, woman drinking tea. Marey's approach was to superimpose separate stages of movement by multiple exposure on the same plate. To reduce the resultant complexity into terms that made strict analysis possible he devised means to simplify the forms. He covered his figures with black cloth and drew lines in white along the axes of limbs – he used lights to indicate paths of travel. Marey's concern was less with changes in anatomical structure than with changes in relationship between parts of the organism.

The schematic approach of Duchamp is clearly derived from Marey and not from Muybridge whose influence remains strong in art less as motion study than through the bizarre character of his images (see Francis Bacon[1]). The *Nude Descending* is anonymous and neutral; although we tend to think of the subject as female there is no evidence of sex for all the nudity. A pin figure illustrates a diagram of the phases of descent. If the picture incidentically looks like analytical cubism it is because the cubists modified form into straight lines and flat planes and used a palette restricted to browns and ochres. Gleizes was absolutely right in thinking that the painting was in conflict with cubist theory. It shocked the 1911 Salon des Indépendants Committee so much that they requested its removal, not because they thought it a bad painting but because they misinterpreted it as a bad cubist painting. There are passages which are Cubistic in the worst sense. The top right hand corner and the bottom left corner are filled in with Cubist style marks. The diagonal movement of the composition left these holes to be covered – Duchamp filled in a decorative coating to the margins of his real concern.

---

[1] Francis Bacon's images of men grappling on a bed are derived from Muybridge – as is David Hockney's painting of nude ladies taking tea.

2 Nudes: One strong and One Swift, 1912

Duchamp's is a curious mind – if his personality were not so perfectly integrated one might be tempted to think of him as schizophrenic. The dichotomy which accounts for the widely contradictory assessments of his motives begins now to emerge, less as contentiously paradoxical, more as detached and universal. A dual yet balanced attitude emerged early and completely in the *Nude Descending.* Its complexity derives from the fact that although the conception is primly pseudo-scientific, aesthetic control is precisely applied, until even pure delight in coincidental abstract relationships can be exploited. The statement of the dynamic programme is beautifully exact. The staircase is spiral so that we are presented with views of all sides of the subject, as well as with varying degrees of elevation. There are frequent cross sections and the diagrammatic simplifications of separate phases are allowed to build themselves into simulations of solid form. It wasn't long before the marks took over, assumed a life of their own and indeed began to create a world in which the schematic space was populated by beings whose character was defined by the arbitrary functioning of style. This is one reading of the paintings which succeed the *Nude Descending.*

They stem from drawings (such as *Two Nudes: One Strong and One Swift*) which exploit the abstract calligraphy to the point where personages are born, personalities develop: King, Queen, Virgin and Bride. Psychoanalytical criticism of Duchamp always leaves me a little cold (the overt motivations have yet to be examined), yet there is something to be learned from the dream which he experienced at Munich, where he made these pictures, for it provides an apt analogy with his fears at the practical level of creation. He said that he awoke in a sweat after a nightmare vision in which he was being eaten by the creatures of his paintings. No wonder, for *Virgin No. 2* resembles nothing so much as a praying mantis. Duchamp opposed this calligraphic autonomy of his Munich period by injecting new content into each work. The *Passage from the Virgin to the Bride* uses the same plastic language as the *Nude Descending,* though the 'passage' is not only through time and space. The title also refers to a change of state at a metaphysical level. In one sense the painting can be read as a transition between the *Virgin* drawing and the *Bride* painting; purely at the plastic level it has formal echoes of both in it. The *Passage* also makes a visual pun on that which determines the difference between virgin and bride; in this sense it is an image of an event without temporal or spatial significance.

If the *Passage* is transitional the *Bride* is firmly conclusive. Taking the *Passage* as its starting point the *Bride* tightens down into structure; forms arising from visually descriptive analysis of a dynamic situation now resolve into an organism with a new and fixed identity, an emblem of the transformed personage. At the age of 25 he has made a painting which is a final achievement in terms of the painting tradition offered. As always the reaching of an objective is decisive; for him there can be no retracing of the path. Duchamp's swift accomplishment in that year took him to an extreme limit of creativity which the classic techniques of art permitted – as far out in its way, as Malevitch's ultimate of *White on White* – a point of no return and at the same time a situation in which forward progress is frustrated.

With frightening perceptiveness Duchamp found his solution. He simply changed the terms by which painting had lived for centuries. In changing the rules, in re-inventing art as though it had never existed, he re-opened the possibility of working. The new rules were these: Art is conceptual – that is to say it has nothing to do with visual stimuli external to the artist's mind. It was to be as absolutely conceptual as much art of the past had been retinal – provoked by stimuli received through the eyes. Its contact with the real world would be through analogy; there was no real world anyway, there were no real dimensions, there was no real space. The facts of life are an imposed coherence – other invented facts could provide a causality of another order. Some notions elude graphic presentation so the scope of the medium must be stretched to include semantic expression. It wasn't a question of throwing off the shackles and enjoying a release into another world of free expression, the alternative disciplines he imposed were rigorously ascetic. At the same time, art (Duchamp's in particular) was in danger of taking itself too seriously, so the new art must be 'hilarious'.

All interpretations of the *Large Glass* painting are forced back to the texts that Duchamp prepared as a preliminary to work on the glass itself, and before executing separate studies on glass of components of the picture. The terms ascribed to the subject matter, nomenclature and

descriptions of activity, lure the commentator to their use. When rehashed the language seems more wildly surrealist even than it appears in the context of diagrams and sketch notes that accompany it. The notes have a value and purpose which can only be adulterated by using them in a new context; yet discussion of the theme demands the use of Duchamp's invented terms for there is no possibility of identifying the parts except with his notation. If the language seems at times irrational, it is because knowledge of his private systems of laws and sciences has first to be absorbed. Fundamental to the appreciation of Duchamp is acceptance of contradiction, of paradox, as a first premise. The picture requires the adoption of certain basic tenets, i.e. beauty can be expressed through precision or indifference, or both simultaneously. Unlikely as it may seem that two such incompatibles should be integrated we must accept (in accordance with a 'general note') that 'Painting of precision, and beauty of indifference' is an aim, and 'ironic causality' is the tool selected for its achievement. Irony used in 'affirmation' rather than negative irony.

'In general, the picture is the apparition of an appearance'. The distinction between an apparition and an appearance isn't easy to grasp in spite of the fact that Duchamp has made several attempts to define his attitude to subject/object by redefining these terms. We have, I think, to consider any visual knowledge of a subject as given contributions to our perception of that subject/object. Visually derived information (seeing) is very likely to delude us into an acceptance (believing) of the packaged mental facts as definitive and permanent. Duchamp resists a static conception of reality by thinking of all form, all existence, as transitional. All his work is an undermining of belief in absolute values. From *Portrait* into the complexities of the *Large Glass* and beyond to the later works this is true – nothing binds Duchamp's output together as successfully as this unifying theme. Incredibly, he attempts to express his understanding of the nature of our world in the media of the visual arts, however augmented they may be to accommodate the thoughts. At a level of extreme banality Duchamp is prepared to say that if a wooden table is painted white we have an appearance of a white table – an apparition of the table would embody knowledge of the wood colour concealed by paint. Any physical being of an object presupposes a

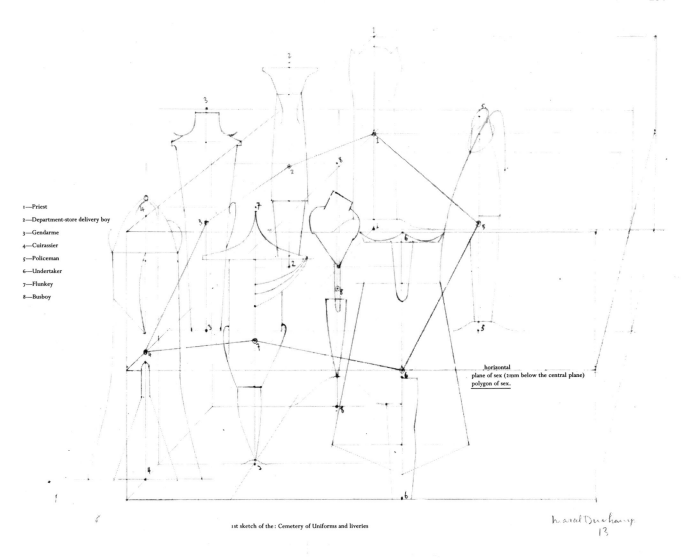

1—Priest

2—Department-store delivery boy

3—Gendarme

4—Cuirassier

5—Policeman

6—Undertaker

7—Flunkey

8—Busboy

horizontal
plane of sex (2mm below the central plane)
polygon of sex.

1st sketch of the: Cemetery of Uniforms and liveries

Marcel Duchamp
13

Cemetery of Uniforms and Liveries, 1913

reverse existence. The table standing in air impresses its form upon the substance air in the same way that a chocolate Santa Claus implies a metal object, the negative of its form, which moulded it. Moulds symbolise the fortuitous aspect of our perception of the universe; recognition of concave, convex, inside, outside, entity, nonentity relates to the state of the observer.

The 9 Malic Moulds (part of the 'bachelor apparatus' of the *Large Glass*) mould 'illuminating gas'. The gas is contained within cells each of which has a different character. The moulds are uniforms – Priest, Undertaker, Gendarme and so on. When the illuminating gas is within the mould the gas is cast in the character imposed by the livery. It is therefore imbued with some of the attributes of Priest or Flunkey or Undertaker or Busboy. The temporary nature of this endowment is stressed by the volatility of the moulded substance; once it is allowed to leave the mould it assumes a shape determined by its new environment or it dissipates into air. A chocolate Santa Claus is almost as susceptible to change as the illuminating gas for it is quickly modified through consumption, digestion and excretion.

As chance determines what the world is for us, so other nonexistent perceptions can be deduced. Existence operates within conventions; the possibility of one conventional existence suggests innumerable other existences related to it. A three-dimensional object can be translated, by means of perspective or isometric projection or any other conventional system, into a two-dimensional statement of its existence. Therefore, Duchamp says, we may regard the three-dimensional statement as a projection of a four-dimensional construct and this of an n-dimensional system.

Duchamp's disdain for fixed conventions is elegantly demonstrated by the *3 Standard Stops*. The metre, a metal rule held under controlled temperature by governmental custodians in a vault in Paris, is a powerful image of immutable dimension and a perfect butt for Duchamp's constructive irony. In taking three lengths of thread one metre long and releasing them from a height of one metre to fall, as chance would determine, on a surface, he effectively symbolized the doubts cast upon the absolute veracity of the measure by Einstein. The most remarkable quality that Duchamp possesses is his ability to find

expression for notions which, at first sight, seem totally devoid of plastic interpretation. He finds a visual poetry for ideas which appear essentially abstract and non-visual. Each part of the *Large Glass* is fabricated lovingly to these unlikely ends. Elaborate description of its elements introduces the danger of missing their overall relationships; all that can be done is to give examples with an explanation that every one of many components is nursed with equal care to demonstrate profoundly reasoned concepts in terms of aesthetic experience, each unit playing its part in a larger cycle of operations and inter-relationships. The mist which obscures our comprehension of the work is often due to our own deficiency because the evidence for understanding is always provided. The notes to the *Large Glass* contain all the clues, once we are prepared to accept all statements as meaningful. The beauty and charm of his solutions are often felt only through appreciation of the problem and the effort of learning his game and its rules is amply repaid. At risk of further destroying the unity of the Glass, I quote another example of his method. The sieves, the set of seven cones that appear below the centre of the glass are described as 'a reverse image of porosity'. The sieves are permeable because the needles of solid illuminating gas pass through the cones from left to right and in doing so are disorientated. When he says that they are the reverse image of porosity he may be referring to the traplike sequence of obstructions. To understand the reason for the way in which they are coloured it becomes necessary to return to the idea of 'apparition'. Light in this sense is not reflected from a painted surface as we so often see colour – some wave-lengths of light being absorbed and others, which affect our retinas, being reflected – what Duchamp wants is a kind of emitted colour. We must see the substance, its 'apparition' not its 'appearance', by being connected optically with a light-emitting body. 'The colour effect of the whole will be the appearance of matter having a source of light in its molecular construction', to quote from his notes. In this way the pictorial matter might become more real. His solution for the sieves (I confess I am knitting notes together) was to allow dust to fall on the Glass for three or four months and to fix the deposit with transparent varnish. The way the sieves are painted/made symbolises the 'reverse image of porosity' in the sense that we see matter, not what is reflected after absorption, though we see something that is eminently porous because we see only

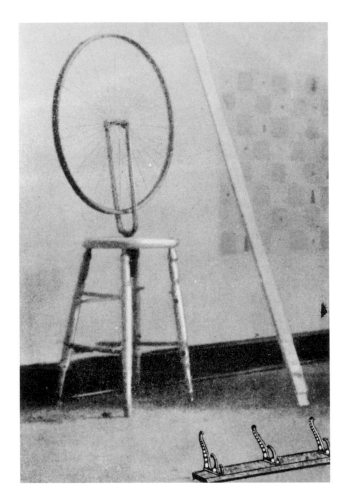

Bicycle Wheel, 1913

light transmitted through the glass partially veiled by dust. The aesthetic nature of our response is confirmed by our awareness of contradictions which defeat every attempt to define the experience in logical terms. His intention to make something real, something which is not merely an appearance, is continually confounded by his insistence on the fundamental insecurity of the 'real'. The *Large Glass* is a fantastic metaphysical construct; its qualities can only be hinted at in commentary. One stands in awe of the overwhelming intellect, the humanity it embodies and, even more surprising, to be in its presence is to feel its great artistry.

Art is often the outcome of iconoclasm. Rejection of currently accepted forms gives the incentive for new production. The history of art is more a narrative of battles with the immediate past than of the entrenchment of traditional patterns. Duchamp is, above all else, iconoclastic – he is even his own best enemy. The private revolution of 1913 was, more than anything, an attack upon his own past work, in particular the role that his talented hand played in it. His skilled hand had to be paralysed and his eye dimmed. If he used the tools of an engineering draftsman, T-square and compass, in the years that followed, it was to reject his painterly flair; if his images operate in the mind it is because he chooses to deny the sensuous pleasures of picture-making.

The large room at Pasadena given over to the period covered by the *Large Glass* 1913–1921 (these are the dates of the activity, not those given for the Glass itself) enables us to see something of the meticulous development and cross-referencing of ideas. There is the chocolate grinder in its three forms. First the 1913 *Chocolate Grinder No. 1* ; a 'still-life' in that it *represents* an object standing on a surface in space. It is hardly 'still' for the object can have no other function than to rotate. It cannot be 'life' for it lived only as a symbol of movement for Duchamp. Near by is the *Chocolate Grinder No. 2* which takes the symbolic object into another frame of reference by translating it from a represented object into a constructed object made with string and paint, still two-dimensional but more real because it no longer has painted shadows, no longer an illusion of a surface upon which it stands. We see it also in its third appearance as the central prop of the Bachelor Apparatus, made more a 'thing' in its newly elaborated perspective context and in the negation of the opaque two-dimensional panel through the use of glass. This has a *trompe l'œil* effect in allowing us to read the object as occupying space behind the glass.

The readymades, often common objects nominated to the status of art, must also be seen in the context of the *Large Glass.* There are a number of notes about readymades among the documents on the Glass; although contact is circuitous they often relate to some aspect of the larger work. The *Bicycle Wheel* of 1913, antedating the idea of readymades by two years, is evidence of Duchamp's concern with motion. If we look for intention it seems to have little significance other than as an enjoyable homemade toy. *Bottle Rack* has the presence, even something of the structure, of the *Malic Moulds* and was contemporary with their production in 1914. *Comb* (1916) is about control mechanism. *50cc of Paris Air,* a gift brought back from Europe to Walter Arensberg, is a nice aside on the theme moulded gas/ephemeral reality. An old geometry book left hanging to weather in wind and rain is an *Unhappy Readymade* with poignant overtones of time ravaging scientific 'truths'. Above all, the readymades satisfy the desire to suppress his artistic hand, leaving the mind in command.

If the readymades severed the instruments of making ('to make' is Duchamp's favourite definition of 'Art'), the rotary devices of the early 1920's destroy the artist's role as interpreter, as middleman who stands between us and nature telling us how to see. The effects of the Rotoreliefs are insinuated through the eye into the mind, for the designed image doesn't exist until rotation builds an illusory three-dimensional space within the observer. The two large rotating machines and the later set of flat discs are not a digression but an attack, from the flank, at the problems which had obsessed him for many years. Certainly, disturbance of optic processes had been the aim of *To be looked at with one eye, close to, for almost an hour,* a study, dated 1918, for the only part of the Glass which was not included in the overall conception of 1913. This was to become the three-tiered group of discs called Oculist Witnesses drawn in silver on the *Large Glass.*

The lesson of the Pasadena retrospective lies in the demand it makes to see Duchamp as a whole; as an entity so infinitely complex that his work resists attempts to transmit adequate experience of it. If I say 'look into this convex mirror', can the reflected thin man see the fat man who is projected on the other side of the glass? When I quote Duchamp as saying 'I am nothing if not an artist' I may divert you from the whole purpose of his life.

Not seen and/or less seen of/by Marcel Duchamp/
Rrose Sélavy

It is a common fallacy concerning Marcel Duchamp that, for all his brilliance, he has been a pretty indolent fellow. Jasper Johns in his review of Duchamp in a journal called *Scrap* was reminded of a caption to a *New Yorker* cartoon which said 'O.K. so he invented fire – but what did he do after that?'. Two hundred and eight items are given in Lebel's catalogue raisonné, a list containing works which pinnacle even in the mountain range of masterpieces produced by the great men of this century.

Perhaps we are to be excused our greedy demand for more from one who has given so much, since surprisingly little has been seen. A pilgrimage to the Arensberg collection in Philadelphia is greatly rewarding. The Museum of Modern Art in New York has proudly exposed its Dreier bequests – a bounty from which Yale also benefited. What has been seen is due only to two generous and far-sighted individuals, Walter Arensberg and Katherine Dreier. Just over a year ago the first major retrospective was held at Pasadena in the artist's seventy-sixth year; indirectly we owe that occasion to Arensberg through the devotion of Walter Hopps, the Museum's Director, to ideals learned from him in California.

We have seen the accomplishment of a decade only, for the Arensberg and Dreier collections hoarded just what they could get from Duchamp (the things that were closest to him when he was closest to them) and these were all from the years 1912–21. What we see now is the result of raids into other territories and times. It is a little surprising that anything survives by this artist, a man who refrained from putting a price on himself, who made a gift of his genius for every act of friendship rendered him, who was indifferent to the objects which he wrought with unbelievable care. Now it is apparent that little is missing – practically everything that Duchamp made has been treasured by someone – the losses are those things that he happened not to give away.

There are two major sources of this new assembly, the collections of H P Roché and Gustave Candel. Roché, a close friend of Duchamp for many years, acquired almost everything that he painted between 1905 and 1910 – a stack of work left behind in Jacques Villon's

Bibliography: 30

house when Duchamp went to America in 1915, which had been left undisturbed for thirty years. Candel's collection is as fortuitous. He can rarely have left Marcel without carrying off some gift. In the period of the regular meetings between 1907 and 1912 he accumulated a large group of drawings and paintings. Whatever justification there may be for the widely held view of Duchamp as 'anti-artist', these early works make it abundantly clear that he had fully mastered the artistic concepts and technical skills that he was soon to forcefully deny. The qualities stifled in every mature product sing out in those of the teenager and the young man. It comes as a shock to remember that Duchamp was twenty-four when he painted the *Nude Descending a Staircase*, twenty-five when he embarked on the *Large Glass*. But here we discover that he painted and drew marvelously when he was eighteen. What astonishes is the way in which his talents first emerged. He was a great natural colorist with a typically French sense of 'métier', a draftsman of easy fluency and commanding sense of style. The qualities that dominated the life's work of his brother Jacques Villon were those that Marcel turned his back upon, this at an age when many young painters are desperately straining after just his kind of flair. The reason that the early work has not been seen is probably that it stayed in France and France has been slower than the place of his voluntary exile in acknowledging Duchamp's eminence.

In the fifties and sixties Duchamp has been king – the wise man respected by his own generation, held in awe by its sons and wildly adored by theirs. The Midas touch was his – if he had cared in the slightest for gold. Incredibly placed, having simply to point a godlike finger, to bestow on any object the nearest thing to immortality we know; he had only to sign to confer the status of high art on a dustbin. He could have laughed himself to death on the way to the bank without affecting the issue one jot. Instead, he gave life to clay – he made Man *(Object Dart)*, Woman *(Female Fig Leaf)* and symbol of their union *(Wedge of Chastity)*. Strangely, the conjunction is not to be fruitful; the nesting 'wedge' fits its mould with a sure finality, polarity is brought to negation by their intercourse, master is lost in matrix.

What followed were elegant, restrained, small things appearing every two years or so in gratuitous compliance with friendly requests, pleasurable additions to the world's inheritance from a great artist. More than we knew – less than we had hoped. But Marcel Duchamp performs on his own terms or not at all.

Object Dart

Given the Illuminating Gas and the Waterfall

Female Fig Leaf

Wedge of Chastity

The Bride stripped bare by her bachelors even, again

In the Autumn of 1912 Marcel Duchamp, at the age of 25 and after the production of a body of painting that would in itself earn him a place of high honour in twentieth century art, began to conjecture a new work which would press beyond the bounds of art as then known, one that would be a compound of literary and graphic forms. By the end of 1914 a mass of notes had been made which describe in mechanical terms, often poetically irrational, a project entitled *The Bride stripped bare by her bachelors, even.* The pictorial embodiment of these ideas had been conceived as a composition on glass to be executed in lead wire, oil paint and lead foil. Many perspective studies had been made and parts had been tried out in the form of independent paintings.

In 1915 Duchamp went to America. It was there, soon after his arrival, that the large painting on glass was started. By 1918 a good deal had been done. Some new ideas were incorporated subsequent to that date until by 1923 the painting was complete, or rather, Duchamp decided that he would leave it at that. In 1926 it was displayed in Brooklyn; a first public appearance. While being returned from exhibition it was accidentally smashed. Ten years later Duchamp put the shattered pieces together. It was installed permanently in the Philadelphia Museum of Art in 1954, a gift from Katherine Dreier who wished to see it reunited with the great collection of Walter Arensberg who had been close to the work since Duchamp first arrived in America.

The *Large Glass* is in two halves on separate sheets of plate glass, one above the other, making an overall size of 108 × 67 inches. The lower glass, slightly larger than the upper, contains the Bachelor Apparatus which breaks down into five major units: Chocolate Grinder, Glider, Malic Moulds, Sieves and Oculist Witnesses. The Bride Machine above consists of three main parts: Bride, Blossoming and Shots. This nomenclature is elaborated in the textual component of the work – a documentation published in 1934 as a collection of 94 items, facsimile notes, drawings and photographs; the publication known as the *Green Box.* Each of the elements subdivides into smaller units having their own precisely described character and functioning – a network of complex interrelating activity that only the

Bibliography: 31

Pendu Femelle

Malic Moulds and Capillary Tubes

Glider

Oculist Witnesses

Sieves

Chocolate Grinder

Shots

notes can fully communicate. The *Large Glass* is thus a construct surrounded by a cluster of associated productions each having its own validity and each contributing hugely to our understanding of one of the most mysterious works of art of all time.

When the Arts Council of Great Britain proposed to organise a major Duchamp retrospective at the Tate Gallery for June 1966 it seemed so desperately unfortunate that our British audience should be denied any experience of the Glass that we decided to fill the gap with at least some semblance of the great painting. A precedent had been established for, in 1961, Ulf Linde made a version for the Moderna Museet in Stockholm. Prompted by a full size photographic copy on film for a BBC programme on Duchamp I had, that same year, thought about the possibility of making a replica. In June '65, with the enthusiastic support of William Copley, an American painter and friend of Duchamp, a start was made on a new version of the Glass in the Fine Art Department of the University of Newcastle upon Tyne.

It isn't possible to approach this task in the way that copies are usually made of paintings – to set up a canvas beside the original and reproduce the marks stroke for stroke. To work from photographs isn't satisfactory because much information, even at the straightforward level of fabrication, is lost. The alternative method, that of using the detailed documentation of the *Green Box* to cover the ground again – to reconstruct procedures rather than imitate the effects of action – was the one adopted. Duchamp's attitude to painting after 1912 moves progressively to a point where the act of creation can be no more than the nomination of a mass-produced object to the status of art. This seemingly perverse proposition is the logical extension of a point of view which caused Duchamp to divorce the sensual and manipulative aspects of painting from his purely conceptual interests of that time. The techniques of the Glass – the craftsmanship and even the planning method – are devised to isolate the artist from any emotional relationship with his medium. Drawing is mainly draughtsmanship of a geometric kind. Paint is applied in flat areas contained by boundary lines of lead wire. There are no passages where the Duchamp hand cannot be followed quite

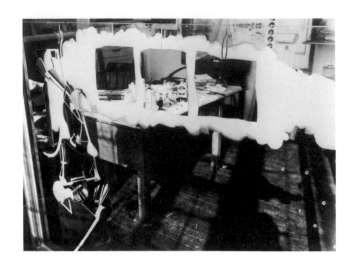

Bride: reconstruction

Bachelors: reconstruction

faithfully without the least consciousness of forgery. The most crucial decision in the reconstruction was that of opting to avoid a copy of the present appearance of the Glass. Severe deterioration has taken place quite apart from the fragmentation of the glass itself. In its fifty or so years of life it has succumbed to drastic changes. Our efforts have been directed at a recapitulation of intention – to make the glass as it was conceived, allowing for the possibility of change but accepting the inevitability of a different life for this echo of a masterpiece. The most obvious feature of the Philadelphia Glass, caused by the accident which ran sparkling fractures in a thousand rivulets across it, we have not attempted to repeat. Duchamp did use chance in three closely controlled sequences in his planning of the *Large Glass*. The breaking was an unpredicted calamity which caused, however, little distress in its victim. This new version is made on armour plate glass – a provision likely to preserve the appearance of its model's youth.

The parts of the Bachelor Apparatus are precisely located as though they existed in the space behind the glass. Within the *Green Box* is a pair of drawings, a *plan* and an *elevation* of the objects situated in the lower glass. Duchamp used these to produce a *perspective*, first in one tenth scale, then half size on canvas, then full size on the plaster wall, now destroyed, of his studio in Paris. My first task was to make the lost full-size perspective drawing from the dimensioned plan and elevation. References were made to the Philadelphia Glass more to gain knowledge of the construction of subject matter than to copy delineations on the surface of the original. There are slight differences – deviations accepted to maintain an integrity in the reconstruction equalling that of the original. Tracings were made, from the new perspective, of each of the elements with key lines added to relate them to each other. These tracings, reversed, were attached to the front of the glass to give the positioning of lead wire, formed to the drawing, then cemented to the back of the glass with mastic varnish.

Two studies were made on glass by Duchamp. So unusual are the techniques that it seemed sensible to repeat these – not only did we gain experience in handling the medium but we acquired more exhibits whose originals were too fragile to be loaned to the Arts

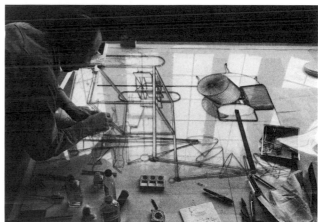

Bride: reconstruction

Bachelors: reconstruction

Council. Duchamp's first trial was of the *Glider* on a semi-circular piece of glass (his only glass painting to remain unbroken) now in the Philadelphia Museum entitled *Walter Mill within Glider* (*in Neighboring Metals*), dated 1913–15. The second study, *Nine Malic Moulds,* dated 1914–15, is still in the possession of the artist[1]. Duchamp permitted these studies to be repeated for our reconstruction. Further studies to explore method (practise runs not found necessary by Duchamp) were made in Newcastle: a small glass of the Sieves, trying out a specified 'dust raising' process, and another of the Oculist Witnesses. The Oculist Witnesses, unlike the rest of the Glass, demanded a technique not used by Duchamp. The right hand area of the lower glass had been silvered on the back and a drawing transferred to the silver by Duchamp through a piece of carbon paper. The silvering was then scraped away up to the drawn lines leaving the brilliantly reflective image. The long process was shortened in the remake by means of a silk-screen made from a blocked-in redrawing of the carbon paper. Pigment screened on to the mirror formed a resist which allowed the redundant silver to be etched away.

The upper half of the Glass is less precise in its drawing; Bride and Blossoming are free organic constructions. The outlines were taken from photographs, a technique which has itself perfect antecedents, for the Bride in the Philadelphia Glass derives directly from Duchamp's 1912 canvas called *Bride.* Parts of a photographic enlargement of the *Bride* painting provided a new configuration for the Glass. The Shots, nine holes drilled at spots located by projecting a paint-dipped match from a toy cannon, were plotted from the Philadelphia Glass.

Duchamp's labour, extending over thirteen years, has been repeated in about as many months in Newcastle. His problems were not ours – mental effort was exerted only in the direction of detective work, deductions from signs marking a path to be followed – the creative anguish was erased from the trail. We were speeded by adequate funds for the venture and our University ambiance made assistance available as needed. Duchamp's lonely nourishing of ideas into form was a far cry from the appreciative co-operation provided fifty years later and which is gratefully acknowledged here.

[1] Now owned by Teeny Duchamp, the artist's widow.

Sieves: reconstruction

Oculist Witnesses: reconstruction

The Bride stripped bare by her bachelors, even: reconstruction, 1965–6

The almost complete works of Marcel Duchamp

No living artist commands a higher regard among the younger generation than Marcel Duchamp. Appreciation of his activity and its historical consequences is now fervently demonstrated throughout the world though the evidence, the work itself, has not been easy of access. The myth of the man has overshadowed a confused picture of the artist. Until the present only a handful of his paintings have been shown outside the U.S.A. This is the second major retrospective anywhere, the first was held in Pasadena in 1963. Last year the Mary Sisler Collection shown at the Cordier and Ekstrom Gallery in New York well merited its title 'Not seen and/or less seen of/by Marcel Duchamp/Rrose Sélavy'. The present exhibition is remarkable not only in presenting the work of this major artist for the first time in Europe, it is unique in showing him nearly complete. Most of the extant works are here, if the original was not able to travel we have a replica. Only six important things are missing (reproduced unnumbered in the catalogue). A lifetime of art is laid before us to experience in moments. We can at last clearly see the artifacts and relate them to their maker.

The pace at which we scan the pattern is enormously accelerated so that even the fast headlamp of Duchamp's intellect is speeded by the compression. We see the tradition from which this life stems, ties with family and friends, teenage influences, its roots in the bohemian art of Montmartre. We are thrown almost immediately into a group of paintings of brilliant assurance. The canvasses of 1911 must be rated among the greatest products of a period that will be marked as one of the most distinguished in the history of French art. *Nude descending a staircase* and *Bride* are achievements of such authority that it is startling to remember that these were made by a young man of 24 years. Duchamp's intense search for personal expression had reached its goal early but the accomplishment induced no satisfaction, only a crisis of self-doubt which set off the long labour of planning and constructing *The Bride stripped bare by her bachelors, even,* at the same time initiating the programme of rejections and denials which cut away with surgical precision all the hard gained attributes that designated him 'artist' and asserted that art is a fact of mind.

With this realization of Duchamp's work firmly bedded in

Bibliography: 32

the past we can see the growth that has fed so much art of the present. All the branches put out by Duchamp have borne fruit. So widespread have been the effects of his life that no individual may lay claim to be his heir, no-one has either his scope or his restraint. Duchamp's refusal to repeat himself has persuaded others to follow one or another of his indications. He can have no true progeny because his wisdom has led, ultimately, to neutrality. His greatness lies in the completeness of his understanding – his ability to triumphantly reverse his stand or even to find plastic expression for concepts of negation. His detachment is observed with such scrupulous exactitude the wonder is that the precipitate of his thought, the made, the nominated works of Marcel Duchamp, can communicate so successfully an idea that occurs in the *Green Box :* 'painting of precision and the beauty of indifference'. This paradox is the key to Duchamp. If his objective of a precise formal statement which encompasses a dedicated rejection of commitment fails to strike a chord then the last forty years of his work will seem little more than a jest. Those who do perceive the value of this enigma may well be surprised by the second half of this exhibition for they will find that 'indifference' provides a 'beauty' unintended by Duchamp. His search for an object without aesthetic merit, one 'with the least virtue' that he could find to allege his conviction that 'taste is the enemy of art', has proved futile. For the Duchamp personality, his essentially artistic genius, has defeated him. Time has mellowed his readymades, given them a hallowed aspect that welds them into a vision of implausible unity. In his purpose of 'changing the definition of art' Duchamp had no power to exclude, he could only widen the language, only make us more aware that art is all pervading.

It was with just a tinge of sadness that Duchamp admitted in 1961, 'I'm nothing else but an artist . . . I couldn't be very much more iconoclastic any more'.

The Large Glass

The Bride stripped bare by her bachelors, even, 1915–23: Photo. 1926

La Mariée mise à nu par ses célibataires, même (the *Large Glass*) is most of Duchamp; earlier paintings feed its voracious capacity, and half a century later the saga of the stripped bride was painstakingly pressed into new moulds to build another astonishing perception, *Etant donnés.* Duchamp's incomparable mind disdained the role assigned it by Parisian art; he saw through every sham, subjecting his own talent to no less fierce a distrust. This aggressive humility (it might be mistaken for arrogance) nourished the little inventor. If he could conceive of something, then he could try to give that thought form; insisting that 'art, etymologically speaking, is to make', his occupation was to tinker. An artisan's approach to fabrication freed his mind to soar way out of sight while the constructs remain gloriously unpretentious. Discussion of the *Large Glass* will involve a good deal of description of techniques and methods; though its prefiguration – a leap of the imagination that is, in some minds, the ultimate heroic feat of Modern Art – was accomplished in some few months, twice as many years were to be devoted to laborious detailing and execution.

There is a well-marked starting point. The drawing made soon after Duchamp reached Munich for a visit in July–August 1912, on which was written *'Première recherche pour: La mariée mise à nu par les célibataires',* nearly the title given to both the *Large Glass* and to the boxed annotations that are an integral part of the total work, can be seen as an illustration of its legend. It shows a central female figure attacked at either side by two rampant males. Ulf Linde first observed that the drawing bears a resemblance to an illustration in a treatise by Solidonius – an insight which proliferated into the fashionable notion that alchemy provides a key to iconography of the Glass. Ingenious and amusing as later cross-referencing with esoteric texts and images may be, it must be said that Duchamp gave this no credence. An inspiration (frequently mentioned by the artist) was his enthusiasm for the work of Raymond Roussel, whose play *Impressions d'Afrique* he attended in the company of Apollinaire, Gabrielle Buffet, and her husband Francis Picabia during its run in May–June 1912 – an excitement carried fresh to Munich. But the *Large Glass* is born of Duchamp's perversity. It springs from the intensity of his

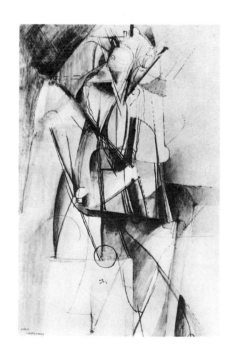

The Bride stripped bare by her bachelors, 1912

Virgin (No. 2), 1912

Bibliography: 51

will to seek only within himself the rules of a game of his own devising. Unquestionably the Munich drawing coincides with the purpose and the graphic language of the works that immediately precede it (*King and Queen traversed by Swift Nudes*, for example), which owe something, in both intention and style, to the *Nude Descending a Staircase.* Two subsequent drawings, both called *Virgin,* lead to the small painting *The Passage from the Virgin to the Bride,* which in turn acts as prompter to the climactic Munich painting, *Bride.* The chronology is plain, and that sequence is vital to an understanding of the creative mystery of those fecund weeks in Germany. The logic of Duchamp's purposeful progression, his persistent questioning of these products of his own fantasy, offers the best clue to the genesis of the Glass.

In Munich, his interest in chronophotographic representation of movement, most rigorously applied in the descending nude, went beyond the brisk graphic style of the intervening works to engage in a new inquiry. If the subject is time and space, in what way, he asks, can such a subject be pictured as a formal entity? And then, what attributes, what functions, what desires and psychological peculiarities does that time-generated structure possess? The crisis occurs with *The Passage from the Virgin to the Bride.* Its figurative language stresses spatial movement; yet the transposition from virgin to bride cannot be a displacement from here to there, nor is it an illustration of defloration. The subject undergoes a metaphysical change, and a search for the identity of that change is the motivation of the *Bride* painting. The *Passage* configurations are here crystallized into well-defined forms, indications of transference are firmed into volumes, kineticism gives birth to a new formal state.

Returning home in August 1912, he was very sure that, for him, painting was over; the extremity of effort, the conclusiveness of the *Bride* were traumatic. Paris provided a convalescence from the fervour of Munich and relief from his isolation there. A key event followed: he made a weekend trip to the Jura mountains, arranged by Gabrielle Buffet, with Picabia and Apollinaire (the group that had attended *Impressions d'Afrique* together). Duchamp was moved by the fast

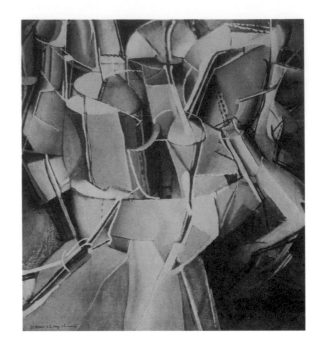

The Passage from the Virgin to the Bride, 1912

car ride across France to produce a prose fantasy. A machine, with an animal component, is described as absorbing the long, straight, empty road, with its comet-like headlights beaming out in front toward a seeming infinity. The text turns to a speculation on the graphic means by which to express this mechanomorphic object in a limitless one-dimensional space; only at the end does it become evident that a painting is being proposed, one that will require detailed planning.

Although resolved that painting, per se, was untenable, he was nevertheless stuck, for the moment, with the pictorial modes he so firmly rejected. His Jura-Paris text was full of vague notions about the possibility of using materials other than artist's pigments, but another painting was made in January 1913. It portrayed a chocolate grinder he had seen displayed in the window of a well-known confectioner in his home town, Rouen. *Bride* was the first canvas for several years in which physical motion was not illustrated, though movement is its rationale. *Chocolate Grinder, No. 1,* a literal picture of an odd object, stands three-square on a tabletop; its formal existence is so totally dependent on function that motion is implied without explicit representation.

The stay in Munich had been a period of separation from friends, and isolation was the more complete for Duchamp because he spoke little German. Another period of similar containment followed with a visit to Herne Bay on the south coast of England in the summer of 1913, ostensibly as chaperon to his sister Suzanne. It was here that *The Bride stripped bare by her bachelors* began to take shape in written notes which establish the chemistry and mechanical performance of the complex apparatus to be depicted. These notes, together with others made over the next few years – none more than a single sheet of paper, often a torn scrap – were to be published in 1934 as facsimiles of the originals in a green box. Though a sequence for the notes was never prescribed by their author, it is fair to assume that among the first was the longest and most ambitious. This text, on a piece of paper concertina folded five times to give ten closely written numbered pages, establishes the interelationships of the main characters. It is headed 'the Bride stripped bare by the bachelors' and it begins:

Bride, 1912

Chocolate Grinder (No. 1), 1913

2 principal elements: 1. Bride
                                     2. Bachelors
Graphic arrangement.
a long canvas, upright.
Bride above –
bachelors below.

There follow detailed descriptions of the two elements as machines. They have interrelationships, but the Bride's domain is strictly separated from that of the Bachelors by a 'cooler'. Above the earthbound, 'fat and lubricious' Bachelors hangs the Bride, 'an apotheosis of virginity' who has reached the 'goal of her desire' and emits a 'cinematic blossoming . . . the sum total of her splendid vibrations . . . the orgasm which may (might) bring about her fall'. A thumb-nail sketch indicates the composition with its three glass fins which forever divide MARiée from CELibataires. Quotation from the notes unfortunately distorts their quality; intimacy with all the texts and diagrams of the *Green Box* is the best, indeed the only, way to achieve true understanding and enjoyment of the Glass.

The annotations for the upper half of the *Large Glass* begin with a consideration of the Munich *Bride.* They are an after-the-fact determination of a possible physical nature and operation, justifying the fortuitous disposition of forms which would be abstract if they did not give a strong illusion of existence and if some alien causality could not be read into them. Duchamp crosses into this other reality, reducing its fantastic character by playing it very straight with descriptions as precise as those of a patent engineer. Each constituent is named, and its function and interactions with the whole are stated with inexorable logic. The Bride in the Munich canvas floats vacuously in her mesh of paint – in the new work she will hang free on the glass 'The Pendu femelle is the form in ordinary perspective of a Pendu femelle for which one could perhaps try to discover the true form'. In spite of his precision, or maybe because of it, Duchamp sees any configuration as arbitrary – it is one fixed state in a flux of time and space. The images of the Glass are a 'Delay in glass . . . not so much in the different meanings in which "delay" can be taken, but rather in their indecisive reunion'.

As the *Bride* canvas gives birth to the upper half of the

Note from the *Green Box*

Glass, so the only pure painting to follow it, *Chocolate Grinder, No. 1,* is the starting point of the Bachelor Apparatus. Duchamp thought always in terms of oppositions, so the Bride's irregular organic shapes and hinged, flexing relationships are contrasted with the Bachelor's predetermined, mensurated, rectilinear planning and simple mechanical movements. *Bride,* painted with the artist's fingers directly, a perfect tactile communion with *matière,* had induced a disgust with sensual aspects of painting. The Bachelor Machine, conceived after the Bride, would be drafted with measured care, its members plotted to a millimeter, the hand distanced from the surface with instruments. The most remarkable aspect of the arrangement of the lower part of the Glass is that it was not composed in perspective. The Bachelor features were conceived from above, for the first drawing of the whole Bachelor Apparatus is evidently the 'plan' included in the *Green Box.* The circular platform of the Chocolate Grinder occupies a central position; its stem is the core from which all other dimensions are generated. Parallel with the plan is, of course, an 'elevation' which carries all vertical information to complete a three-dimensional record of the apparatus. With these figures at hand, two-dimensional composition consisted of positioning the central vanishing point (nicely judged at 11.8 cms left of the grinder's centre, roughly the viewpoint of the original grinder painting), which locates the spectator relative to the objects depicted, projecting the perspective, and then deciding where to place the edges of the glass. No perspective treatments were necessary for the Bride panel.

The next two years were spent in consolidation and refinement. With the aid of the *General Plan – Perspective,* the elements of the Bachelor Apparatus could be treated separately. Duchamp returned to the grinder and made a new painting, redrawn to marry it perfectly with the general plan. *Chocolate Grinder, No. 1* was visualized as an object standing on a surface with a fixed point illumination, a classic perspective exercise; indeed, shadow cast by curved forms on curved surfaces is pure textbook study. *Chocolate Grinder, No. 2* takes the image to another realm, where it becomes a philosophic statement concerning the nature of two-dimensional

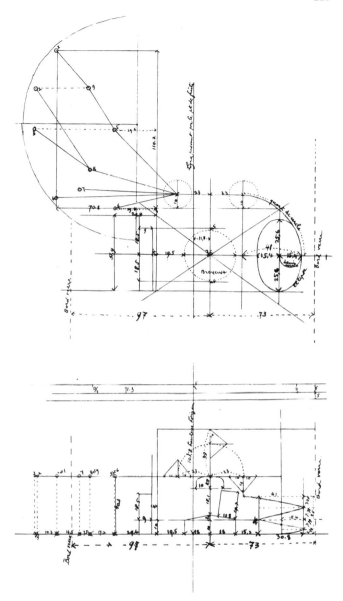

Bachelor Apparatus 1° in plan

Bachelor Apparatus 2° in elevation

representation. The subject is no longer illuminated from a point source, colour is applied flat and unmodulated, additional lines made with thread sewn through the canvas radiate from the centres of the rollers and turn across their slightly tapered sides – no longer a likeness but an object flattened, re-created in two dimensions on a background painted in the flat blue tint he used to symbolize a neutral, vacant ground. By this time (winter 1913–14) the perspective of the whole Bachelor Apparatus had reached full size, drawn on a plastered wall in his studio. Thread is very helpful in making a perspective drawing of this size. Since the vanishing points are a considerable distance from the image, a ruler would have to be long – and therefore clumsy. The simplest method is a nail driven into a vanishing point; from the nail a thread can be pulled taut to the position required for any particular line. The technique of drawing with the thread itself on the *Chocolate Grinder* canvas is an invention more plausible than its concurrent use to make *Three Standard Stoppages*.

Einstein's theory of relativity was just then being discussed at a superficial level in the popular press, and Duchamp gave an ironic twirl to the notion of the standard metre being modified by movement through time and space. 'A horizontal thread one metre in length falls from a height of one metre onto a horizontal plane while twisting as it pleases and creates a new image of the unit of length'. This process was repeated three times with the thread falling on a canvas painted blue (the Prussian blue of the Grinder background), and drops of varnish were gently applied to fix the curve as it lay. Each canvas was cut into a strip, and these were glued individually to long pieces of glass. The three curves were then inscribed on wooden slats so that a profile of the curve could be cut to make three templates, boxed as a set of tools.

To the left of the Chocolate Grinder, attached via the Scissors which pivot on the central stem, or Bayonet, of the grinder, is the Chariot, Sleigh, or Glider. This element received separate treatment as a study on glass (the first work on this unforgiving material and the only one to remain unbroken). The technique derives in part from Duchamp's use of plate glass as a palette in the studio. The reverse of the palette showed flat brilliant

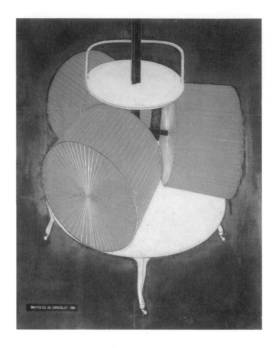

Chocolate Grinder (No. 2), 1914

3 Standard Stops, 1913–14

colours, and it occurred to him that the problem of impermanence of oil pigments could be solved by using glass as a support. Paint seen through glass would be isolated from contact with the air, so that oxidization, the main factor in deterioration, would be prevented. Another virtue was that he would be freed from the 'demeaning' task of actually applying colour to an area coincidental to the form – a negative activity he disliked. Finally, and most important, the background would be provided by chance, by whatever environment the picture happened to be in.

Work on the semicircular *Glider* began with an unsuccessful attempt to etch the drawing with hydrofluoric acid. A long period of dangerous discomfort from fumes produced a barely visible line. At that time in Paris it was customary to keep a supply of lead fuse wire at hand, in various sizes for different amperages. It is a malleable, strangely sculptural material that may be shaped to follow a laterally reversed drawing placed underneath the glass. The wire, precisely positioned, might then be fixed to the glass with mastic varnish, another handy commodity in the studio, already successfully used to fasten the threads of the Standard Stoppages. The technique worked well and was slow enough to satisfy Duchamp's painstaking deliberation. Once the wire was fixed in place, the glass could be painted within the wire boundaries, and a sealing layer of lead foil pressed to the wet paint – a final optimistic protection of the pigment, sealing it in an envelope of glass and lead. The *Large Glass* and its studies have undergone a dramatic change, for Duchamp's contriving of permanence was thwarted by two factors: an unexpected chemical interaction takes place when lead foil is in contact with the lead pigments used (white lead as a base and pure red for the Malic Moulds); and the glass, though chemically resistant, is very liable to fracture. Chance has run with unwitting abandon through the fabric of these works.

A study on glass was also made of the *Nine Malic Moulds*. Originally eight moulds (the ninth had been added before the glass study), they are hollow shells each representing a different professional uniform, surmounted by an appropriate hat – Priest, Delivery Boy, Gendarme, Cuirassier, Policeman, Undertaker,

Glider Containing a Water Mill in Neighbouring Metals, 1913–15

9 Malic Moulds as they appear in the *Large Glass*

Flunky, Busboy, Stationmaster. Their function is to mould Illuminating Gas. (Duchamp liked to turn to account readily available utilities, so what more natural than to resort to the water and gas supplied to all floors of Parisian apartment houses of the time, proudly advertised as having *Eau & gaz à tous les étages,* for the two 'given' requirements of his Bachelor Apparatus?) The moulds endow the gas with a particular character – rather as clothes make the man. A strange feature of the Malic Moulds is that the figures do not stand on a surface; Duchamp's perspective is never less than cunning. The common denominator linking them is the 'horizontal plane of sex' – the crotch of each mould is at the same level, while head and feet vary in extension above and below that plane.

Illuminating Gas, given a particular character by confinement in the livery moulds, seeps along Capillary Tubes joined to the hat of each mould. A large canvas was at hand, the unfinished *Spring* painting discarded in 1911, on which had been superimposed a pencil-drawn enlargement of the 'General plan' to half the full size. Overlying these earlier uses, the positions, in plan, of the Nine Malic Moulds were located full-size with the centre of vision of the Large Glass perspective carefully noted. Each template of the *Standard Stoppages* was used three times to trace the network of Capillary Tubes so that all paths meet at their termination on the right. This painted map derives from an idea to place the canvas at such an angle relative to a camera that a photograph would provide a perspective projection of the lines to fit accurately into the existing master perspective. Camera lenses proved inadequate to the task, so a conventional method of drawn projection was used. All the elements of the Bachelor Apparatus would have to be in reverse, so that the wire on the back of the glass would be seen right way round from the front. The only reversed drawing that survives is that for the Malic Moulds, which shows the 'network' in perspective.

In its passage through the Capillary Tubes, the Illuminating Gas solidifies. When it reaches the opening, extruded by pressure from the mould, it breaks into short 'needles' which will ascend (since coal gas is lighter than air) through the Sieves (seven cones in a semicircular arc behind the Grinder). Duchamp's conceptual subtlety, as recorded in the notes, could

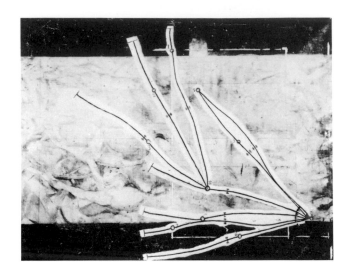

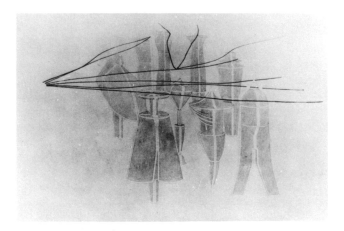

Network of Stoppages, 1914

Cemetery of Uniforms and Liveries (No. 2), 1914

hardly be matched by execution; such elegance and refinement of thought made impossible demands on the technical resources then available – which meant that a great many ideas got no further than words. The Sieves drawing carries a text which describes how the disposition in plan of the Malic Moulds, as seen in the 'network', could be marked on a thin rubber disk. If the membrane were pushed at its centre to make a cone, the cone might be photographed for each of the Sieves so that the original relationship of the fragments of solidified gas would be maintained throughout their 180° disorientation in the Sieves – in other words, the distribution in plan would be inverted; the scheme was abandoned, however. During their circumnavigation the 'spangles' of solidified gas are converted into a 'liquid scattered suspension' sucked out, in its later stages, by a 'butterfly pump'. From the pump, the liquid spirals down to create a great 'flow' to the orgasmic splash.

Another cycle of activity takes place simultaneously at a purely mechanical level. The Chariot, Sleigh, or Glider slides back and forth on its 'runners', powered by the Waterfall through the Water Mill. The right-hand side of the Chariot's box frame has extensions up to the Scissors so that sliding connections allow the arms to open and close in unison with the movements of the Chariot, while the opposite ends relate to the splash. There were problems in converting the rotary motion of the Water Mill to the reciprocations of the Chariot. Springs (a 'Sandow') were finally assisted by an ironic solution – a weight of oscillating density (in the form of a bottle of Benedictine) adds its impetus.

In 1915 Duchamp left France for America, arriving there as something of a celebrity. The *Nude Descending a Staircase* had been illustrated in the Armory Show press. He had contacts, through Walter Pach, with the organizers of the show and with the poet and collector Walter Arensberg, who became a lifelong friend. Nobody in the United States, and hardly anyone in Paris, had knowledge of Duchamp's extraordinary new project. The whole work had been elaborately studied in notes, a perspective of the lower half was fully prepared, technical solutions were developed for the fabrication of the image on glass, and trials made of three main features of the Bachelor Machine, but as yet work on the *Large Glass* itself had not been started. Soon after

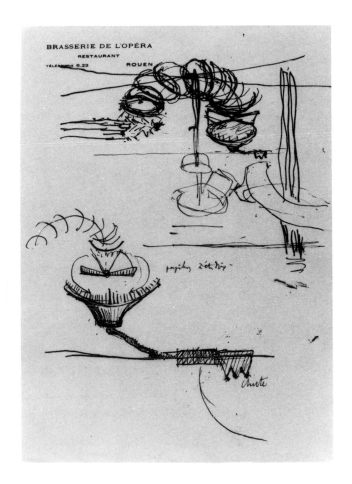

Sieves and Butterfly Pump, note from the *Green Box*

Duchamp's arrival in New York, plate-glass panels were bought and work began. There were limits to the amount of material Duchamp could transport across the Atlantic in 1915; he could carry his notes, but the large glass study of the Chariot remained in France, as did the *Bride* painting, which he had given to Picabia. The full-size perspective on plaster had to stay where it was; but the full-size details of most of the Bachelor Apparatus existed on paper, so that execution of the lower glass presented the least problems. Duchamp began to grapple with the unresolved upper panel – the Bride's domain.

We know that the Pendu femelle of the *Large Glass* derives from the Munich *Bride* painting. In fact, those organs of the bride to which Duchamp had been able to ascribe a function reappear unchanged except in colour. It is possible to isolate the Pendu femelle by cutting her silhouette from a photograph of the Munich *Bride.* A remarkable note on the 'blossoming' proposes that the glass be prepared with a silver bromide emulsion; indeed the technique was tried in an unsuccessful attempt to print the Pendu femelle by projecting a negative of the *Bride* directly onto the glass from a photographic enlarger. Only a thin, elusive image was produced, so the wire-drawing procedure was put to use again; but instead of filling in with flat colour, as in the lower glass, Duchamp painted the Pendu femelle in black-and-white gradations simulating a photograph of the *Bride.*

Though manipulation of paint had become repugnant, the 'halo of the Bride' is given due lyricism in its handling – 'this cinematic blossoming is the most important part of the painting (graphically as a surface)'. The treatment, however, is no less conceptual than the flat pigments used as substance in other parts of the Glass. As the colour of the Grinder is chocolate, so the hue of the blossoming is flesh, rich, sumptuous, Renoiresque: the rose pinks and pale peach tinged with emerald green of the classic female nude. Buried in glass and lead, the colour has an actuality richer than its appearance from the front, modified by the overall *eau de Nil* tinge that plate glass adds.

Within the blossoming are three rectangular openings, Draft Pistons or Nets, a Triple Cipher, terms that explain

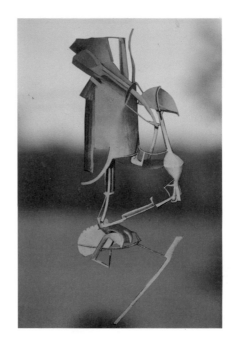

Simulation of Pendu femelle from *Bride* painting

Reconstruction of Blossoming

their role in the allegory and that also stress the importance of method in the Glass. Duchamp used the number three throughout his work, so much so that one might be tempted to suppose that he ascribed to it some magic property. But his mind is Cartesian and the predilection for three is rational. One is unity, two's a pair, three is number (n). To make three of a thing is to mass-produce it. Triplication deprives the art object of a factor he found deplorable – that reverence given to a unique work for no other reason than its singularity. There is another, equally important application of number in the *Large Glass;* the number three is 'taken as a refrain in duration', so that it binds the elements of the composition together in a repeating rhythm. Three rollers grind chocolate, Three Standard Stoppages, each used three times, form the Capillary Tubes coming from the Nine Malic Moulds, and they fix, 'preserve' or 'can' a chance-modified line. The three Draft Pistons apply the principle to a plane, while the Shots (to be discussed later) are a three-times-three chance distribution of points. Point, line, and plane are all submitted to systematized hazard – a triple use of triple chance.

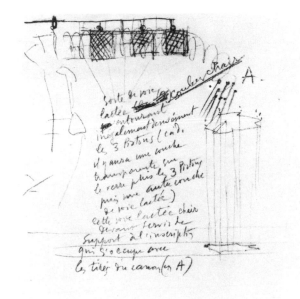

Draft Pistons (planes moved by air pressure) were fabricated by hanging a one-metre-square Net (net curtain or veiling) above a radiator. Rising currents of warm air disturbed the material, so that three photographs of it produced three different profiles for the plane. Since the Net had spots distributed at regular intervals, the photographs record not only the contour but the topology of the entire surface. Naturally the Pistons have their function: they are to determine the terms of the Top Inscription which will run over the blossoming like news flashed across Times Square in letters of light. A text must have its 'alphabetic units' readily available, so a 'letter box' is situated at the junction of the Pendu femelle and her blossoming from which the Draft Pistons sort the ciphered messages. This 'moving inscription' crosses toward the Shots, a group of nine holes drilled in the top right.

Duchamp's manipulation of chance always has a profound philosophical content which finds expression in play (Von Neumann's mathematical treatise on chance is, after all, devoted to *Theory of Games*). For the Shots he takes a toy cannon, with a match dipped in

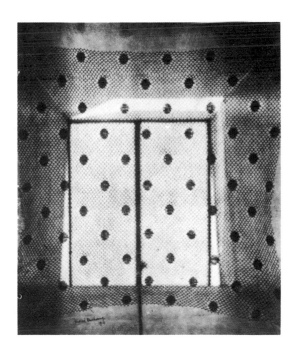

Blossoming and Shots, note from the *Green Box*

Draft Piston, 1914

paint as a projectile. A carefully aimed shot is fired at a 'target' point – the target is missed but a mark is made by the paint. Two more shots from the same position produce spots at varying distances around the target, since neither his skill nor the instrument is unerring. This process operated from two other positions gives nine points. The target is, according to Duchamp, 'demultiplied' – a phenomenon then developed metaphysically. If the nine spots are joined in sequence, in the manner of a numbers drawing, the result is a jagged plane. If lines are drawn vertically below the points of this plane we get a fluted column. Therefore the one-dimensional target is said to embody 'the schema of any object whatever', in much the way that a single living cell carries within it the potential of complex organic development. This is just one elegant demonstration of a major obsession of the Glass, dimensionality. The question continually posed is: If the Large Glass is a representation of a three-dimensional world on a two-dimensional surface, then could a three-dimensional representation be a conventional projection of a four-dimensional world? One is tempted to continue this speculation and to ask: Is *Etant donnés* (the recapitulation of the saga of the Stripped Bride that occupied the last twenty years of Duchamp's life) the three-dimensional construction forming the centre of a trilogy awaiting the final unimagined, probably unimaginable, restatement, the four-dimensional Bride?

We must stay with the Glass and turn, as Duchamp did, to the lower panel. Four of the Bachelor features presented no problems. Chocolate Grinder, Glider, Malic Moulds, and Capillary Tubes required only the patient labour of remaking them as grouped on the glass and linked by the Scissors, following the methods used in the studies. In the way that it is applied, the paint on the lower panel is quite different from that on the upper. The Bride presents the appearance of a three-dimensional object attached to the top edge of the glass with *trompe-l'oeil* loops and hooks. Another intention prevails in the Bachelor Apparatus: pigment is used to create an 'apparition of an appearance', By this Duchamp seems to mean that the colour we see is not a semblance of something; it is not a colour decision, nor is it a skin of paint on the surface of an object. A

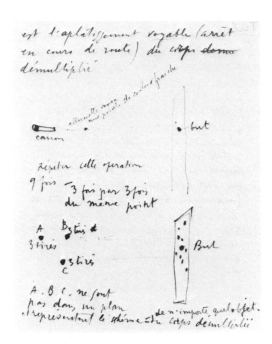

Shots from canon, note from the *Green Box*

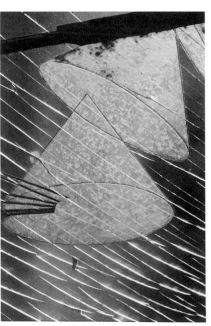

The *Large Glass,* Sieves, 'a reverse image of porosity'

two-dimensional layer of pigment does not merely represent the metal frame of the Glider, but is the substance itself; oxides of lead and cadmium actually compose the metal framework of the Chariot. An arbitrary colour choice for the Malic Moulds is avoided by the application of an undercoat of 'provisional colour.' They wait, primed with red lead 'like croquet mallets', for each to be allocated its final coat.

A full-size drawing of the Sieves was done in Paris, but there were no trials of an idea for their execution. Since the Sieves permit the passage of Illuminating Gas, they must be permeable. The fabric is to be a 'reverse image of porosity' so dust might be allowed to settle for a period of three months (Man Ray's famous photograph shows the 'dust breeding' process) to be finally fixed with varnish. This 'breeding of colours' takes us closest to his ideal – the Glass seen as a 'greenhouse' in which transparent colours, as ephemeral as perfumes, will emerge, flourish, ripen, and decay like flowers and fruits.

By 1917 all of the developed aspects of the *Green Box* notes, the 1913 conceptualization, were completed. Two proposed components had been abandoned: a Boxing Match attached by Rams to the top right of the lower panel and above that a Juggler of Gravity at bottom right of the upper panel. Duchamp was bored by the need to cover the same ground repeatedly. He had also perfected another art, that of the Readymade, which removed the need for manual skill altogether. Life was exciting, and the Glass must have appeared an overworked private obsession to the man who presented a urinal to the Independents' exhibition, New York, 1917, with the title *Fountain.*

A third significant opportunity for isolated introspection occurred in 1918, when Duchamp went to Argentina. As the Bride appeared secretly in a Munich pension, as the intricacies of the great Glass were figured out in a seaside boarding house in Herne Bay, England, so the conclusive effort was made in a Buenos Aires apartment, where a new contribution (the Oculist Witnesses) was added to the original scheme. From the Sieves, the Illuminating Gas converted to a fog of 'spangles', is sucked down by a 'butterfly pump' which ejects it through a 'chute' to make a great splash, the

Dust raising, photo: Man Ray

To be Looked at with One Eye, Close to, for Almost an Hour, Buenos Aires, 1918

orgasm of the Bachelors ('a liquid elemental scattering'), which makes such a 'din'. The splash ascends above the 'planes of flow' and finally relates to the Shots; thus the issue of the Nine Malic Moulds is 'regularized by the 9 holes' which terminate the Bride.

The 1918 supplement to the project was a witness to the events of the glass – a Peeping Tom. A *témoin oculiste* is, in French law, an eye witness. But it is also a chart used by opticians for eye testing[1]. Duchamp, exploring as always the ambiguous character of any one *reality,* the fortuitous nature of any one existence, was intrigued by devices that play visual tricks. He enjoyed optical illusions as he loved verbal puns which question the validity of language. In Buenos Aires a new glass study was made – *To be Looked at with One Eye, Close to, for Almost an Hour.* It is a direct study for the Large Glass (the Scissors, at their free ends, enter from the side of the small panel), though not all of its new material was used. The relevant part of the image is a series of reflecting lines, in mirror silver, which radiate from the vertical axis of the splash. This is a standard, readymade oculist's chart placed horizontally in a precise relationship to the scissor arms and the central vanishing point of the Large Glass.

On his return to New York Duchamp took this element and multiplied it. Of course it had to be three charts, so two other designs were chosen, to be placed one above the other, as a column of shimmering disks surmounted by a vertical ring at a central position between the terminations of the Scissors, a place occupied by a magnifying lens on the *To Be Looked at . . .* glass. Projection of the perspective was, in itself, a most demanding task, no less difficult than that of transferring it to the back of the Bachelor panel, now silvered on the right-hand side. To work in negative, scraping away the surplus silver, was a long and difficult process.

Walter Arensberg owned the unfinished glass in 1918. When he moved to California in 1921, ownership was transferred to Katherine Dreier, for the piece was rightly thought too fragile to travel. By 1923 Duchamp had decided that no further work would be done, and *The Bride stripped bare by her bachelors, even* was publicly exhibited for the first time in 1926 at the International Exhibition of Modern Art in the Brooklyn

[1] Oculist's charts can be seen in Man Rays's photograph of the *Rotary Glass Plates* in Duchamp's New York studio.

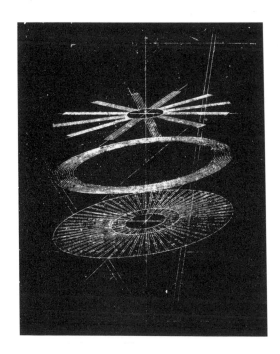

Rotary Glass Plates (Precision Optics), 1920, photo: Man Ray

Oculist Witnesses, 1920 (The carbon paper used to transfer the image to the mirrored glass)

Museum. Returning to the Dreier home in a truck, the two sheets of glass, lying face to face in a crate, bounced and shattered in great symmetrical arcs – a disaster hidden until the box was opened some years later. Duchamp, undismayed by this unplanned intervention of chance, reassembled the fragments in 1936, aided by the lead wire and varnish which had helped to hold the pieces together.

With the publication of the notes in their *Green Box* in 1934, the story seemed at an end, until another batch of notes, covering roughly the same period and almost equalling their number, emerged in 1964. Duchamp's involvement with words is extensive –as unique in itself as it is uniquely integrated into his art. In much the way that he defeated pomposity of pictorial expression, he attacked explicit formal language. *La Mariée mise à nu par ses célibataires* was a sentence with too clear a meaning; *même* made nonsense of its grammatical structure. Why a green box when he detested the colour green as much as he disliked the name Rose? Perhaps, in pursuance of his creed to make determinations other than aesthetic ones, a *Boîte Verte* should accompany a *Grand Verre,* Duchamp's writings equate in spareness with his images and have all their concentrated power; together they are an experience unmatched in art. One sheet in the *Green Box* is headed 'General notes for a Hilarious picture': this says more about Duchamp and the Glass than twenty pages of criticism or explanation. The stripping is hilarious because if it were solemn it would be laughable. His keenest tool is irony, 'ironism of affirmation: differences from negative ironism dependant solely on Laughter'. He doesn't avoid decision – 'Always or nearly always give reasons for the choice between 2 or more solutions (by ironical causality).' What he does is to devise systems by means of which choice is no longer an expression of ego. Everything he attempted is accomplished meticulously, with 'precision, and the beauty of indifference' for Duchamp saw detachment as the greatest human virtue. As the Bride hangs stripped yet inviolate in her glass cage while the Bachelors grind their chocolate below, so Duchamp is remote and alone with his high art that he held to be artless.

The *Large Glass,* reassembled in the Dreier home in Connecticut

The complete works

Marcel Duchamp's *The Bride stripped bare* continues to haunt us. Not merely Duchamp's masterpiece but a work of such timeless power that its mythic significance will continue to obsess when its author is as unknown as Homer. Crammed with incident and riddled with blind alleys, it is as hard to get into as it is to get out. It is one of those open-ended aesthetic mysteries that hold their magic through ambiguity and paradox, it is all things to all men because it can never be truly understood.

The work consists of two parts: an image on glass now housed in the Philadelphia Museum of Art which is known as the *Large Glass,* and an accumulation of working notes which were envisaged as a component of the entire work of art *The Bride stripped bare by her bachelors, even* (to give it its full title) that occupied the artist between 1912 and 1923. Duchamp himself published ninety-four documents in his *Green Box* of 1934. In 1964 a further seventy-nine similar notes from the period were found and these have also been published as loose fragments in a very limited edition beginning to be called the *White Box.*[1]

Notes and Projects for the Large Glass
(Thames & Hudson) puts most of this 'literary' concomitant of the Glass into a single book and it does the job superbly in giving a near facsimile of the original handwritten note in French opposite its typeset English translation. It is a book essential for the understanding of art at the present time. Arturo Schwarz has selected, ordered and introduced the notes. What a pity it was found necessary to 'select': all the notes of *The Green Box* are included, all those of *The Box of 1914* (a dry run, in an edition of only three copies, for the *Green Box*), a couple of notes that had been published separately and something over half of those in the *White Box*. The notes missing from the Schwarz selection are mainly concerned with perspective and with gropings for a visual representation for four-dimensional concepts, so the person who is after the complete documentation will still have to wait.

Parallel with *Notes and Projects* is a monumental effort by Schwarz himself: **The Complete Works of Marcel Duchamp** (Thames & Hudson), a heavyweight running to 630 large, thick pages. It is really three books. The first is a discussion of Duchamp's work and interests apart from the *Large Glass.* This is followed by a lengthy commentary on, or analysis of, the Glass – elaborately cross-referenced with

Bibliography: 42

[1] A third group of notes, as extensive as those already published, has now been issued under the title *Marcel Duchamp, Notes,* arranged by Paul Matisse and published by Centre George Pompidou, Paris 1981.

its notes. More than half of the volume consists of a third book, a section of illustrations, catalogue raisonné and comprehensive bibliography. Schwarz's zealous catalogue, which roughly doubles the number of items listed in the first great cataloguing by Lebel is, I am sure, as accurate and scholarly as we are likely to get, Duchamp is quoted extensively throughout the three books of the volume; so much so that one is reminded that Joseph Beuys (the only artist in sight worthy to succeed him) titled an 'Action' of 1965 'The silence of Marcel Duchamp has been overestimated.'

The labyrinthine Glass has attracted many would-be guides. Duchamp's intricate metaphysics includes everything from the profound to the banal. It is a total statement, none the less so for being uncompleted. He uses chance techniques with rigorous logic and exactitude, meticulously opening doors to the irrational at every opportunity. The most astonishing thing is the utter precision of his contrived anarchy. Duchamp stripped himself bare, as all great artists do, so it isn't surprising that a good deal of the investigation to which he has been subject deals with the *Large Glass* in terms of Freudian analysis.

The *Complete Works* has the potential of a fashionable book; its esoteric mixture of alchemic studies, Freud, Jung and Trotskyism couldn't be much smarter, unless a touch of astrology were to be added. In spite of two chapters which contain the best and most complete gloss on the Glass yet available the book isn't the last word it aims to be. The trouble is that well versed as Schwarz may be in Freud he seems fundamentally lacking in any visual sensibility or even expertise. He seems incapable of reading images other than semantically.

This blindness, coupled with an awesome lack of humour, makes him less than competent to define a work of art which Duchamp called, among other things, a 'Hilarious' picture. Not that Schwarz is without his moments of burlesque. In discussing an early picture called *Young Man and Girl in Spring* which shows two figures each standing on a tangential quadrant in the bottom (forgive me) of the canvas he says, 'If this painting is looked at upside down the merging of these two semicircles unmistakably suggests the buttocks' and *proves* the artist's anal obsession. It is more serious when he misreads the forms of the 'Nine Malic Moulds', seeing them as 'headless' figures (they not only have heads, they are even wearing hats) and thus clear evidence of a castration complex.[2]

But these are mere details, along with narcissism, onanism, hermaphroditic bisexuality, exhibitionism, voyeurism and homosexuality. The meat of his thesis, the juicy bit, is incest. He pins it down to Marcel's sister Suzanne. It all gets a bit boring, like certain Sunday newspapers – though even they might not be so lacking in taste as to detect, with final glee, in the exquisite work of art *Wedge of Chastity,* given by Duchamp to his wife Teeny on their wedding day, a symbol of impotence. To give Schwarz his due he does confess in his 'acknowledgments' that he owes Duchamp 'more than gratitude – understanding him has enabled me to understand myself'. If I may be permitted an amateur diagnosis I would suggest an aberrant case of 'scoptophilia'.

Octavio Paz's elegant little book **Marcel Duchamp or The Castle of Purity** (Cape Goliard) is the perfect antidote to Schwarz. The paperback version is a bargain. Paz, a wise as well as learned man, warns us of the danger of accepting readymade interpretations of the Glass. Correspondences with medieval alchemy, with Tantric imagery or a reading as the Virgin Mother pictured at her Assumption can only be opinions on facets of a multilayered creation. This essay is the best introduction to Duchamp I have read, for it will excite the reader to enter deeper but it arms him with knowledge of the key to be found at the centre of the maze – irony.

---

[2] Perhaps the point needs clarification. The Malic Moulds do not have 'heads' any more than they have 'hands' or 'feet' to cut off. They are hollow liveries, clothes without wearer, headed by hats and in no sense 'castrated'

Letter to Alison Knowles

Dear Alison

What a difficult question you ask – but I must try to answer. Not that I feel confident that my reply will be in any way definitive, even as far as I am concerned. I'm as open to argument as you are. However, this is the way I see it now.

If everything that Marcel signed is to be regarded as a Readymade by Duchamp, then we are in deep water. This is clearly not the criterion in this context. Two young men once went to see Marcel in Cadaques, they knocked at the door and pleaded a meeting. One of them, a big chap, became so excited in the presence of the great man that, when he was invited to sit down, he threw himself with such violence into the chair that it collapsed completely under him. This provoked more hysteria and he begged Marcel to sign the chair, which Marcel did with his usual kindness. Marcel and Teeny saw the chair being carried off triumphantly.

When Rita first met Marcel we were staying with Marcel and Teeny. One day Rita was sitting alone with Marcel at a cafe and she asked for Marcel's autograph (she didn't know that she would be seeing him again quite often in the future and she wanted a token of the occasion), so he wrote his name on the nearest piece of paper, Rita's cigarette packet. She still treasures it.

Another example relevant to this issue is a signature that Marcel sent to me in 1959. I needed a signature to reproduce in the Green Box book that I was just completing. He sent it to me on a piece of paper headed 'DONT FORGET'; you may have seen this as a postcard that Hansjorg Mayer and I made recently. We were careful not to say on the postcard that this was a work of art by Duchamp. Yet, although I asked Marcel for the signature, I am quite sure that his placing of it on the 'DONT FORGET' slip was a deliberate and beautiful thought. He could have used any scrap of paper and, no doubt, the pad was the handiest thing available but I see it as an entirely typical Duchamp image.

None of these cases, from an endless number, is similar to the one you describe. I understand that there was a quite voluntary signing of the object and that it was in no way prompted by a request. Marcel's answer to

Alison was making an edition of Duchamp's *Coeurs Volant*. The colour match is crucial, so she made up seven colour swatches so that Duchamp could choose the inks. Teeny Duchamp, seeing him with the definitive swatch, asked him when he had done the piece. 'He smiled and signed it.'

In December 1972 (after Duchamp's death) Alison wrote to ask if, in my opinion, this made the swatch a work of art by Duchamp.

Teeny's question is characteristically witty and the signing in these circumstances does sound like an aesthetic decision. However, I would be chary of saying 'this is a work of art by Duchamp' because Duchamp did not have the opportunity to confirm that statement by agreeing to its being exhibited or catalogued as just that.

The danger of adding to the catalogue, a game that Schwarz plays with great enthusiasm, is that the balance of the total oeuvre is changed. A criticism that I would have of the Schwarz book *The Complete Works* is the even weight placed upon things. The wide extension of the catalogue, at both ends, immature scraps in front and slight gestures filling the rear, devalues the great body of work. Or, at least, makes it more difficult to see it properly.

It is for this reason that I would suggest leaving well alone and not making the swatch a work of art. It was a theory of Marcel's that the more things he signed the more he devalued the unique object. Perhaps it would be a pity to give the swatch a unique value because he signed it.

DON'T FORGET

Marcel Duchamp

Reminder

Whom do you admire?

The answer's pretty obvious – Duchamp. In the first place, I've found his work more interesting, more exciting, more durable, than any other; the more I know and think about it the more interesting it becomes. I've spent more than four years of my life working on his *Large Glass* and his notes for it; the *Large Glass* has to be an extraordinary work to survive that degree of attention and that amount of time without being boring. It's never palled.

Also, the variety in his work. He covered so much ground. It's as though he's had any idea one encounters oneself, which gives one a yardstick to relate to. And his overall approach – his detachment, his unwillingness to overdo things. Once he'd done something, he was likely to turn his attention to another thing. The many solutions he discovered are valid and right as far as my own experience of painting is concerned.

But the major influence he's had on me is a kind of reaction against him – not in any sense of being anti-Duchamp but in accepting his iconoclasm, the fundamental aspect of his work. There's one way to be influenced by Duchamp and that's to be iconoclastic – against him. He was, for example, always anti-retinal. Now I'm turning away, becoming more 'retinal' in my painting, and thinking, that's the way Marcel would like it.

ARTnews, November 1977 (75th anniversary issue) asked nearly 100 artists: what specific work(s) or artist(s) of the past 75 years have you admired or been influenced by – and why?

Other artists

Di(e)ter Rot(h)

Typography is more a craft than an art – the graphic designer using type will need to be something of an artist but the typographer of today is a logician whose job is to distribute given information in the most rational way possible. His skill is demonstrated through his ability to organize information, his knowledge of modern printing techniques, his precision when ordering and specifying and by the taste he exhibits in the selection and patterning of elements. The typographer's task is clearly to present the ideas provided in the copy with sympathy and understanding. The best of typographers attempt no more, nor need they.

Prior to the invention of printed type a rather more intimate association existed between the meanings of words and their mode of expression in written form. And during the last fifty years there has been a revival of interest in the possibility of making the visual form of a word, or group of words, convey some part of the message inherent in the literal sense. Poets like Apollinaire, Marinetti and Mayakovsky used type layout to reinforce poetic ideas and some even made pictures with type as, for example, in the calligrams of Apollinaire. Artists such as Schwitters, Picabia, Boccioni, van Doesburg and Lissitzky used type to create messages as much pictorial as literary. These onslaughts against the prim barricades of printing technique have left some indents in the vocabulary of graphic design, but, it is as art objects each with its own unique merit that the original manifestations must be judged.

The work of Diter Rot must be placed in this context of type as a medium of high art. What distinguishes his work from that of other artists who have attempted to render aesthetic propositions in type is that he does so as typographer per se. For the first time we find the roles reversed: an evidently typographic mind ordering type into a poetry rather than the essential poet wrenching the printer's form into art. For Diter Rot manipulates the limitations of the mechanics of modern print to construct his aesthetic; the instruments of his poetry are mathematics, the micrometric assemblage of metal units and a language that seems to consist of twenty-six letters instead of 50 000 words. He can write an essay with 2304 full points and a poem with a single i.

Bibliography: 19

Diter Rot's language and attitude are esoteric and isolated and so is his situation. Since 1957 he has lived and worked in Reykjavík, Iceland. From Box 412 (his address is a mere box number) have emanated a few books, published from his own miniature publishing house. The Diter Rot *bok 56-59* consists of 72 pages, 9½ × 8⅜ inches, with a spiral wire binding. It is the result of three years' work, averaging out to two pages impressed with surgical tenderness every month. The monotype fount was bought by the artist and left with a printer in Copenhagen who then worked upon instructions sent piecemeal by Rot from Iceland. The book, for Rot, isn't simply a form which provides the means to a continuous sequencing of text. The book is a plastic entity which can be entered from back or front – it can accept the limitation of attachment of sheets along a common edge or not. It gives a multiplicity of surfaces which project a set of precisely conditioned variations. In his bound books the page is a rectangle with one attached and three free edges – the sheet can be considered as a single continuous surface or as two related surfaces. Paper, the fabric of the book, can be subjected to a range of operations – it can be cut, perforated, folded and crumpled; inked metal can be pressed into it. The pieces of metal that Diter Rot uses in *bok 56-59* are of one fount, lower case only and only of one size; his technique is contrapuntal and its harmonies and reverberations derive from a carefully restricted range of units. Fundamentally Rot's interest in words is plastic rather than semantic – the palindrome and the anagram are two of his favourite devices, for him the visual pun has great significance, the verbal pun less. His work, for this reason, easily crosses the barriers of language; it is written in an Esperanto of the eye but, like the poetic language of Kurt Schwitters, it is a tongue susceptible to universal comprehension but one which only its creator can utter.

Better known than the printed books of Diter Rot, because they have been exhibited as works of art in galleries, are the albums made from separate sheets of perforated paper. The perforations are slots of different widths laboriously hand-cut by Diter Rot for a limited edition. The reader of these works simply examines the consequences of laying one sheet over another until the vast range of possibilities is exhausted – a more rewarding experience than it sounds, a sensuous and physically creative pleasure which readers of *Typographica* cannot fully appreciate from the photographs of the loose sheets. Other books have been made without type: Diter Rot *bok 2a,* made by overprinting a standard grouping of pieces of monotype rule; *bok 2b,* a similar project but using a modified sequence of shifts and turns of the basic unit; *bok 4a,* made with two kinds of triangular blocks with slots in the rubber face – fourteen pieces of each kind were variously composed on the machine bed to give a range of combinations, using either single or double impression.

Despite the remoteness of his present location and the refinement of his vision Diter Rot moves freely and frequently throughout Europe. His talents have been directed to furniture, textile and graphic design, painting and engraving, poetry, films, books and commercial typography. No doubt his influence on typography will be felt whether he chooses to operate in many fields or not. We must hope, though, that the book as art form, the book within his newly invented terms, will continue to obsess him.

Two pages from *bok 4a*

```
        t r              t r              t r
        oa               oe               eo
       o  e             o  a             e  a
        ae               ea               oa
        t  r             t  r             t  r
        t   r            t   r            t   r
        t  r             t  r             t  r
       o  a             o  e             e  o
       o  e             o  a             e  a
        a e              e a              o a
          t r              t r              t r
         t  r            t  r             t  r
         t r              t r              t r
        oa               oe               eo
       o  e             o  a             e  a
         ae               ea               oa
         t t r            t t r            t t r

          t r r            t r r            t r r
         oae              oea              eoa

         oae              oea              eoa
           t r              t r              t r
         t                t                t
           t r r            t r r            t r r
         oae              oea              eoa
             e                a                a
        oa               oe               eo
           t r              t r              t r
         t     r          t     r          t     r
          t r              t r              t r
         ac               ea               oa
        o    e           o    a           e    a
        oa               oe               eo
              r                r                r
        t t    r          t t    r          t t    r
         t r              t r              t r
         ae               ea               oa
       o  a e           o  e a           e  o a
         o                o                e
              r                r                r
        t t r r          t t r r          t t r r
          t                t                t
          e                a                a
       o aa e          o ee a          e oo a
         o                o                e

         t  t r r r       t  t r r r       t  t r r r
          t                t                t
          e                a                a
       ooaa e           ooee a           eeoo a


        t t t r r r      t t t r r r      t t t r r r

       ooaaee           ooeeaa           eeooaa

    t t t      t t t      t t t     t t t       t t t       t t t

 r
```

Horizon-Animals at Work, Collotype 1974

The pious wish expressed in the final sentence of the above, written sixteen years ago, before I had met Diter Rot and some time before Dieter Roth had returned to the scene, now sounds a little naïve; certainly it was unnecessary. Of course his obsession with the form was to endure and pour out a rich torrent of books. What could hardly have been anticipated was the direction that these publications took. But, with hindsight, one sees that what was to emerge had, given Dieter's genius and technical mastery, to follow the pattern of the technical revolution in printing that took place over these years – the replacement of hot cast metal by lithography and photo-graphics. The simplicity, lower cost and technical freedom offered to the commercial printer by planographic processes were all virtues to be swept enthusiastically into Roth's aesthetic bag. If Diter Rot's typographic works are an ideal expression of the technical character of letterpress, as I believe they are, then Roth's are as pure a manifestation of the technical character of offset.

Another departure from the books discussed in Typographica was an increasing involvement with language, both poetry and prose. Not many of his contemporaries are as devoted to the sonnet. Could the Bastel novels have been foreseen from bok 1956–59? It is this heightened 'literacy' of his output that has, unfortunately, taken it way out of my reach for I have been unable to take the advice given in the first edition of Schelsse to 'Force your German up to date'. Only in those rare moments when he chooses to write in English (even when he is not using his mother tongue his linguistic originality is obvious) can I fully appreciate his later books – yet, it is always possible to gain pleasure from the form and substance alone.

One pervading feature of Dieter's work is its constant capacity to surprise. Having proved his meticulous dexterity, anything goes. When you've got to the point of thinking that some, maybe even surprisingly silly, series of apparently thrown off productions must have come to an end he will astonish by pushing on to some other unlikely extreme, so perverse that it would be silly to doubt the purposeful course. Sometimes it doesn't seem to matter to him what he does, though that too is a deception, as long as productivity is evident. Creative energy gushes not as single images but in a massive

Bibliography: 57

bulk of them, not merely in a fat book but by the series of volumes. A drawing on an occasional page can be so offhand as to present an impression of disinterest. It is the intricate development of his total plot that counts. More than any other artist of his generation he illuminates Duchamp's dictum 'precision and the beauty of indifference'. The exquisite refinement of his early books was misleading, though I suppose that a clue to an understanding of his later strategy lay within them: the key is in the use of permutation, an everpresent concern. Permutation is a tool with which Dieter Roth reaches the unthinkable. As he discovers every possible manipulation of his triangular units in bok 4a to be of equal interest he logically concludes that any image or any grouping of words, in any conceivable order, or disorder, will merit as much attention as any other. So what differentiates good shit from bad shit? You could start by considering what Dieter Roth makes and what he, miraculously, does not make.

A blurb for Emmett

Emmett Williams' **Sweethearts** is a breakthrough. It is to concrete poetry as **Wuthering Heights** is to the English novel; as **Guernica** is to modern art. **Sweethearts** is the first large-scale lyric masterpiece among the concrete texts, compelling in its emotional scope, readable, a sweetly heartfelt, jokey, crying, laughing, tender expression of love. It moves. Miraculously, the formal limitations of **Sweethearts** enabled Emmett to prove that, with both hands tied behind his back, gagged, just nudging letters out of a regular grid with his nose (look, no mirrors), a real artist can write the Book of Life all over again.

Concrete poetry has a comparatively short history (Emmett Williams, by the way, edited the newly published **Anthology**) and, as the label suggests, its exponents have been busy with structures and techniques. Emmett himself makes poetry with the precision of a mathematician, what he writes can often best be described in numerical terms, yet it is these crisply ordered equations that declare his endearing humanity so extremely.

Emmett's large reputation as a poet derives from a tiny oeuvre of exquisite refinement and restraint. He would not complain, too bitterly, that his active profession of words has been so often directed at descriptive writing, journalism and editing, jobs he does with a sweet art that distinguishes many publications. His translation and annotation of Daniel Sporri's **An Anecdoted Topography of Chance** is one of those rare cases where the English version contains its unique perfections.

Browsing through the now considerable documentation of twelve years' of happenings in both Europe and the US we become aware of Emmett Williams as a glowingly unassertive personality enlivening that scene too (who put real maggots on Oldenburg's fake meat during Claes 1964 show in Paris?). He is the misfit patiently demonstrating his own gentle nature in a genre notable for aesthetic violence. I'm sold on Emmett.

Dick Higgins asked if I would care to compose a publishers 'blurb' to use on the dust-jacket of his Something Else Press edition of Emmett's wonderful book. My interest in pastiche pervades the writing genres I've attempted as it also colours my paintings.

t h e
h e a r t
t h a t
h e a t s
h e r
h e a r t
h e a t s
h e r
s w e e t h e a r t s
s w e e t
h e a r t

t e a r s
a s
s w e e t
a s
h e r
s w e e t
s w e a t

a s
h e
w e t s
h e r
e a r s
h e
h e a r s
h e r
t e a r s

t h e
s w e e t
t a r t
s t a r t s
h e r
s w e e t
a r t s

Pages from *Sweethearts*

Roy Lichtenstein

Roy Lichtenstein, Oldenburg, Warhol, Rosenquist and Jim Dine have gained their exalted position in the international art scene very rapidly. It wasn't so long ago that a curator of painting at the New York Museum of Modern Art was publicly complaining that whatever it was that they were doing it wasn't making art. The basis of Peter Selz's contention was that an artist must transform his source material in some very tangible way and this necessary transformation was not evident in the work of the so-called 'Pop' artists. I doubt if any museum official anywhere would now be so rash as to suggest that 'Pop Art' is not art or that an aesthetic transformation has not occurred. Most artists dislike the label 'Pop' when it is applied to them but Lichtenstein accepts it fairly happily. Of the Pop artists, I suspect Lichtenstein is the only one who would have some interest in this question of transformation, in particular of just how little of a transformation will make sense, because he has been more concerned than the others with consideration of this issue as a factor in his work. Between Dine – deeply involved (so much so it worries him) with the sensual aspects of his medium, whether paint, object or plumbing – and Warhol, who would regard the whole controversy as silly, there is a lot of room for manoeuvre.

Lichtenstein's early work, or at any rate the earliest by which his present style can be recognized (he thinks of himself as schooled in Abstract Expressionism), pedantically excludes attributes that we normally expect in a work of art. His method of composition then (*Roto Broil, Tire, Ice Cream Soda, Hot Dog, Ball of Twine* are examples) was to ignore the problem by placing the image centrally and symmetrically on a stark ground in the middle of the canvas. What he paints is often a whole object offered in such a way that we resist thinking of it as 'Still Life' – there is no support for the illustrated object so the canvas bears the blazon in a quite heraldic manner. His forms are described in a fashion consistent with this style – linear treatments, coarse as in naïve illustrations for line reproduction or the more skilfully explicit old-time mail order catalogue draughtsmanship. There is no encouragement to think of the line as painted at all. The mark imitates a line drawn with a pen but magnified. Although it must be painted, all brushstrokes, or indeed any signs that the marks are made by hand, are smoothed away. Where colour is applied, usually through a

Bibliography: 36

Ball of Twine, 1963

perforated screen, it is invariably an even tint filling in an area enclosed by a line that has grown to the proportions of a form in itself. His major concern appears to be with the task of depicting a figurative subject in such a way as to adhere to the two-dimensional integrity of the canvas and in these preoccupations he poses as an abstract artist like Mondrian or Vantongerloo (a disguise from which he later emerges). The clinical picture planning, in which he parallels these artists, repudiates physical virtuosity in aggressive conflict with his immediate New York stock.

Warhol also specifically rejects the Abstract Expressionist's love of paint. Oldenburg, Dine and Rosenquist all used the language of Pollock and de Kooning, albeit for very different purposes. Both Lichtenstein and Warhol betray awareness of their predecessors only by a meticulous contradiction of their attitudes and techniques. Warhol, in the Campbell's Soup series, set aside subtle pictorial arrangements and exquisite paint quality as though they were an extrovert self-indulgence. In their preference for banal themes they even go some way to eliminate subject matter. The familiarity of hot dog or Coke bottle makes choice an irrelevance; they are more concerned with the style of its intermediary treatment than the object itself. Curiously enough, if Warhol's aim is frankly seditious, to pervert and destroy older aesthetic viewpoints, another aura is given off by Lichtenstein. This is partly the consequence of his technical detachment but not less it is due to the emotional remoteness of his pictures. Under the flippant surface Warhol seethes like Goya; Lichtenstein is more like Ingres. Though the comic strip heroines drip tears in great blobs he doesn't move us to pity. There are many sad and sadistic images (a boot smears flesh on a hand that grasped a gun) which merely cause us to smile – they are like the old horror comic joke of a man hanging by his fingers from the top of a cliff while his tormentor stands over him with a knife saying, 'If you want to die with your hands on, drop'. His aerial battles and explosions are no more a condemnation of war than a glorification of it. They excite a purely aesthetic response. He's really cool.

An objective of making art without actually seeming to try pervades Lichtenstein's work at every level. After proving that composition is unnecessary he went on to make rather careful organizations of his pictures using an almost photographic technique of close-up. Composition starts with the definition of boundaries, the relationship of the

Foot and Hand, 1962

Live Ammo, 1962

formal elements to the edges of the canvas. After the very first of the comic strip paintings whole frames are no longer treated as autonomous objects. What Lichtenstein gives is part of a frame, as though he drew boundaries around a detail before blowing it up. At this point choice is exercised in a very critical way, as for a photographer the options are manifold. Using a readymade drawn environment filled with ersatz human incident he can zoom into these dramas isolating an expression, a mood, an event, even a thought. It's like pressing the button, but, since this pseudo world is static he can really get those edges where he wants them and his refined skill in the artistic placement of the image within the frame carries a great deal of what we recognize as quality in a Lichtenstein.

A feature common to all Pop Art is a readiness to move freely between different conventions and different imagery. A Rosenquist gives an experience analogous to that of looking through a magazine. The jolt from page to page doesn't come as a shock because we know the form. Each page is another story told in a new way. Rosenquist, Wesselmann, Kitaj and Peter Blake tend to make their statements in this discretely sequenced way, but Lichtenstein opposes the narrative character of his sources, the progressive frames of a real comic strip, by making his pictures a completely integrated whole. His two-panel pictures, even the diptych *Step-on can* where an action is demonstrated in two successive frames, don't deny this principle –nor does the use of text in balloons; the image is always treated as a totality.

Most art of the past accepted a role as provider of a simulation of direct visual experience of nature – until the twentieth century, when a complete revision of our understanding of what perception was affected art so profoundly. Artists then retired from nature into conceptualizations and abstraction and failed to notice that the visual world was becoming something radically else. The surprising thing is that it took until the mid-fifties for artists to realize that the visual world had been altered by the mass media and changed dramatically enough to make it worth looking at again in terms of painting. Magazines, movies, TV, newspapers, and comics for that matter, assume great importance when we consider the percentage of positively directed visual time they occupy in our urban society. So much of what we look at is sieved and screened and scanned in the process of conversion to

We rose up slowly, 1964

Step on Can, 1961

another dimensionality. TV has only one dimension most of the time for the linear stream of electrons needs to be reconstituted into two dimensions before a picture can be made. It is its appreciation of the multi-dimensionality of our modified world that makes recent art exciting, and the more important figures have all contributed to that understanding. Even Oldenburg, whose sources are entirely in the round, harasses our sensibility with the squeeze he can put on space by warping it with false perspective. Pop mainly uses source material that has been already processed into some two-dimensional medium. Most of this processing is photographic and photography has some status as a stimulus for art – Lichtenstein's sources are graphic and as such haven't the same degree of respectability. They were that much more shocking at first sight.

More than anyone, Lichtenstein is true to the mass media because of the way he persuades that his sources are flat. When he works in three dimensions he does so only to examine the paradox of applying flat conventions to a more elaborate surface. His cups and saucers and the bust of a blonde girl are about two-dimensional language interacting with three-dimensional structures. One of his most haunting images is of a girl's head seen from the back- she holds a hand-mirror reflecting her face so that the conflict between the flatness of treatment and the requirement of reading the picture in spatial layers is very disturbing. The remarkable series of print multiples in which he uses flat treatments on a plastic sheet with a built-in stereoscopic depth continue the play with that paradox. Another example, quite devastating in its simplicity, is the 1965 painting *Landscape with column*, which consists of a canvas divided horizontally into two nearly equal flat areas; from the side of the lower half a piece of column protrudes an end in crude perspective projection.

Lichtenstein has said that his choice of subject matter has something to do with realism. Yet his realism seems to have less to do with 'a preoccupation with everyday life' than with his steadfast candour of treatment. What is realistic about the versions of Mondrian or Picasso is that they are not copies of paintings – they have been removed from that reality by the processing they received in the course of reproduction. What Lichtenstein makes perfectly clear is that all his subjects are made as one before he

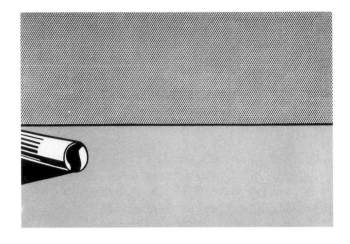

Landscape with Column, 1965

Girl in a Mirror, 1964

touches them. Parthenon, Picasso or Polynesian maiden are reduced to the same kind of cliché by the syntax of print: reproducing a Lichtenstein is like throwing a fish back into water. The *Brush-strokes* are more real (and at the same time less consistent) because they appear to derive from an actual brushmark rather than a secondary source. It is also difficult to concede that Courbet-type realism can be a strong motivation for an artist whose attachment to ideas about style seems inevitably to lead to a high pitch of mannerism. Moments in 'Rebecca of Sunnybrook Farm', revived on television the other evening, displayed how apt is his appreciation of style; I could have sworn I saw his *Modern sculpture* behind Shirley Temple.

The wonderful things in his work are notions about the conflict of flatness and illusory space, but superficially the concern is with style. It is a curious fact that these obsessions, a Baroque love of decoration and a delight in illusion, often go together. In any essentially mannerist art it is in the extremity of the stance that the glory lies – Lichtenstein is marvellously extreme.

Big Painting No. 6, 1965

Miscellaneous

In a Little Hotel by the Deserted Sea – A Landscape

Once upon a time S. Anchor and Sancho Panza, that legendary and plumply tiny supporting player to the cosy supporting beasts turned busted performers, aware of skinny and lovable (though a bit batty) Don Quixote, are at their sausages; i.e. facing an audience, called 3 Sausages. Clearly upstaging his theatrical buddies (placed as the audience's support centrally and impressively) he is delivering the opening 3 lines of sausage bearing busts in '3 Sausages Dell'Arte', an ancient Spanish pantomime. It isn't called '3 Sausages too Difficult to Do'. It was a second opening. On the three first occasions that the busts had performed for the audience, plenty of them had departed. Guardia Civil (drawn by aromatic fumes from sausages of whom the number cannot be named – where there's smoke there's fire), had burst in and dealt summarily with the whole cast. But why can the number of those 3 self-busting sausages not be named? It cannot be named because it is unknown. O. K., Buster, (gay Thespian, thank you.) don't bother. They were well and truly busted. Why mention it Sauce? o. k. I will not m. i.

The performers bore a marked similarity. As the curtain went up and down we might have been brothers. A tiny wondrously small curtain that went up and down before it did not fall down again on any scene. In any case, it must be regarded as more than mere coincidence that the busted characters, supporting a deserted landscape when the curtain fell, are regularly distributed across the stage, in a disturbingly simular posture, and all wear a sausage down hat. The hats are not, of course, made of sausages. Again, it is we simples that see the wide rolling brim and the small tassels at each prologue of the side-play (and how deceptively that was played) called 'Concern for the Life of Sancho, S. Anchor and D. K. Hotel'. Living sausage-like colour, conveys us to a hotel called Donkey Ho Tell. And are we living in that hotel through the Quixotic illusion that the busted actors are balancing gross wursts? Not at all –that would be absurd.

Now we are by the sea called 'The Life of Whom it May Concern', or 'The Shortcomings of Donk Hey Hare', in that little harbour where the knobs are now set for the continuation of the account. We need not dwell on the

Dieter Roth and I collaborated on the production of 74 pictures exhibited under the title *Collaborations of Ch. Rotham.* We produced some text for the catalogue (bibliography 58). A group of 'pictures for dogs' provided a narrative on which we both, independantly, wrote a story. Dieter proposed that we make a chance mix of these. We then alternately offered random numbers. The listed numbers were then applied to the two texts, extracting 7 words from Dieter's, 6 from mine, 3 from Dieter's, 5 from mine and so on. A minimal amount of editing, prologue. D. Donkey is there, extremely carried away by his blind companion S. Arbor, who, in short, came just for the view. The introductory play curtain is up, completely down, or on the sides, set to stanzas, the (divided in the middle) scene establishes the period. Can you see her over the rim of the deserted landscape? Yes, the scene is set to put the audience in a receptive mood – on a discarded landscape where the spectator can see poorly. Primarily it is intended to ensure that Sandor is falling out of the window onto the paying customers. That the pityful donkey, standing in front of his bucketfull of desert sand, called D. S. R. T. Sand, grinding desert sand with his unreal (a play) teeth, used to grinding sausage-busting, not sand grinding, is only a picture in the mind. Even that bust over there knows the sort of thing:

'If we pale shadows cause offence
to a bucket of desert sand,
a wish to please will not grind sand
and that is our defence.'

'But no Buster, it CAN grind sand with its teeth.' 'Oh! OK S. Anchor, we believe you.'

Act 1 scene 1: The spectators looked at the performers and found A. S. Sandal there in a deserted landscape in which the spectator was impersonating poor Naposolion, called N. P. Lion and brave Sancho, standing beside a pityful donkey; the pityless sun glares into smiler's face down from the sky. Brave compiler of stories as radiantly blue as only Valentine's Azul Radiante can be, blistering the parched earth of la last Mancha. Sancho Panza bears a strange resemblance to Napollomisius Buonaparte, but also to Buster, soldier of sable. Dead Josephine's second glance reveals that it is the crescent shaped shoulder hanging almost down to the Napoleonic hat (which has replaced the wooden floor of the stage). She is seen well, sausage-like, which has created the illusion. There she is, as D. H. Ocelot hallucinating. It is true some similarity between a moon and N. A. P. Osio exists, a sausage, the crescent Gin Tonic full of it, moon is much more pointed. How curious it is that the human mind, which cannot see anymore (P. J. O. Cean swept the stage with it), and its ready propensity for fantasy which will play on, will be led to suppose that

this is, that the regal-looking lady standing beside Sancho IS Josephine. The simple difference is between the busted full point of a crescent moon and the tasseled bulb at the terminations, at the ends, of a sleek pork sausage widow. Do we? Yes, we do, but who can see the donkey called Killer? But it has introduced another mean character into our sausage saga. You will, patient reader, P. B. Rhinoceros by name, be wondering how it is that this desert of skill, called Y. O. S. Landscape, can be so buster of image and heavily populated. For who is stretching it? Not only does Sancho stand beside him but we hear the snapping itself in the donkey and see that Josephine is standing beside Sancho. But it is a crazy unnamed person disporting on a tightrope whose angry tape we have been hearing, though we cannot hear above them all. I hope that it will not stretch anymore, it is way out now. But the image of your credulity is too far pressed even to propose what is, after all, quite plausible, a Hercules, pressing on the table a fairly logical explanation. No, leaning over a table, imitating Hercules, pressing these characters like a giant, or dreaming of them actually there; they emanate from the mind of a gin tonic on a table. A giant, by the sea hotel, thinking himself mythic, who imagines not only the hotel in the play but also the audience and, dare I say it, you, yourself, dear reader.

Meanwhile, by the sea backed by mountains, in his Spanish castle, the giant king is sitting by the window by the sea in Spain, which, incidentally, he has never left, beside a pityfully shaking little table. On its lie, resplendent, a Gargantuan desayuno, a mammoth sausage, like an image of Hercules: an Immense Platter on a table groaning under the enlarged pressure of its enormous load.

Herr Cul is a hearty eater, quite capable of consuming a whole dead pig, minced and photographed. He is devouring the pathetically shaking little table, stuffed into its own entrails, at a gulp. No doubt, to the giant, such a gigantic breakfast could be bettered only by a more gigantic sausage. One even large enough to dwarf the great pleasure steamer cruising by, trembling, falling, shaking hands with or shaking the window of the breakfast room, would be no more than a light snack. As sausage (whose pen name is often Herr

largely punctuation and omission, was done to assist readability. *In a Little Hotel by the Deserted Sea – A Landscape* is the resultant mix.

Lester C. Cules) spare a collation as it may be to the giant, just a tiny fraction to Herrn Cul. We may think of poor Buster Useless, known as Utter L. Tit-bit Sausage, who would provide a generous repast for any number of lesser mortals – such as M. I. Morsel, devourer of breakfasts, lunches, loaves and fishes, oy Veh! So there it is, the Wunderwurst, bracing itself like liquid or frozen food, frozen butter, for the onslaught, sweating slightly and coming out in sage-green spots (whether from malt or beer, dog's goulash made with the admixture of herbs to its filling, or the decay to which waiting roasted malt or beer and dog's goulash, not the dog's goulash made from sausages, are all too prone we shall never know) for envious eyes, green as a cat's, have fixed upon the phallic form. A sausage lover, heavily and steadily enlarging, is without, intent on evil and conscious of the weight of gigantic sausages, ready to do his wurst – or so it seems.

Yes, you have guessed, it is the batty-for-food-like knight himself, the dear, instant-frozen-goods old Don, aiming at getting into the busting scene for a spoonful of bursting frozen Panza sausage in his hotel. This apparently churlish stratagem is a symptom of the sea, a Herculean labour, the worthiest of motives. Also be it known that under the name Don Quixote, in the taken name of TH. D. Donkey, a vow has been taken, standing under a window, to rescue his lady Josephine from what we can now see is the giant's spell. One or two is imagining oneself unsuccesfully, indeed unnoticed, tempting other heavy eaters to use their oversize measurements, with nothing but spoons so far, on the gigantic person's person. With pressure, they found that they were able to administer a Herculean weight and Hercules. Herr Jee Mighty-Thwack, is exerting it on that thickly skinned sausage, the right hand toe. The Cyclopean giant's weighty attention is on the breakfast table, busting his fingers thrown in the gauntlet, ordering his invitations so as to be able to do a duel, bearing upon the huge depth of our enormous darling breakfast-sausage. Old Don BUT devised, at that moment, a brilliant plan. A ship craftily appears, conceived in schemes. There was window to seize, and the wee sausage-can, and so it starved, riding the big horizon fellow into distant submission.

In riding the delicious breakfast-table by the dreamy little hotel, suddenly the next item in this fair tale is to be Creamy, Blue by name of pen, also called A. D. Mutton, or called C. B. Ballpen or Pinball or Spinball. In the pink of the deserted landscape old baldy head has sausage on his mind. Shambling great hulk he may be, but that framc, unbeknownst either to S. O. B. C. Neither nor M. (great cranium) Barcley's son, Fritz B. Son Tag or her daughter, contains no mean cerebral cortex. Sensitive, intuitive, apt to fancy and hallucination, as you well know, head in the clouds, yet with a pretty cute daughter, often called confusingly Nick or Mos Mostel. But the stage is getting too full for all that. He has figured out the vulnerability of his position, after all, all his sausage was on a plate and open to attack. He reckons it's time to take (what else can be done now!) a gander at the bloated bladder. Little does he know what a dreadful scene awaits his homecoming.

We are glad to announce that big hunks have fallen out of the story, as actors spill from stages when overcrowded. We see space everywhere. The sly knight has engineered, like, for instance, Josephine, his self-appointed task. We find her singing the part of Mox Mortimer, or Morton the Sticker, with consumate skill. Admittedly with Sausage B. Client as well as Ham. B. Cheeseburger, Nutburger, Chesseburger with Ham or Hamburger Cold – it took a little help from many friends, in particular side-kick Sancho, who, with Mister M. Mustard, is singing under a nice little hotel window by the sea while wielding the giant wooden spoon leverwise. We have also found her singing; though many of you think this is not what happens, you think it is Don Quixote himself, cooking whatever you think him fit to cook, playing an heroic role in undermining all the while the bucket of Miss C. Tigers. Now, the sausage is off the plate, off the table onto that long suffering structure's paw, or is it a bird's paw, or claw, writing monstrous installments of the famous novel 'Blood'? Already (Tiger's time-table gave plant-pain relief) out of the hotel – the roughly cylindrical form being 'perfectly', said Mademoiselle Liverwursht, partaking the sausage, 'suited to the operation; much more under the table you know'. It did stand up under the evil pressure of N. Apuleyan, called Donkey, singer of like. Difficult was the second stage of the better her be – better let be – butter her better, so let's have Sly staying inside with gigantic, and outside with gigantic, but which, rather a jape, required ingeniously devised outside, with his flattening every time out of comparatively unbearable time already unbearable, namely, called DF. GJ. Spoon. Suddenly, having done already, comes that tackle to raise one of the giant's giant words 'THINK', which, having been named, turned out to be where he was aware of. Discarded boots up onto the table, plans where are they now? And from thence to the plate, a bit of fun is there where we need another word, namely the giant's name. We need the name of the word 'giant' to bear pressure on the giant's breakfasts. That will cause more heartache than the loss of his monstrous morsel.

Since they were, and are, fearing for their breakfast that was not there, and is not there and will not be, not theirs, they had had them before. What a shocking sight – sure enough. Business calls. Their boot called, in a nighty some think 'Bright'. The giant saw red. He was apoplectic. Why do they think 'Bright boot'? A is a. A boot being a. His is a. Was this the trouble? Was there. . ., was his. . ., had he stolen a. . ., had he nothing left to cook for her in the mighty cupboard? Was there nothing left in his mighty house to. . . Ah! Cruel the night that now we see, magically one might say, now and forever in the mind's eye, shining on in a great, in THE great mind, in the mind of minds, stroking, encircling the boot on the sorry-looking table. Himself, boot-looking, thinking that it might be recalled, or replaced under the eye called Ample. The pabulum-bearing halo brought down, crunching the huge Brobdingnagian hunks of sausage, following down, falling through to the earth-window, but with not a hint of a bump. The mind's march in time evoked his despair, he saw that ghostly sausage levitated above the miserably singing mind's ear (famous for footwear), thus conferring on Hercules G. Table-Pressing Giant, or CRUNCH, a saintly dignity (a distinction often mistaken by B. Dinner Mishap and quite lost to others), a blank fatso to go on that terminal cladding. So this is what we must heave out of the window. What? Out of the window our deflated friend? Breakfast falling out

to the sea? Rough diamond, though he be, some are talking some of the time of maybe butts, boots, busts, spoons, sausages, victims (surely the salt masters) voicing their lament late though it is (is it too late?): because doleful night was with us it was a trifle too late. Hard though, taking him on to its image with its mind's eye, to be dealt so. The table is empty, a dire blow.

Don Quixote's jolly crew were in a very different mood under the window, the spot on which Buster fell, called Tabula Rasa. They rolled their prize teller of the tale, standing under the mountain to the North called Lamentator. Delighted by Fierce (or Barker) the Dog, and at the success of the sausage appropriation little hotel project and feeling full of the sea, which we see with our joy of life (not to mention sausage) they went their merry way. Aye, regaling we see the sea, the South Mediterranean. We ask: what do passers by the we see? We see a story of the exploit, we see the menu to the dinner. The men say 'yes, this is the menu to which Sancho had contributed so much of his burly vigour'. The menu's mouth said a bucketfull.

In truth, lettered words show the letters, such stress was put upon Sancho's part in the enterprise. His mouth, yes, what do you see in the MENU? The hat's contribution padded out more with every retelling. Biped's Goulash (pickled corrugated bipedal cardboard). Second. That he soon accepted the adulation of the admiring crowd, in corrugated slippers on corrugated floorboard. Third. Dessert Sausage Paint on Corrugated board. There was no holding his ego when it was proposed (I suspect it was Sir Vantes who first had the idea) that so valiant an exploit of chivalry should be marked by the bestowal of a coat of arms. Kippers, and unknown paint. The design might be thought crude by College of Heralds standards but their was a rustic felicity in the image of the great sausage buster, on corrugated slipperbords, duly invested in slippers (complete with sausage-type hat, though faintly corrugated) painted on Doggy Chews falling out of a shield supported by rampant sausages in bed.

Bounced out of it, it is not surprising, what with the saga of the window, our daring Don fallen into the sea, assumed eaten by P. Pike the First, of mythic proportions. As Sancho's sausage slips back (whereupon P. Pike the First had been eaten by P. Pike the severe) also into the mists of time you can still hear of Sancho, a legend in tiny pueblos hidden deep in the majestic valleys. Hell, go tell it to the Pyrenees. Old men, faces heavily lined with fissures that echo. Was it Sancho? There to tell the same crevasses of their mountain fastness. Whoever yet tells the tale of a great However, his face is hers, and his sausage of around 5 km (that means in length). His face was hers abducted and partly his (or her) own from the seablown castle of an evil giant who preyed upon us, or, according to taste, our populace. Hell, how happily they lived ever after!

What a surprise! So what a surplus surprise. What did you say? I said 'so prevalent has the sausage cult become that what a sure surprise that was'. Thats what I, the most notable of Catalan intellectuals, said. There he goes now carrying (and the sausage he carries with him is an enormous surplus sausage), as on ceremonial occasions, a can of unknown Paint of Sausage in his beak. What? But sporting the familiar hat and carrying in his teeth the symbols of our hero's valour: Surplus Pain of Sausage, and unknown pain paint. Actually you might find persons of any station, or any degree of aesthetic pretension, affecting these patriotic appertenances and/or doggy chews and beverages.

B.C. bearing coat with hampton rampant, 1976

A question of censorship

That the Arts Council is now in a pathetically submissive situation is revealed by the absurd exchanges leading to the bowdlerisation of my collaborative exhibition with Dieter Roth.

I approached Barry Barker last year to ask if the ICA New Gallery would consider the possibility of taking the show Dieter and I had made in Cadaques in July and for which several other European locations had been arranged. The ICA space, elevated to a new respectability in Barry Barker's hands, was an obvious choice for London. We were fortunate in the response we got from the ICA and also the Arts Council who were required to give the show its blessing. Hansjorg Mayer was already involved with us in the publication of an ambitious catalogue for the tour and we had embarked on a literary development of the visual material. The Arts Council expressed interest and support for this too. Dieter and I had produced bibliographies for the initial showing in Spain. Mine was very short, offhand and laconic. By contrast, Dieter's was a marvellously bitter scatological tirade. We wrote a lot of additional text for the Hansjorg Mayer publication; narratives which had absorbed as much energy as the painting sessions, and which we regarded as essential to the literary/pictorial whole. Part of Dieter's contribution is as brilliantly anal as his biography, and these grossly ribald sections contribute perfectly to a literary quality with which I am proud to be associated. Using any of the standard definitions of pornography, the exhibition and catalogue would have to be discharged as 'clean'. Not only is it intensely aesthetic but it could not possibly be thought to possess any capacity to corrupt. One pair of pictures among the 74 exhibits schoolboy graffiti – a crudely and arbitrarily drawn prick on an otherwise fully clothed figure. Any obscenity is offset by it's humorous charm.

It was evident that the Arts Council, in view of recent attacks on it by the piss-ignorant press, couldn't stomach the text. Dieter Roth provided the perfect answer – he would obliterate every word that the British press could possibly find objectionable by hammering the type into rich illegibility. Word came from a high authority that this solution would make the Arts Council look silly. Our opinion, that a blatantly self-censored version specially created for the British

Letter to *Art Monthly,* March 1977, on the removal of a painting from the *Collaborations* exhibition (bibliography: 58).

public could only make the critics of the Arts Council look ridiculous, did not prevail. We were prevented from making the catalogue available at the exhibition in either a full or censored version.

As for the picture entitled *B. C. bearing coat with hampton rampant*, this had been offered for a legal opinion which deemed it 'libellous' and therefore not exhibitable. I proposed to put a fig leaf over the offending member, yes, under the glass so that it could not be lifted by the public. On second thoughts, and presumably after further legal advice, the Arts Council decided that the prick would still be there 'by implication'; the painting could not be hung.

While I can enjoy the comic aspects of all this nonsense it does seem that things are getting a trifle out of hand. Censorship of the visual arts has reached a stage where the Arts Council of Great Britain is so shit scared of unfavourable press comment that it can't even see what's coming out of its own trouser leg.

The Arts Council's predicament arises from a single persistent issue, 'Should public money be spent on . . . (porn, rubbish, bricks [sic], diapers etc?)'. It appears a dubious case to make a stand on – but is it? The trouble is that the visual arts have no outlet at all without Arts Council backing – unless you imagine that the commercial galleries make a significant contribution to a wide freedom of expression. All right, Claes Oldenburg gets away with pricks and girlies at the Mayor Gallery – if the curtains are kept drawn. Censorship barely exists in the visual arts if you care to include in that category the gaping, glycerine-coated cunts stacked up in almost any newspaper shop. The open acceptance of so many stupid obscenities makes Britain look free.

Where censorship does operate is in the area given most protection in law, where the artistic intention is clear. And specifically it is the work of the younger artists, those who are not likely to get a secondhand Tampax show at the Marlborough, whose used diapers won't be snapped up by Waddington. The Arts Council now controls the Hayward, Serpentine, Whitechapel and ICA galleries. It could withdraw finance from Butlers Wharf or Acme at the drop of a pair of knickers if the *Evening Standard* happened to catch them

coming down. Can British Art be confidently put in the hands of old pro press-persons who know that they cannot only satisfy their power mania but make more money selling papers with every new 'art scandal' they can invent? Now, when the Arts Council anticipates press reactions and censors or blocks or sweeps under the carpet what it supposes others might find distasteful, the problems and the effects become amplified. If the Arts Council does not see itself as the one institution whose duty it is to give strength and support to the creative arts then it might as well pack up and go home to the Royal Ballet.

The Artist's Eye

Forty years ago I had to make choices in the National Gallery. As a student at the Royal Academy Schools I was required to attend the Gallery to make either one full-size copy or three sketch studies each year for the annual examination. I recall the pleasurable hours of deliberation before the intimate act of copying went some way towards explaining the magic that had generated a commitment to a particular work. When I realize that it has taken half a lifetime, and another 'set task' to renew that more than casual involvement with our heritage I feel a trifle oafish. An invitation to select a group of paintings from the National Collection is irresistible. To dispose of such riches is an undreamed of princely power – be it only a Medici for a day. But the arrogance of transplanting masterpieces from their accustomed places into a new situation must be justified: just what is the point of this dislocation if it is to be no more than a personal whim?

When narrowing down on the many possible inclusions it became clear that some concordance was emerging. The paintings that were least willingly relinquished had something in common; they all appeared to me to derive from a concern within the artist himself; they pander to no patron's ego, nor even to a public taste; they are without bombast and all attain a high personal ambition. There is no rhetoric, only a calm resolution in the undertaking of a remarkably daring endeavour.

The stance I have tried to describe is demonstrated perfectly by Jan van Eyck, the creator of a painting that is not in the exhibition though it was first on my list, the *Arnolfini Marriage*; an easy option dropped without demur. The picture was recently given prominence in a 'Painting in Focus' special exhibition in the Gallery and to disturb it again was not essential. The *Marriage* does embody all that I most admire in art: incredible technical mastery (in a medium that van Eyck was himself inventing) set to the service of an arcane symbolism that moves its audience with profound simplicity. It is an epiphany, a crystallization of thought that gives us an instant awareness of life's meaning. No other art has this capacity to be entirely there, totally existent like a phenomenon of nature. When this enduring presence is charged with the spirit of one such as van Eyck, God himself can look a little ham-fisted.

Bibliography: 60

Time measures an artist, not his peers. Few of the painters represented in this selection would have lived free from abuse by parochial bigots or the disdain of society as a whole, yet these works are now undoubted masterpieces that have been relished for generations by historians, art experts and the larger public. It is unnecessary to write, were I indeed competent to do so, about the reasons for the choice of specific paintings. What I would like to communicate is my sense of wonder that human beings should possess this capability of utterance through the unlikely methods of any art form: for the practitioner this wonder will, as often as not, be tinged with despair. Perhaps the setting, the exhibition itself, can make its own commentary.

My hope is that to encounter these classic works in a context that differs from the usual museum arrangement will reinforce our appreciation of them. It may be thought gimmicky to place an operating television set in the same space as a Mantegna, Goya, Poussin or Turner, but the degradation, and I do not use this word in its pejorative sense, of our normal 20th century visual field is a fact to be understood. Why not consider the significance of a reproduction of Van Gogh's *Sunflowers* in the home of its original? How is it that this most banal of contemporary objects can echo such a sublime source, and conversely, how does Velázquez cook poetry from his eggs and fishes? The pictorial skills that have been the stock-in-trade of artists for many hundreds of years are out of fashion. Marcel Duchamp's success in the half of his personality that was so brilliantly iconoclastic is, in some measure, responsible. When Duchamp put a snow shovel into an art gallery he questioned those values which placed manipulative talent above all artistic criteria. If a domestic object becomes a work of art by displacement to another environment then a reciprocal process would postulate the use of a Rembrandt as an ironing board. A gentle reminder of Duchamp's trust in 'grey matter' may not be out of place. For we must recognise that it is the mind of the artificer, not the artifact, that we are touched by.

An assortment of seating is provided, not to suggest that these particular chairs should be viewed in a museum of modern art 'good design' sense. They are to be used and, with the carpet (another kind of art), give a hint of homely warmth.

The suggestion that I should have the privilege of putting one of my own paintings beside some of the greatest ever made was alarming. But this can be put to some negative purpose. My inadequacy can help to sharpen the understanding of real achievement. At least this choice can be explained.

In order to avoid invidious comparison I settled on a picture that would be sufficiently alien. *My Marilyn* can be used, with other props in my staging, as a device to stimulate response to the main performers. Which is a roundabout way of saying how awesome, how ludicrous, but how interesting it is to have the brief pleasure of seeing a painting by myself among those from minds that I respect enough to suffer no serious qualms. They would, I am sure, be generous and tolerate not only my presence as an artist but also the presumption of my role as connoisseur.

Propositions

A work of art is a vehicle for the transmission *of* information concerning *the* mental, or physical, activity *of* an artist.

The vehicle, or medium, need not transmit *information* (a message) – it can stand as a symbol *for a message.*

The work of art may be structured *or not – it can be a* concept.

An artist can propose that his *work of art* shall *be structured by someone other than the artist – or it can be structured by* chance.

Structures (and non-structures) *may be* characterized *by a* style (*or* non-style).

The style of a structured (or unstructured*) message (or* symbolic non-message*) can* serve to identify *the* individuality *of an artist.*

Art can be structured in *the style of* another *artist,* either *in* sincere emulation *or as* ironic parody.

A work of art is evidence *that an artist* has proposed *a work of art.*

An eye witness account *is evidence that an artist has proposed a work of art.* But documentary *evidence* (i.e. *a* photograph) *is* more conclusive.

A painting *is documentary evidence that an artist has proposed a work of art.*

The *Propositions* were a response to a request to provide a 'statement' for the catalogue of the Biennale Nürnberg exhibition (August 1971) *Künstler – Theorie – Werk.* A British postal strike prevented its inclusion there. Printed later (bibliography: 47).

A conceptual exhibition

A proposal concerning the 'presentation and conveyance of the experimental art of today', i.e. An International Exhibition of Experimental Art

1. Criteria for an Exhibition

a) Relevance of stance in relation to a wide range of activity in avant-garde art.
b) Ability to present high quality examples of work in the field of experimental art.
c) Value of its documentation of the area covered – theoretical information and representation of works.
d) Success in creating an audience for the ideas and images presented. (Success is usually measured by attendance figures.)

2. Possible organization for a regular International Exhibition of Experimental Art

A *symposium* would discuss all current activity in the visual arts that could be regarded as experimental, regardless of style or medium. It would create a *Selection Committee* whose duty would be to propose *Artists* to be exhibited. The artists would assist in preparing a documentation of their contribution to the *Exhibition* and its presentation in the *Catalogue*. During the course of the exhibition, artists might participate in an extensive programme of *Seminars* to inform the public about the theoretical basis of their 'experiments'.

3. Difficulties that might arise in organizing an International Exhibition of Experimental Art in Berlin

a) There is no large ready-made audience in the Berlin population itself to provide an audience. The location does not encourage a large transitory tourist traffic.
b) It is becoming increasingly difficult to organize large shows of high quality in any location. The heavy demand for works and the reluctance of owners to lend, cause many problems.
c) The budget required is very large.

4. Conclusions

The circumstances operating against success could be overcome by removing only one element from the organization (2), namely the physical *Exhibition* of works – all other factors remaining intact.

A symposium was organized in Berlin to discuss the hypothetical exhibition. This was my contribution.

The benefits of this apparently perverse suggestion are considerable; notably budget economies, no transport, insurance, space, installation nor maintenance costs. Selection would not be limited by availability of specific works. 'Difficult' projects would not be excluded for scale or other reasons.

The disadvantage of such a scheme is that the audience would be deprived of direct communication with the 'work of art', whether it be painting, sculpture or performance.

More than fifty years ago, Marcel Duchamp made the daring proposition that the conceiving of a work of art is more important than its formal realization. A good deal of experimental art in recent years has accepted his notion – hence 'Conceptual Art'. An artist might textualize his thought about a work of art so we have 'Art Language'.

However, it is not the idea of a conceptual exhibition that is attractive, it is rather the gaining of the pragmatic advantages of programming.[1] The proper formulation of questions has as much value as answers. A large part of the value of a large international exhibition is in the demand the form makes in evaluating, selecting and documenting a period. The experience of the objects by a privileged few need not be regarded as the *raison d'être* of an exhibition.

[1] Charles Eames, on a visit to India, was asked by President Nehru what could be done about India's deficiency in computer technology. Eames said, 'You have a great papier mâché technology. Make a simulation of a computer in papier mâché and prepare programmes for it.' If the question is developed to a programme a good deal of the answer is available.

Composition

Get a coloured postcard in the Chicago area of a subject in Chicago. Either get it yourself or, if you are worried about the aesthetic responsibility of choosing something, ask a friend to provide it.

Take a piece of paper and cut a hole in it 1 inch high by 1½ inch wide. The hole should be square with a corner of the paper, 1 inch to the left of the right hand edge and ¾ inch from the bottom edge. Place this in the bottom right hand corner of the postcard. Get a photographer to enlarge the area of postcard revealed in the hole to a size of 2 feet 8 inch × 4 feet, preferably on sensitized canvas but if this isn't possible have a print dry mounted on hardboard (Masonite).

Leave 20% of the surface untouched, black and white.

Paint 40% in roughly the colours apparent in the postcard.

Paint 40% in complementaries of the colours that appear in the postcard.

Either use transparent stains or opaque colours, some thick, some thin, which areas are at your discretion.

Instruction telephoned from London to Ed Paschke in Chicago to paint a picture for the *Art by Telephone* exhibition at the Museum of Contemporary Art in 1969.

Statement

Although some of my pre-Pop pictures may seem to the casual observer to be 'abstract' I believe it is true to say that I have never made a painting which does not show an intense awareness of the human figure. In the case of earlier work it was the human configuration (two eyes situated at a certain distance from two mobile feet) confronting the picture that determined its composition. Assumptions about the human figure were fundamental to the location of elements within the painting and the painting's relationship to the viewer was prescribed. That is to say, one justification for the picture was its value as a contribution to the total perspective of the spectator: a candid demonstration of the platitudinous concept that a work of art does not exist without its audience.

Later pictures of mine have absorbed into this external concern a recognition of the potency that representation of the human figure adds to this dialogue between image and witness. A fellow creature in the viewer's environment, either artificial (a semblance) or real, must be the strongest, most emotive, factor in it; he will command attention for no other reason than his figurative identification with the ego. The force with which this *dramatis persona* can provoke displeasure is no less great than its capacity to provide companionship or to alter the construct of our lives. It, another self, real or semblance, revealed or implied, will always be a major factor in my art.

Statement in response to the question 'What kind of significance and/or importance does the image of the human figure have in your works?' put by Yoshiaki Tono from Tokyo in January 1971.

Name games

SAD
FACES
STARE
GRIMLY
FROM
VACUUS
PRISONS.
STERILE
CAPSULES
THAT
ENCLOSE
UNBORN
PAIN

Compliance with a request from Dario Vilalba to make a contribution to a catalogue.

Mallarmé
Apollinaire
René Magritte
Carroll
Edgar Allan Poe
Lautréamont

Baudelaire
Rabelais
Oscar Wilde
Offenbach
Duchamp
Töpffer
Hegel
Aesop
Erasmus
Renard
Swift

Wo50f 5oste5050

An obituary for Marcel Broodthaers published in *Art Monthly* No 1, October 1976

Greetings to Wolf Vostell on his 'L'th birthday (1982)

Selected bibliography

1 Institute of Contemporary Arts, London, July 1951, *Growth and Form.* Exhibition devised and designed by Hamilton.

2 Hanover Gallery, London. January 1955. *Paintings 1951–1955.*

3 Hatton Gallery, Newcastle-upon-Tyne, May 1955; Institute of Contemporary Arts, London, July 1955, *Man, Machine and Motion.* Exhibition devised and designed by Hamilton. Catalogue commentary by Reyner Banham.

4 Whitechapel Gallery, London, August 1956. *This is Tomorrow.* Group 2 environment devised by Hamilton, John McHale and John Voelcker.

5 Hatton Gallery, Newcastle-upon-Tyne, June 1957; Institute of Contemporary Arts, London, August 1957, *an Exhibit.* Exhibition devised and organized by Hamilton with Lawrence Alloway and Victor Pasmore. Catalogue text by Lawrence Alloway.

6 'Hommage à Chrysler Corp.', *Architectural Design.* March 1958, pp. 120–121.

7 'U-L-M Spells H.f.G', *The Architects' Journal,* July 17, 1958.

8 'Towards a Typographic Rendering of the Green Box', *Uppercase 2,* 1959.

9 'Ulm', *Design,* June 1959, pp. 53–57.

10 'Diagrammar', *The Developing Process,* Newcastle, 1959, pp. 19–26. 'Work in progress towards a new foundation of art teaching as developed at the Department of Fine Art, King's College, Durham University, Newcastle-upon-Tyne and at Leeds College of Art'.

11 'Glorious Technicolor, Breathtaking Cinemascope and Stereophonic Sound', 1959. Unpublished typescript of lecture on technical innovations in the leisure industries.

12 'Persuading Image', *Design,* February 1960, pp. 28–32.

13 'Artists as Consumers; the Splendid Bargain', 1960. Unpublished BBC transcript of discussion between Lawrence Alloway, Basil Taylor, Richard Hamilton and Eduardo Paolozzi, in the series *Art-anti-art;* produced by Leonie Cohn, recorded January 18 1960, broadcast BBC Third Programme, March 11 1960.

14 'Art and Design'. *Popular Culture and Personal Responsibility,* October 26–28, 1960, pp. 135–155. Lecture followed by transcript of discussion, verbatim report of National Union of Teachers Conference, Church House, Westminster.

15 'First year studies at Newcastle', *Times Educational Supplement,* c. 1960.

16 Diagram and 'The Green Book', *The Bride stripped bare by her bachelors even,* Lund Humphries, 1960. Typographic version by Hamilton of Duchamp's Green Box.

17 'FoB + 10', *Design,* May 1961.

18 'For the Finest Art try – POP', *Gazette,* no.1, 1961.

19 'The Books of Diter Rot', *Typographica 3,* June 1961. pp. 21–40.

20 Statement on 'Glorious Techniculture', *Architectural Design,* November 1961, p. 497. Part of 27 pages devoted to buildings and art assembled on the South Bank for the Congress of the International Union of Architects, London, July 1961.

21 'About art teaching, basically', *Motif 8,* Winter 1961, pp. 17–23.

22 'An exposition of $he', *Architectural Design,* October 1962, pp. 485–486.

23 'Artificial obsolescence', *Product Design Engineering,* January 1963.

24 *Ark,* 34, Journal of the Royal College of Art, London. Summer 1963, pp. 4, 14–16, 24–26, 34–37. Texts and illustrations on commissioned theme of incidence and selection of images experienced in daily life.

25 'Urbane Image', *Living Arts 2,* 1963, pp. 44–59, inside and outside cover photographs.

26 'Duchamp', *Art International,* January 1964, pp. 22–28.

27 Hanover Gallery, London, October 1964. *Paintings 1956–1964.*

28 Interview with Andrew Forge, 1964. Unpublished BBC transcript produced by Leonie Cohn, recorded November 3, 1964, broadcast in part on 'New Comment', November 1964 in full on April 5, 1965. Both broadcasts BBC Third Programme.

29 *Portrait of Hugh Gaitskell as a Famous Monster of Filmland,* 1964. Unpublished typescript.

30 Cordier & Ekstrom Inc. New York, *NOT SEEN and/or LESS SEEN of/by MARCEL DUCHAMP/RROSE SELAVY 1904–1964 (catalogue of the Mary Sisler Collection)* January – February 1965. Introduction and notes on works.

31 *The Bride stripped bare by her bachelors even again,* Newcastle-upon-Tyne, 1966. Account of Hamilton's reconstruction of Duchamp's Large Glass.

32 The Tate Gallery, London, *Marcel Duchamp,* Arts Council of Great Britain retrospective, June 1966. Introduction and catalogue notes.

33 'Son of the Bride stripped bare', *Art and Artists,* July 1966, pp. 22–28. Interview with Mario Amaya on Hamilton's reconstruction of Duchamp's Large Glass.

34 'What kind of art education?' *Studio International,* September 1966. Interview with Victor Willing.

35 Galerie Alexandre Iolas, New York, May 1967. *Paintings 1964–1967,* first New York exhibition.

36 'Roy Lichtenstein', *Studio International,* January 1968, pp. 20–24.

37 Interview with Christopher Finch and Anne Seymour. Unpublished BBC transcript produced by Leonie Cohn, recorded May 3, 1968, broadcast BBC Third Programme, May 15, 1968.

38 Studio Marconi, Milan, November 1968. *Work 1957–1968.* Contains Italian translation of 'Urbane Image'.

39 Conversation with Christopher Finch and James Scott, 1969. Unpublished, pre-edited transcript made for Arts Council/Maya Film Productions.

40 'Photography and painting', *Studio International,* March 1969, pp. 120–125, cover.

41 Galerie Hans Neuendorf, Hamburg, November 1969. *Paintings and graphics.* Contains phonetic translation by Dieter Roth, of 'Urbane Image'.

42 Review of 'The Complete Works of Marcel Duchamp' by Arturo Schwarz, *The Sunday Times* February 22, 1970.

43 The Tate Gallery, London March 1970, *Richard Hamilton.* Catalogue introduction and commentary by Richard Morphet.

44 The National Gallery of Canada, Ottawa, September 1970 and Canadian tour to December 1971. *Prints.* Separate French language version of catalogue.

45 Studio Marconi, Milan, January 1971. *Recent Editions,* contains Italian translations.

46 Stedelijk Museum, Amsterdam, February 1971. Prints and multiples, contains Dutch translations.

47 'Propositions', *Catalyst,* May 1971.

48 Galerie Rene Block, Berlin, July 1971. Contains German translations.

49 Whitworth Art Gallery, Manchester, January 1972. *Prints, multiples and drawings.*

50 Studio Marconi, Milan, December 1972. Contains Italian translations.

51 Museum of Modern Art, New York, 1973. *The Large Glass,* in catalogue of the Marcel Duchamp retrospective.

52 Solomon R Guggenheim Museum, September 1973. *Richard Hamilton.*

53 Davison Art Center, Middletown, Connecticut, September 1973. *Prints.*

54 Nationalgalerie, Berlin, July 1974. *Richard Hamilton.* Contains German translations.

55 Serpentine Gallery, London, October 1975, *Paintings, Pastels, Prints.*

56 Stedelijk Museum, Amsterdam, February 1976, *Paintings, Pastels, Prints.* Contains Dutch translations.

57 The books of Dieter Roth (part 2), *Sondern 2,* Berlin 1977.

58 *Collaborations of Ch. Rotham* (with Dieter Roth), Edition Hansjörg Mayer with Galeria Cadaqués, January 1977.

59 Kunsthalle Bielefeld, *Studies,* April 1978.

60 The National Gallery, London, July 1978. *The Artist's Eye.* Catalogue introduction.

61 Interview. *Vanguard* (the magazine of the Vancouver Art Gallery) September 1978.

62 Waddington Galleries, London, February 1980. *Interiors 1964–79.*

63 Letter to P. Fuller, *Art Monthly,* October 1981.

64 'In Horne's house'. Commentary on etching illustrating the 'Oxen in the Sun' episode of James Joyce's *Ulysses.* Waddington Galleries, 1982.

Contents